HIS WORD IS LIFE

VIMA DASAN S.J.

HIS WORD

IS

LIFE

Daily Homilies for
Advent, Christmas, Lent,
and Easter Seasons

And Days of
Solemnities, Feasts and Obligatory Memorials

ST PAULS

ST PAULS PUBLISHING
187 Battersea Bridge Road, London SW11 3AS, UK
www.stpauls.ie

ISBN 085439 660 8

Printed by Biddles Ltd, Guildford, Surrey.

ST PAULS is an activity of the priests and brothers
of the Society of St Paul who proclaim the Gospel
through the media of social communication.

CONTENTS

CHRISTMAS

LENT

EASTER

SOLEMNITIES, FEASTS AND OBLIGATORY MEMORIALS

PREFACE

The Word of God is Life. 'I will feed them from the tree of life" (Rev 2:7) is the promise of the risen Christ to those who have ears to hear him as he speaks in the Scriptures. God's Word is living water to the thirsty and light to those in the dark. It guides and counsels, comforts and supports, defends and heals. Therefore the Church has always venerated the divine Scriptures and unceasingly offers from them the bread of life to the faithful, especially in the sacred liturgy.

Through the cycles of the liturgical years, we are brought closer and closer to the fountain of life flowing from the inspired divine Word. In everyday life, there are high points and low points, peak days and ordinary days. So too, in the life of the Church, there are 'Ordinary' days and 'Special' days. The special days occur during the Seasons of Advent, Christmas, Lent and Easter. Advent grace helps us to let go of our mistaken dreams, our conceited poses and other pretences, so that Jesus, who was born once according to the flesh may be born again in each of us according to the Spirit. The light that shone on the first Christmas night still shines, for it can never be extinguished. The Seasons of Lent and Easter which we observe amidst blood and sorrow, foreshadow our re-entering into Paradise with the risen Christ. Unlike the three-year cycle of Sunday readings, the weekday readings for these holy Seasons are the same every year. This book, *His Word Is Life*, offers short homilies on these weekday readings.

In my preparation of these homilies, I had uppermost in mind the immediate and personal needs of the people as they endeavour to live their faith in everyday life. Of course, my preparation always began with a careful reading of the two Scriptural texts for the day, which allowed me to discover a theme common to both readings, at least in most cases, and then the theme was 'enfleshed' in the context of people's daily lives. Therefore, I would like to call these homilies 'incarnational'. But in doing so, I hope that I have not sacrificed the exegetical and theological integrity of the Scriptural texts.

At the end of the homilies for the holy Seasons, this book contains brief reflections for days when Solemnities, Feasts and Obligatory Memorials are celebrated. The highest class of liturgical celebration is the *Solemnity*. The next class consists of those which commemorate important saints, days or some events from Christs life and are ranked as *Feasts*. Memorials are divided into two classes. About one third of the saints' days are *Obligatory* memorials, that is, they must be celebrated unless superseded by a higher-ranking celebration. The other celebrations of saints' days are *Optional*. The section on obligatory memorials contains brief preachable comments with a significant reference to the life of the saint and to one or two dominant virtues that shone in his or her life. The saints are special signs of God's activity. The Church recognises them as heroes and heroines worthy to be held up for our inspiration.

Homilies and reflections in this book are meant for different groups of people: those who come for daily Mass, those who attend regularly; those who participate occasionally. There is still another group of people: those who would like to come for daily Mass but can't, and so they spend daily some time privately, prayerfully reflecting on the liturgical readings of the day, thus finding a sense of being more in tune with the rhythms and movements of the liturgical year. The contents of this book are meant also for them.

These homilies and reflections are for busy priests, in particular. Every priest knows that he should make time to study, to reflect and pray as a preparation for his homilies, but a busy priest deserves an aid, a 'starter' for his own preparation. And each of the homilies and reflections in this book is intended to be nothing more than a starter, not a substitute for one's own preparation.

This book *His Word Is Life* is my third in the series of books on Homilies, following earlier ones *His Word Lives* (for all Sundays of the Year for A, B, C, Cycles, for Special Feasts and Occasions) and *His Word for Today* (for all weekdays in Ordinary Time), all published by *St Pauls,* London. Therefore I owe St PAULS Publishing a special word of gratitude for their willingness and readiness to undertake the publication of this series, with all their usual colour and attractiveness in combination with the expertise they posses and proper use of modern publishing techniques.

Vima Dasan, S.J.

Advent

MONDAY – WEEK 1 / ADVENT

WALK IN THE LIGHT

Readings: Is 2:1-5; Mt 8:5-11

Some lament: "We prayed for peace, and God did not answer; we cried, and he remained mute; we wept tears that consumed our hearts; we could have proven to him that our claims are modest, that they are realisable, since he is the Almighty; yet he was silent. Does God exist at all?" How are we going to convince such people that God does exist and he is in our midst and he cares for us? Not by giving a philosophical lecture on the existence of God, but by ourselves living as the children of the light. And so Isaiah appeals: "Let us walk in the light of the Lord" (Is 2:5). What does that mean? It means that we practise in our lives both as individuals and within community the law of love and forgiveness that the Lord has taught us. It is our practice of forgiving love that will draw all people to God and to the knowledge that he does exist and cares. The 'centurion' in the Gospel represents "all nations" (Is 2:2) who are drawn to God, not by the stony symbol of the Jerusalem temple, but by the forgiving and healing love that Christ extended to him (cf. Mt 8:7). We should ask ourselves: Is our Church an effective power for pardon and peace? Are we individually instruments of peace and not of division, advocating reconciliation and not discord and violence? In short, do we walk in the light of the Lord?

TUESDAY – WEEK 1 / ADVENT

LIKE LITTLE CHILDREN

Readings: Is 11:1-l0; Lk 10:21-24

Some animals are natural enemies because of hunger; humans often become mutual enemies because of greed and pride. The result is that injustices flourish and wars escalate. But Isaiah prophesied that the Spirit-filled Messiah will institute an era of justice and peace for all: "with righteousness he will judge the poor, and decide with equity for the meek of the earth" (Is 11:4). Isaiah probably had in mind some ideal Davidic king when he wrote this prophecy. But the Church, reading this passage in the light of further revelation, understands that Isaiah's prophecy was eminently fulfilled in the person of Jesus Christ. Can we, then, dream of world peace based on justice, believe in it, and work for it, by continuing the mission of Jesus Christ? Yes, provided we imbibe the simplicity of children. Hence, Jesus praised children, referring to his own disciples as the first recipients of the mysteries of God thanked the Father "for revealing them to babes" (Lk 10:21). Children seem to trust humans and animals alike. If you visit a zoo with small children, you will see them reaching out to a lion in the desire to touch it. It is the same when a child meets a dog in the street. They really want to embrace all life around them. It is as if the whole world is their friend. If we adults relate to each other in the same way that children do, a world of justice and peace based on equality will not remain a dream, but become a reality.

WEDNESDAY – WEEK 1 / ADVENT

THE QUESTION OF IMMORTALITY

Readings: Is 25:6-10; Mt 15:29-37

Many deny immortality. They argue that a thing or a life that has a beginning must of necessity have an end. This is not true. The almighty God who can make a thing from nothing, can by the power of his Word confer immortality on that which he has made. Otherwise he could not be called Almighty. But what will that immortal life be like? Isaiah pictures that life as a state where there will be unending joy and happiness: "The Lord will make for all people a feast… will wipe away tears from all faces" (Is 25:6,8). When the Lord Jesus fed a huge crowd of hungry people in the desert by multiplying a few loaves (Mt 15:36), he gave out a symbolic message that there is an eternal feast of joy and happiness waiting for all human beings in the immortal life. Therefore the question whether there is such a thing as immortal life should not even arise. Life in this world appears to be liable to decay and destruction, because it is in subjection to those things which are themselves subject to change and decay. But if this life is set free from these changeful and decaying influences and brought under the care of the eternal and unchanging God, it would escape from the clutch of death and attain to eternity. Hence, as the stars descend to rise upon some fairer shore, so we die to rise to immortality.

THURSDAY – WEEK 1 / ADVENT

BUILT ON ROCK

Readings: Is 26:1-6; Mt 7:21. 24-27

St Thomas More was in prison awaiting execution. His daughter came to him desiring to change his mind and do what the king wanted and escape death. But Thomas told her: "I will not mistrust God, Meg, though I shall feel myself weakening and on the verge of being overcome with fear." Cardinal Newman declared: "Therefore I will trust Him; whatever, wherever I am, I can not be thrown away. If I am in sickness, my sickness may serve him; in perplexity, my perplexity may serve him; If I am in sorrow, my sorrow may serve him; He does nothing in vain." To these Christians of heroic trust, God was indeed "an everlasting rock" (Is 26:4). But they could so trust in God, come what may, because they had built their own Christian life on a rocklike foundation. They were not like some people who merely say to the Lord, "Lord, Lord"; but they were those who "did the will of the Father" (Mt 7:21). They did not just profess allegiance to Christ, but put into practice what Christ has taught us. Do we want to have God as a rock on whom we can rely in any situation? Then we cannot just remain in the realm of words. The words that fill our parish committees, subcommittees and reports are necessary, but they are not enough. It is not enough just to talk about what ought to be done for the poor, the homeless and orphans. It is not enough to have a nice feeling, singing beautiful Christmas carols. We have to put our faith into practice and transform our words into deeds.

FRIDAY – WEEK 1 / ADVENT

ABSENCE OF LIGHT

Readings: Is 29:17-24; Mt 9:27-31

People are keen to discover faults in the sun and moon, such as spots and eclipses; but to the spots and eclipses of sin, they give no heed. Just as the body of a leper, by reason of his disease, becomes numb and insensible, so the heart and mind of the person, by reason of sin, becomes dull and insensible to spiritual realities. Thus sin is the cause of spiritual blindness. When Isaiah prophesied that at the coming of the Messiah, "The eyes of the blind shall see" (Is 29:18), he was referring to this spiritual blindness, and hence he added, "The ruthless shall come to nought and the scoffer cease and all who watch to do evil shall be cut off" (v.20). Jesus' life was a continuous struggle against these powers of darkness, not merely against physical sicknesses, but against all the other dark consequences of sin. Therefore when he gave sight to the two blind men (Mt 9:30), he was announcing that he had come to save us from sin and its awful results, bringing us into the light. Light is something which has real existence, but darkness has not; it is only a state, the absence of light. Thus, sin or evil is not a self-existent thing, but simply the absence of good. This dark side of evil is most terrible, for because of it, we miss the right course and endanger our lives. Why should we? Let us come to Christ and enter into his light.

SATURDAY – WEEK 1 / ADVENT

CORRECTIONS FROM ABOVE

Readings: Is 30:19-21. 23-26; Mt 9:35-10:1. 6-8

The boxes that come from some countries may in some ways seem crude and awkward, but they contain spices which fill the air with the fragrance of the Orient. So, too, the sufferings we have to bear on our journey of faith may be hard to bear; but let us not forget that concealed beneath them lies the correction of God. Perhaps we have looked to guides other than Christ; perhaps we have been journeying without Christ's teaching and the sacraments; perhaps we have been living merely for now, for this world, for pleasure, for ourselves and hence the good God corrects us by sufferings, telling us, "This is the Way; walk in it" (Is 30:21). What is more, the same Lord who corrects us, comes to "heal the wounds inflicted by his blow" (v.26). For he is a loving Father of infinite mercy. Let us see how his Son Jesus reacted when confronted by people in misery. "When he saw the crowds, he had compassion for them, because they were harassed and helpless" (Mt 9:36). He even called for "more shepherds" (v.37) in order to alleviate the burdens of suffering humanity. By virtue of our baptism in Christ, we too are expected to be shepherds. But before we can go to comfort others, we ourselves should willingly bear our own sufferings. In this we have to be like Christ. His hands were generous in gifts of healing; his touch has its ancient power even now; his hands were magnanimous in blessing. Even today his hands are saving hands. But his hands can save only because they are pierced hands.

MONDAY – WEEK 2 / ADVENT

LIFE IN ABUNDANCE

Readings: Is 35:1-10; Lk 5:17-26

"Life" and "Life abundant" are not the same thing. A man is lying ill in hospital – he has life but not life abundant. A snake comes on to his bed, but he has no strength to kill it, so it bites him and he dies. But a healthy man has life abundant physically. A rich man owned many estates but lost them all in war, and can live now only in a hut. He tells his friends that when he was rich he had no peace, but now in his poverty his heart is full of peace. In other words, as a rich man he had life only; but as a poor man he has life abundant spiritually. What is the source of life abundant spiritually? It is Christ. He claimed that he has come that we may have life abundantly (cf. Jn 10:10). Announcing the coming of Christ to give to every human being life in abundance, Isaiah rightly called the world to rejoice, for "everlasting joy shall be upon their heads" (Is 35:10). Life in abundance is human wholeness and that is only possible if our body is freed from its maladies and our soul is delivered from sin, which is the root cause of sickness and death. Therefore, Christ not only healed the man in the Gospel from his epilepsy, but also forgave his sin (Lk 5:20). Life in abundance will be ours in its fullest sense when we enter into everlasting life. But even here on earth, we can enjoy a fortaste of it, depending upon how closely we are united with Christ. Perhaps at Christmas we can hope to catch a glimpse of this life abundant for which Advent prepares us. It may be only a glimpse, yet it is worth preparing for it.

TUESDAY – WEEK 2 / ADVENT

EVERYONE IS GOD'S FAVOURITE

Readings: Is 40:1-11; Mt 18:12-14

God is relentless in his attention to the human family for he is its Father. He loves and cares for everyone in it, big and small, rich and poor, good and bad. When a little daughter of a woman was asked which child was her mother's favourite, the little girl replied: "She loves Jimmy best, because he is the oldest; and she loves Johnny best, because he is the youngest; and she loves me best, because I am the only girl." God like the little girl's mother, loves each of us best. Isaiah compares God's tender love for each of us to a shepherd. "He will feed his flock like a shepherd, and he will gather the lambs in his arms, he will carry them in his bosom" (Is 40:11). Taking the same image of a shepherd, Jesus says that, like the shepherd who goes after one lost sheep leaving out the ninety-nine, so he goes after every sinner who strays from his care, for it is God's will that not "one of these little ones should perish" (Mt 18:14). This parable does not say that the one lost sheep is equal to the other ninety-nine, but rather insists on the responsibility of the shepherd to each individual in the flock. So too, God cares for each of us, even the little ones. It is our task to imitate the Good-shepherd-God. We are all 'small' people spiritually speaking, all in need of being cared for by others, all called to look after others, all committed to seek out and serve the poor and the weak in our society, whether local or global.

WEDNESDAY – WEEK 2 / ADVENT

THE OIL OF COMFORT

Readings: Is 40:25-31; Mt 11:28-30

It is of no help to a train if its axles run hot; the heat generated is only a hindrance. It does not generate steam. Because of unnecessary friction, the axles get heated. Dry surfaces grinding together can be kept in smooth co-operation, thus avoiding friction, by a delicate cushion of oil. So too, we must seek the smoothing grace of Christ through daily prayerful communion with him when we experience life's pressures. "Come to me", he invites us, "all who labour and are heavy laden, and I will give you rest" (Mt 11:28). Stress caused by our grinding daily task, often by uncomfortable and un-loving circumstances, by the ingratitude of others and by disappointments in projects undertaken, can lead us to fretting. But through daily communion with Christ, we can obtain the necessary strength to keep our cool under stress. Isaiah assures: "They who wait for the Lord shall renew their strength; they shall mount up with wings like eagles" (Is 40:31). Sometimes, we come across a place polluted by filth, but then we notice flowers blooming and giving out a sweet fragrance that overcomes even the stench around them. Likewise, if we turn our hearts regularly to Christ, the difficulties of the day may even come to nourish our hearts and minds, bringing deep peace and inner contentment.

THURSDAY – WEEK 2 / ADVENT

IT TAKES COURAGE

Readings: Is 41:13-20; Mt 11:11-15

In Christ's own time, there were men known as the party of zealots who were trying to achieve Jewish freedom through the use of violence and armed force, attempting at the same time to accelerate the coming of the kingdom of heaven. Did Jesus have these men in mind when he said,

"Men of violence take the kingdom of heaven by force" (Mt 11:12)? Or, did he mean that the kingdom makes violent entrance into the world taking the field against forces of evil? In all probability what Jesus meant was that anyone who wants to enter into heaven must force their way in, through, that determined and courageous action. For example, it takes courage to touch a sick person in order to offer consolation, as the Lord did; it takes courage to speak to unbelievers about Christ; it takes courage to share things with the poor when we have just enough for ourselves. Thus, entering the kingdom takes unwavering courage. Crossing the ocean in a rowing boat is a courageous act, for there are some who have risked their lives doing it, and to what end? To become famous and popular. But the Lord expects us to muster spiritual courage, even risking our personal and family welfare, in order to enter into eternal life. Perhaps we are afraid of taking such risks. But God says, "Fear not, I will help you" (Is 41:13). Hence, hold on to God's hand and walk trusting in his help. The farmer buries good seeds in the earth trusting that they will grow and provide increase. The merchant places his money in the banker's care, trusting in the honesty of the bank. So too, trust in God. His word is true. He has never forsaken one who has trusted him.

FRIDAY – WEEK 2 / ADVENT

MANUFACTURING EXCUSES

Readings: Is 48:17-19; Mt 11:16-19

A man was reading the Bible. A friend came in and said, "What in the world are you doing?" The man did not ordinarily read the Bible. He said, "I am looking for loopholes." If half the ingenuity spent in finding excuses for not doing what we ought to do were exercised in finding means to do what ought to be done, the world would be a different place. As someone has said, "We are all manufacturers: making goods, making trouble, or making excuses." Many of the contemporaries of Jesus refused to recognise God's coming in either John the Baptist or himself, though both of these envoys showed, by their behaviour, that the promises of the Old Testament were accomplished in Jesus. Their excuse was that John the Baptist was too much of an ascetic, and Jesus mixed with sinners and led an ordinary life. Exasperated by their tendency to find excuses, Jesus lamented: "To what shall I compare this generation" (Mt 11:16)? God gave us ten commandments and assured us that, "I am your Lord, God, who teaches you to profit, who leads you in the way you should go" (Is 48:17). But some of us have our excuses not to follow God's commandments. One excuse is that the ten commandments are too negative, full of "Do's and Don'ts. But we forget that the basic thrust of the commandments is to lead us to life in abundance. The person who really wants to do something, finds a way, the other kind finds an excuse! An excuse is worse than a lie; for an excuse is often a guarded lie.

SATURDAY – WEEK 2 / ADVENT

WINTER OF SUFFERING

Readings: Ecc. 48:1-4,9-11; Mt 17:10-13

Pain and suffering are bitter as poison, but it is also well-known that sometimes the antidote to poison is itself poison. And thus God sometimes employs pain and suffering as bitter medicines in order to promote our spiritual health and vigour. As soon as our perfect health is secured there will be an end to all suffering. Our pain is no pleasure to God, for his one object is our eternal wellbeing. That is why Jesus who came to open for us the gate of eternal life, himself had to suffer and die on the cross. This was not only to take away our sins, but also to give us an example. He foretold, "The Son of Man will suffer at their hands" (Mt 17:12). It goes without saying that those who went before Christ as his messengers such as Elijah and John the Baptist, had to suffer. Elijah possessed extraordinary spiritual powers, so much so that the Scripture exclaims: "How glorious you were Elijah, in your wondrous deeds" (Ecc 48:4). The prophets predicted that he would return to inaugurate the messianic era; but he suffered, living on the edge of society, on the poorest of food, and constantly pursued by his enemies. John the Baptist was no exception. The price he had to pay for preparing the way of Christ was his own head, on a plate. We too, as Christ's disciples need to learn that to follow Christ means suffering and sacrifice. But that is not all. Spring follows winter, so resurrection followed Christ's crucifixion. May we then courageously go through our winter of suffering in order to enter into the spring of heavenly joy.

MONDAY – WEEK 3 / ADVENT

SUPERSTAR

Readings: Num 24:2-7,15-17; Mt 21:23-27

Each day our society bombards us with a myriad of images, sounds and words, in all sorts of sizes and colours and with all sorts of gestures and noises. They yell and scream at us: "Eat me, drink me, buy me, hire me, look at me, talk with me, sleep with me." We simply can't go far without being engulfed by words and images, forcibly intruding themselves into our minds. But do we really want our mind to become the rubbish bin of the world, to be filled with things that confuse us, excite us, depress us, arouse us, repulse us or attract us? Do we want others to decide what enters into our minds, what is right or wrong, good or bad? Clearly we do not and cannot, for we believe in Jesus as the Way, Truth and the Life, and so we want to be led by the star of Jesus Christ. Balaam, prophesying God's determination to save his people, said, "A star shall come forth out of Jacob" (Num 24:17). Balaam probably had David in mind; but we know that Christ is even a brighter star than David. Indeed, he is the Superstar. If we are among those who are still searching for the Superstar, let us be at least honest in our search, and not like the Pharisees who asked Jesus questions about him out of mere curiosity, and hence were turned down by Jesus with the words, "Neither will I tell you by what authority I do these things" (Mt 21:27). The questioners were foolish for they thought the secret of happiness lies in curiosity. But God gives the happiness of truth only to those who seek after it with sincerity.

A FORMIDABLE FOE

Readings: Zeph 3:1-2,9-13; Mt 21:28-32

All religions warn us that pride is a formidable foe, for it is the root of sin and woe and the giver of constant pain. Hence they advise us to kill it and replace it with poverty of the spirit. What is poverty of the spirit? It is born in a reliance on God's strength and not on our own: the humble and the lowly people "shall seek refuge in the name of the Lord" (Zeph 3:11). The poor in spirit are honest and truthful with others, unlike the second son in our Lord's parable who said that he would go but did not (Mt 21:30). The poor in spirit will acknowledge their faults but will repent like the first son in the parable (v.29). The poor in spirit also suffer. They hurt, they still feel incomplete, but they do not hide their pain, as conceited people do. The poor honestly and even openly mourn their losses. They will not live as if their losses are not real. They will not blame someone else for their loss. They will humbly accept their pains for they know that as human beings we are not made to be here for ever, that we are created for heaven, and that we are created with the ability to choose it. They also know that to grieve is to allow our losses to tear apart feelings of security and safety, and lead us to the painful truth of our brokenness and need for God. And the poor in spirit can be patient not only with others but also with themselves, for they are wise in realising that there are rewards for patience.

DEFECTS IN THE UNIVERSE?

Readings: Is 45:6-8,18, 21-25; Lk 7:19-23

God is the creator of the universe. He is omnipotent. Our wellbeing is the result of his creative hand. "Let the earth open that salvation may sprout forth and let it cause righteousness to spring up also" (Is 45:8). Yes. With the enabling power of God, salvation can emerge from the mix of good and bad in the universe. Until then there will be defects in the universe and evil in human society. Fault-finding critics say, "If there is an Almighty Creator of the world, why are there defects in it, such as hurricanes, earthquakes, eclipses, pain and suffering and death?" The folly of this criticism is similar to that of an unlearned man who finds fault with an unfinished building or an incomplete picture. But when he sees them fully finished he is ashamed of his folly. God did not in one day give this world its present form, nor will it in one day reach its perfection. The whole creation moves onward towards perfection. The almighty God continues to create the universe, to shape and to reshape human society, and his work took a definitive turn in his Son Jesus Christ. When Jesus gave sight to the blind, cleansed the lepers, gave ear to the deaf and raised the dead (cf. Lk 7:22), the Lord was shaping, forming and creating a people of his own. And God Almighty has bestowed his own great creative energy on his people in the form of the Holy Spirit, through the death and resurrection of Christ. Thus he is engaged in taking this world to its perfection through us his people, aided by his Spirit. May this grand plan of God take flesh in us.

THURSDAY– WEEK 3 / ADVENT

A POEM OF LOVE

Readings: Is 54:1-10; Lk 7:24-30

What fascinates us in God is his humility. God does not impose himself. He is neither a dictator nor an army commander. He never forces our hand. He is so respectful of human freedom that there are times when he is so silent our hearts almost break. It is all because he loves us so much. He compared his love for his chosen people to marital love. His people broke away from him and were in exile. But God took them back and declared, "The mountains may depart and the hills be removed, but my steadfast love will not depart from you, and my covenant of peace shall not be removed" (Is 54:10). And thus, whatever God does, his first instinct is compassion. The greatest expression of God's love was reached in the coming of his Son Jesus, through whom God has made a new covenant of love with the whole of the human race. We are all blessed people living after Christ for we are living in the new age of this new covenant of God's love. Jesus said "I am the Truth", and we are in possession of this Truth; he said, "I am the Way", and we know that Way; he said, "I am the Life", and we have a share in that Life by faith and baptism. Therefore, we are more blessed than John the Baptist. As special messenger of God, his role was to prepare people for the coming of God's new kingdom in Christ. But we actually participate in the blessings of that new kingdom. Hence Jesus was right when he declared "The least in the kingdom of heaven is greater than John the Baptist" (Lk 7:28). This is how God has loved us, is loving us and will love us to the end. Is it difficult, then, for us to be able to turn our lives into a continuous poem of love for God?

FRIDAY – WEEK 3 / ADVENT

GATHERING LOVE

Readings: Is 56:1-3, 6-8; Jn 5:33-36

On a black velvet cloth lie three beautiful diamonds. They all glisten in the light; they are all cut precisely. But are they all diamonds? No. One is glass; one is zircon; and one is actual diamond. So too, the word "love" is attractive and appetising. But is all love true love? No. There is "if" love which says, "If you meet my expectations, I will love you". There is "because" love which says, "I love you because you are rich, powerful or beautiful." And there is "in spite of" love which says, "I love you in spite of your being ugly, uneducated, poor; I love you because you are God's child like me, created in the image of God." This is unconditional love; it is real love like real diamond. This is the kind of love we need today to bring all people on earth into one family, as God himself planned. Isaiah said in the name of God, "My house shall be called a house of prayer for all people"...Let no foreigner say, "the Lord will separate me from his people" (Is 56: 3,7). It is to this work of gathering all people into one loving family Jesus referred when he said that he had come to carry out the work his Father had given him (Jn 5:36). Therefore let us

endeavour to build close-knit communities of loving people in the milieu
through the way in which we live, so that one day all humanity will become
one loving community. But let us remember that a community is only a
community when the majority of its members are making the transition
from "the community for myself" to "myself for the community."

DECEMBER 17 / ADVENT

WHO IS IN CONTROL?

Readings: Gen 49:2, 8-10; Mt 1:1-17

God can draw good out of evil because while the power of doing evil is
ours, the effects of our evil deeds are outside our control, and therefore
in the hands of God. I once saw a man drawing some black dots. I looked
and could make nothing of them, only a chaotic collection of black dots.
Then he drew a few lines, put a few rests and then a clef at the beginning
and I saw that those black dots were musical notes. Likewise, God can
make a glorious harmony out of good and bad people and succeed in
working out his grand designs. For example, the list of Christ's ancestors as we read in the Gospel (Mt 1:1) contains some outstanding people,
others who were not great followers of Yahweh, and still others who
were not even Jews. Yet God worked through them all to bring forth the
greatest son of Israel as he had promised: "The sceptre shall not depart
from Judah until he comes to whom it belongs and to him shall be the
obedience of the people" (Gen 49:10). Therefore we should never give
up our faith that God works for the benefit of humankind in all circumstances, favourable and unfavourable alike, through all kinds of peoples,
sinners included. The astronomer does not give up his science because
he does not find a new planet every day; the poet does not give up poetry
because he cannot write brilliant verses everyday; but the ideal of science and the ideal of poetry remain. So too, we can not give up our faith
in God's promises because we are placed in unfavourable circumstances
or because we have to live with bad characters. That would be like leaving our faith to the mercy of the stomach.

DECEMBER 18 / ADVENT

FAIRNESS TO ALL

Readings: Jer 23:5-8; Mt 1:18-24

In our world of today, we are only too conscious of the appalling injustice inflicted on people, by people. The injustice done to an individual is sometimes even thought to be of service to the public. Some, of course, are just, but their love of justice is often no more than the fear of suffering injustice. In a world such as this, it is consoling to hear God promising that he will restore all things in a Messiah who "shall reign as king and deal wisely and shall execute justice" (Jer 23:5). A just rule recognises everyone's fundamental right to life, a right to those conditions which make life truly human. Justice cannot be sacrificed on the altar of democracy. Democracy can never be a self-fulfilling justification for policies that are intrinsically immoral. Democracy to be healthy requires more than universal suffrage: it recognises the presence of a just system of rule. Individuals dealing with one another must also be moved by a sense of justice. Joseph was "an upright man" (Mt 1:19) and therefore, when he came to know his espoused wife's pregnancy, he wanted to divorce her privately, in order to save her from public shame. His justifiable attitude towards Mary's situation is far removed from the legal prescriptions of the time which called for stoning. Instead of listening to the demands of the world with its own social order, Joseph listened to the demands of his conscience where the Spirit of a just and merciful God speaks to us. May we not forget that we win justice quickest by rendering justice to others. But let us also remember that justice without generosity may easily become Shylock's justice.

DECEMBER 19 / ADVENT

WE CAN STILL FLOURISH

Readings: Judg 13:2-7, 24-25; Lk 1:5-25

In every garden we notice some patches which never catch the light. Any expert gardener will tell you that there are some flowers which are not afraid of these dingy corners. In actual fact, they may rather like them and flourish in them. Likewise, we have men and women whose spirits flourish when material circumstances become stern and severe. How is it possible for them? It is possible because they believe that, in whatever barren circumstances we may live, we are valued by God. They believe that, however small or ordinary or weak we may be, we have a role to play in the mighty work of God. Manoah's wife was barren, but in answer to her prayers, she gave birth to Samson (Judg 13:24), whom God used to protect his people from the Philistines. And we know the miserable downfall of Samson through his infatuation with Delilah. Yet God used him as one of the charismatic leaders, to consolidate Israel's original possessing of the Promised land. Like Manoah's wife, Elizabeth was barren, but she conceived a son (Lk 1:24) in her advanced age who became great, full of the Holy Spirit, and prepared the world for the Messiah. Therefore, let us never be discouraged by the ordinary, domestic routine of our lives, or by our weaknesses, failures and mistakes. From God's point of view, they are valuable, and he can still use us for his mighty work. Let us not loose heart because life has pushed us into a dingy corner. We can still flourish if we patiently walk holding on to the hand of God.

DECEMBER 20 / ADVENT

GOD WITH US

Readings: Is 7:10-14; Lk 1:26-38

A South African woman prayed thus: "Lord, you are in my baby's awakening, your Spirit fills her. You are in her playful washing, your

Spirit splashes her. You are in the way I feed her, your Spirit satisfies her. You are in the games I play with her, your Spirit delights in her. You are in the song I sing to her, your Spirit soothes her. You are in her time of sleep, your Spirit keeps her." In order to pray like this mother, one has to believe firmly that God is with us in the Spirit of his Son Jesus Christ. This was the promise he gave to Ahaz the king: "A young woman shall conceive and bear a son and shall call his name Immanuel" (Is 7:14). In fulfilment of this promise, Mary conceived a son when she said "Yes" to God's call to become the mother of his Son Jesus (Lk 1:28). Since the birth of Jesus, God is with us in the most intimate manner. Julian of Norwich, a fourteenth century English mystic and all-round practical person, believed so intensely in God's being with us that she said: "God is our clothing." One could ask: Is God in our socks and shoes, our shirts and pants? Why not? Like all other living things, the things we wear are also God's gifts and he must be in his gifts. If we really believe that God is with us, then I will look at a friend who comes in pain and a neighbour who tries to hide her tears and I will see God in them. If I truly believe God is with us, I will look at an enemy reaching out a hand and a stranger crying out for help and I will see God in them.

DECEMBER 21 / ADVENT

LEAPING WITH JOY

Readings: Song 2:8-14; Lk 1:39-45

We are all in some kind of trouble, in darkness of some kind, prisoners of some problems. Some are crippled with jealousy or possessiveness; others nurse deep anger. In some of us, our hidden stress manifests itself in physical diseases. Others are constantly worried that even the small aches and pains they suffer are going to be fatal. Many of us are driven to pessimism and feelings of hopelessness, because we see disaster looming everywhere. There are those who crave acceptance and others who go through the agony of rejection, becoming paralysed by recurring depression. There is a remedy to all this. Allow God to come into your life this Advent, and you will find joy even in the midst of your pain.

When God comes, joy always accompanies him. The lover described in
the first reading as "leaping over the mountains" and "bounding over
hills" (Song 2:8-9) to his beloved, is clearly an image of the Son of God
being carried in Mary's womb over the hill country of Judah, as she goes
to visit her cousin Elizabeth (Lk 1:44). Her arrival brings great joy to her
cousin, for she brings the Son of God with her. Similar joy can be ours
whenever we are visited by God. But we have to pave the way for God
to visit us. One sure way by which we can receive a visit from God is to
offer some form of substantial help as Christmas gift — to some
unfortunate stranger, outcast, or marginalised poor in society. May we
think of them when we go shopping to buy gifts for our own children.

DECEMBER 22 / ADVENT

THANK YOU, GOD!

Readings: 1 Sam 1:24-28; Lk 1:46-56

God who is love has freely bestowed on all human beings those things
which are necessary for both temporal and spiritual life. He has freely
given us the air and water, heat and light without which life is impossible.
But these are lightly esteemed by many, and so they do not stop and
thank God for them. God has similarly provided us freely with the things
for our spiritual life. But many so lightly regard them, that they offer no
thanks to the Creator; but on the other hand, God's gifts of gold, silver
and jewels, which are scarce and obtained with great difficulty, are highly
esteemed by many — though with such things the hunger and thirst of
the body can not be assuaged, nor the longings of the heart be satisfied.
Two women in today's readings teach us a lesson on gratitude to God
and put us to shame for the folly of our thoughtlessness of God's gifts to
us. Hannah had prayed that she might have a son. Her prayer was
answered. Then she returned to give thanks and offer her son over to the
Lord (1 Sam 1:28). Mary conceived a son by the Spirit of God. In the
Magnificat, she praises and gives thanks to God for giving her son Jesus
saying, "My soul magnifies the Lord, and my spirit rejoices in God my

Saviour" (Lk 1:46). We belong to God. All that we have comes from God. Why are we sometimes so full of our own self-importance, that even the God who made us and gave us all, can find no place in our hearts?

DECEMBER 23 / ADVENT

REFINER'S FIRE

Readings: Mal 3:1-4, 23-24; Lk 1:57-66

By definition, fire is the result of combustion, that is, the burning of anything that is capable of igniting, such as wood, hay, and stubble. We too are combustible in a spiritual sense. God knows it and hence when he comes into our life, he comes as fire. He promised that he would send his prophet to prepare the way of the Lord who "will be like the refiner's fire" (Mal 3:2). And John the Baptist was the prophet thus foretold, since "the hand of the Lord was with him" (Lk 1:66). We know well that John preached repentance and change of heart. If we, too, repent and have a change of heart during this Advent, we will experience the salutary effects of God's fire of grace. What are the effects? Fire consumes; to consume means to destroy. The grace of God will destroy whatever is ungodly in us. Fire purifies; the grace of God will cleanse us from sins; his grace can melt the worst rubbish that litters our past lives. Fire softens; the fire of God's presence in our heart can soften even the stoniest of hearts. The result of all these processes is the peace of God. This peace is not like the deadly hush preceding the tempest, but the serene and pure-aired quiet that follows it. But are we prepared to repent? If we lack time to mourn our sins, then we lack time to mend our lives. However, what we need is not remorse but repentance. Remorse is impotence; it will sin again; only repentance is strong, for it can end everything.

DECEMBER 24 / ADVENT

HIS SAVING POWER

Readings: 2 Sam 7:1-5, 8-12,14-16: Lk 1:67-79

It would be possible to take a worthless piece of paper, write a poem on it, and make it worth a thousand pounds; that is genius. Another could sign their name to a piece of paper, and make it worth a hundred thousands; that is capital. Another can take gold, stamp an eagle on it, and make it worth dollars; that is money. A craftsman can take material that is worth only five pounds, and make an article worth fifty pounds; that is skill. But Jesus, and only Jesus, can take the sinful life of humanity, wash it in his blood, and make it a blessing to humanity; that is salvation. Referring to this salvation, Zacharia blessed God for having "raised up a horn of salvation for us in the house of his servant David" (Lk 1:68). David wanted to build a Temple for God (2 Sam 7:5), as if God's continuing presence depended on a building of granite and limestone. But God had his own designs for a spiritual dynasty: he will dwell with us in the saving power of his Son Jesus, born of David's line. The saving power of Jesus "Gives light to those who sit in darkness and in the shadow of death to guide our feet into the way of peace" (Lk 1:79). Although the ocean surface had been whipped into huge waves by high winds, a vessel that remained submerged overnight, came out calm and tranquil. So, too, our life may be buffeted by all kinds of troubles, but if we remain in the peace of Christ, we are safe and secure. That is the secret of Christ's saving power.

Christmas

DECEMBER 26 / CHRISTMAS

FIRST MARTYR, STEPHEN

Readings: Acts 6:8-10,7:54-59; Mt 10:17-22

Not only are there those who lead evil lives and suffer, but there are also those who lead good lives and suffer. Look at the foot of the cross and see who is suffering: good people, particularly our Blessed Mother. When we are tempted to ask: "Why should I suffer?" we need to remember that we are called to share in the redemption of the Lord. St Stephen was one of seven deacons appointed by the Apostles to relieve them of their routine duties of giving alms. But he had a rare gift of preaching. His preaching brought him into conflict with those Jewish Christians who wished to retain the customs of the faith of their birth in their new faith. They argued with him but were unable to counter the wisdom and the strength of his arguments. He was taken to the Sanhedrin where he prophesied the destruction of the Temple, and gave a stirring speech of defence, and told his enemies that he saw the glory of Jesus standing at the right hand of God. At that, he was dragged out of the city and was stoned to death (Acts 7:59). Stephen died as Christ had foretold what would happen to his followers: "Beware of men; for they will deliver you up to councils and flog you in their synagogues" (Mt 10:17). Why do we speak of martyrs, death and suffering, so soon after Christmas? But then, why after the season's greetings are over, do violence, threats, destructions return to the pages of the newspapers? Because such is the real context in which God has become man in Jesus. And hence, the followers of Jesus have to be ready to shoulder their crosses in their struggle against evil and for the redemption of humankind.

DECEMBER 27 / CHRISTMAS

JOHN, THE EVANGELIST

Readings: 1 Jn 1:1-4; Jn 20:2-8

Is Christian faith just a blind leap into the unknown, trusting our life to something we can never be sure of? Or, is there more to it than the proud sceptics of the modern world will admit? The answer is that Christian faith is not a blind faith: it is informed faith, because it is based on evidence that you can check out for yourself. For example, we believe Jesus Christ is the Son of God, the Saviour of the world, who lived, taught, died and rose again. We believe this because of evidence. One type of evidence is constituted by a reliable witness, like John the Apostle and Evangelist. St John belonged to the inner circle of Christ's disciples and was present at the transfiguration and at Gethsemane during the Passion. He sat next to Jesus at the last supper and asked him who would betray him. It was to John that Jesus commended his mother at the foot of the cross. When the news of the resurrection was brought to him by women, he and Peter ran to the tomb; when he saw only an empty tomb with linen cloths rolled up by theside, he "believed" (Jn 20:8). Later writing his epistles, he asserted: "We have heard, we have seen with our eyes, we have looked upon and touched with our hands that which was from the beginning" (1 Jn 1:1), referring to Jesus his Master. Because of such reliable witnesses, Christians believe what they believe about Christ. In other words, there is good and solid evidence for believing in Christ. It is evidence, not proof, of course. Very very few things can be proven, and most of what makes up the world view of today's sceptic is itself unprovable. Most everyday assumptions are held because there is good evidence for them: so it is exactly with Christian faith.

DECEMBER 28 / CHRISTMAS

HOLY INNOCENTS

Readings: 1 Jn 1:5-2:2; Mt 2:13-18

What is human life? Is it a vapour that appears for a little time and then vanishes? No. It is the most precious gift of God to humankind, for he creates in our own mortal selves his own image that we might enjoy eternal life with him. In this sense, life is the childhood of immortality. But for king Herod, life was cheap. He ordered the massacre of innocent male children in Bethlehem and its surroundings, in his fruitless endeavour to destroy the child Jesus (Mt 2:16). Life was so cheap to him that in 34 BC he killed his own brother Joseph. In 29 BC, he killed his wife Mariamne. A few months later, he killed his mother-in-law Alexandra. He killed his two sons Alexander and Costobar. His killing was endless, for life was cheap to him. But alas, a more dreadful thing is happening today. Mothers are killing their own children in their wombs, by abortion. The Church tells us: "From the moment of its conception life must be guarded with the greatest care, while abortion and infanticide are unspeakable crimes." The Church illumines us with the light of Christ who called himself the "light of the world" (Jn 8:12), because as John says in his letter, " God is light and in him is no darkness at all" (1 Jn 1:5). Mother Teresa said to the world: "If a mother can kill her own child, what is there to stop you and me from killing each other? The only one who has the right to take a life is the one who created it. God has created a world big enough for all the lives he wished to be born. It is only our hearts that are not big enough to want them and accept them."

DECEMBER 29 / CHRISTMAS

MELTED BY LOVE

Readings: 1 Jn 2:3-11; Lk 2:22-35

Until a lump of salt dissolves in water and mingles in the pot, not a grain of lentil becomes salted; nor can snow water the thirsty earth, until it is melted by the sun's warmth and turned into flowing water. Similarly, until we are melted by the love for our fellow people, we cannot claim to be in the light of Christ. "He who says he is in the light and hates his brother is in the darkness still" (1 Jn 2:9), writes St John. With absolute clarity, he was calling the members of Christian community to love one another, as themselves have been loved by God. Simeon, holding child Jesus in his hands, declared that this child is to be the light for all peoples, pagans, gentiles, the whole world. (cf. Lk 2:35). But the measure of our knowledge of Jesus and the guarantee that we live in the light of Christ, is the love we bear for those around us. Loving others means helping others. Experience has proved that by helping others and making others happy, we ourselves are helped, and a wonderful joy comes into our hearts. This shows clearly that we are intimately bound up with one another and are dependent on each other's help and service for our mutual betterment and progress. This is the kind of law of our nature. If we break this law, we deprive ourselves and our neighbours of true joy, and that leads us to ruin, and to destroy each other.

DECEMBER 30 / CHRISTMAS

GOD IS THE POTTER

Readings: 1 Jn 2:12-17; Lk 2:36-40

God is like a potter. It is not we who shape God, it is God who shapes us. We must entrust our life into the hands of the potter. By obedience to God's will we must offer the clay of our hearts always soft and workable, so that he can fashion us and make us fit for our glorious future. There is much in our world that lures us away from God. St John warns us: "Do not love the world or things in the world" (1 Jn 2:15). Of course, there are many good things in the world which give glory to God, such as artificial hearts, cancer cures, magnificent architecture, just financial dealings, food distribution networks, the space shuttle, brilliant paintings and poetry. But there is a lot of evil as well: abortion clinics, broken marriages, gulags, drug traffic, ghettos of criminals. This is the world John asks us to shun. If we do that, we will enjoy close communion with God and obedience to him will not be that difficult. That does not mean that God will grant us favours material or spiritual the instant we express our needs to him. We must wait on God as long as he wants, for him to respond. Waiting on God in patience is the basic Christian attitude. This is beautifully typified in the figure of Anna who patiently waited through the trials of a long life, for eighty-four years and was eventually rewarded by seeing the Christ (Lk 2:38). If we easily grow impatient of God's delays, we bring upon ourselves a lot of troubles by restlessness, sometimes by reckless haste. A wise man should not be in a hurry to pluck the fruit before it ripens.

DECEMBER 31 / CHRISTMAS

THE BODY OF THE LORD

Readings: 1 Jn 2:18-21; Jn 1:1-18

Our age is often called the "me-generation", because of its emphasis on privatised spirituality. Hence we have to constantly remind ourselves that Christian life does not grow all in isolation. We draw the energy we need to grow into mature Christians not only from Christ but also from his Church, the community of believers. This has to be so, for the Church is the Body of the Lord, which treasures in its bosom the eternal truths about Jesus Christ. Such truths are: "He was the true light that enlightens every man. The Word became flesh; From his fullness have we all received grace upon grace" (Jn 1:9,14,16). Hence, those who have been born into the Church through baptism, would do well to appreciate their privilege in belonging to the Church, and resist the temptation to break with it for insubstantial reasons. Deploring those who had left the Church John wrote: "They went out from us but they were not of us" (1 Jn 2:19). Those of us who leave the Church because of the weaknesses found in the Church, misunderstand what the Church is. The Church is not the kingdom, it is only its servant. As a human reality, the Church is like a clay vessel, and therefore it will always fall short of the kingdom-ideal, and hence need constant renewal and purification. But the Church is not just human, for it is promised the power of God and the presence of the Spirit.

JANUARY 1 / CHRISTMAS

THE MOTHER OF GOD

Readings: Num 6:22-27; Gal 4:4-7; Lk 2:16-22

As one who stands at the gate and with doubtful hand draws aside the curtain and peers into the unknown, so we begin today by taking our first step across the threshold of a New Year. It is already a beautiful year, because it is another year of the Lord. Hence there are new blessings in store for us. Did not God ask Moses to bless his people in these words: "The Lord bless you and keep you; the Lord make his face shine on you and be gracious to you" (Num 6:22)? Of course, there will also be hills of difficulties on the way. But both hills and valleys are needed in our lives, as in any land. It is the hills that collect the rain for fruitful valleys. So it is our experience on the hills of our difficulties that drives us to the throne of God's grace and bring down showers of blessings. As "Mary treasured in her heart" (Lk 2:19) all the wonderful things God had done to her in the birth of her Son Jesus, so let us treasure in our hearts the gifts that God has already given us in his Son Jesus. This will give us constant hope that all will be well for those who walk holding the hand of God. It is not by accident that we celebrate today the feast of Mary as Mother of God. We need her daily assistance throughout the New Year. Her divine Son cannot refuse her anything that she asks him on our behalf. Her Son esteems her prayers so greatly and is so eager to please her, that when she prays it seems as if it is she who commands, a queen and not a handmaid. A great treasure in any house is a good mother. But Mary does for us more than what the best of mothers can do.

(Note: The following reflections are used until the celebration of Epiphany, which falls on the Sunday after the first of January)

JANUARY 2 / CHRISTMAS

REMAIN IN CHRIST

Readings: 1 Jn 2:22-28; Jn 1:19-28

A man went to make a five-day retreat. When he checked in on Sunday evening, the receptionist asked what he hoped to obtain from the coming retreat. "I don't expect to discover profound theological truths," he said. " I just want to find answers to a couple of simple questions: who is God and who am I?" When leaving on Friday afternoon, the receptionist bade the man good-bye and inquired if he had found the answer to his two questions. " Oh, yes," he replied, "I now understand that Jesus is God and I am not." Indeed, Jesus is God and hence he is the Truth, and so St John asks us, "to remain in him" (1 Jn 2:27). By remaining in Christ, we remain in the Truth. Truth is not doctrine or dogma; truth is Jesus Christ. No doubt, many good things are to be found in books, but nothing in them will make us free, because only the truth of Christ can make us free. There are many Christians anointed in baptism but who are not satisfied with Christ. Why? Because they have not tasted the freedom that Christ gives. They are like those bystanders to whom John the Baptist said of Christ, "Among you stands one whom you do not know" (Jn 2:26). We see many things in the world, wonderful things, man-made things. People are able to fly in the air, control machines and electricity, but they can't control their bodily passions, and therefore they are not really free. They can rule nature, but they can't rule their own selves, and therefore they are not really free. Whereas those who remain in the truth of Christ become truly free, for they can control their passions and are masters of themselves.

JANUARY 3 / CHRISTMAS

CHILDREN OF GOD

Readings: 1 Jn 2:29-3:6; Jn 1:29-34

We are called Christians. Imagine if all Christians today were to be given the official title of "Children of God" (1 Jn 3:1). That would help a great deal to close the gap between different Christian denominations. Scarcely could such a simple statement bear such a monumental truth. Our real worth in God's eyes is not what we do or accomplish but simply who we are. Good parents do not demand that their little children earn their love and affection. So too, we are not going to buy heaven from God our Father. We will simply inherit it for we are his children. But St John cautions: "And everyone thus hopes in him purifies himself as he is pure" (1 Jn 3:3). Purification from sin is not going to be our own achievement. Only Jesus, the Son of God can do it, for he is "the Lamb of God who takes away the sin of the world" (Jn 1:29). Dostoevsky, writing of the days of his exile in Siberia as a time in the underworld says, "O God, could you not let me be a sponge to plug up some dirty old hole?" Well, Jesus the Lamb of God was very much like a great sponge that just wiped clean the sin of humanity. But in order to appropriate the purifying power of the Lamb of God, we have at least to acknowledge our sins. That is our problem. There seems to be no sinners nowadays. Many say they are not responsible; others say they are not guilty; still others say that the Oedipus complex or some other complex is responsible for their wrongdoings. Nearly all put the blame on others or circumstances. If we want to be forgiven by the Lamb of God, this will not do.

PERSONAL INVITATION

Readings: 1 Jn 3:7-10; Jn 1:35-42

Rose and Monica work in the same office. Monica is in endless troubles. But she finds Rose quite happy always and has noticed Rose daily visiting the church for prayer after office hours. Rose one day invites Monica to go with her to church for a short prayer and she does. Stephen is a Christian but does not belong to any church. His girlfriend invites him to join her whenever she goes to Sunday mass and later she introduces him to the priest. A nun volunteers to give fresh instructions to an ex-pupil, who had studied in the convent school, but later gave up her faith in God. Nicholas, a parishioner, pays a home visit to his friend Duane who is a lapsed Christian, and presenting parish bulletins, engages him in a friendly chat about the joy of belonging to the parish. These are all specific instances of how we can personally invite someone either directly or indirectly to come to Jesus Christ. When Jesus was asked by two of John's disciples, "where do you live?" he told them, "Come and see" (Jn 1:39). That was a personal invitation. The next day Andrew, one of these two, persuaded his brother Peter to come and see the Messiah and he came; that was a personal invitation. St John says, "Whoever does not live uprightly and does not love his brother is not from God" (1 Jn 3:10). What better way is there of loving one's neighbours as brothers and sisters in Christ than telling him or her what we have found in Jesus Christ, and extend a personal invitation to come and see him?

JANUARY 5 / CHRISTMAS

CHILD OF IGNORANCE

Readings: 1 Jn 3:11-21; Jn 1:43-51

"Prejudice", said Voltaire, "is the reason of fools." Perhaps that is why we should never attempt to reason the prejudice out of anyone; since it was not reasoned into them, it can not be reasoned out! Prejudice is the child of ignorance. Nearly all of us have suffered discrimination at the hands of prejudiced people: because of our background, status, age, ethnic origin or simply the colour of the skin. Jesus also suffered from people prejudiced against him. When told that the Messiah has come from Nazareth, Nathaniel quipped, "Can anything good come out of Nazareth?" (Jn 1:46). A sure way for a person to shed his or her prejudice is to come to Christ. He will teach us by word and example to love others, whoever they are, for "he laid down his life for us" (1 Jn 3:16). He will teach us that we are all God's children created in his own image. A man was selling balloons. A child was intrigued as she watched the balloon-man occasionally release a balloon and let it float into the sky to attract some attention to his wares. Every now and then, the balloons went up the sky – blue balloon, red, green, white, black and yellow. "Excuse me, sir," said the child. "How come, when you let go of the balloons – green, white, red, even black balloons – they always float up into the sky?" The man replied, "Love, it is not the colour of the balloon that matters. It is the stuff inside." To be prejudiced is to be weak on truth. Let us get strong on the truth that we are all God's children.

JANUARY 6 / CHRISTMAS

(When Epiphany is celebrated on Sunday)

WHAT IS LIFE?

Readings: 1 Jn 5:5-13; Mk 1:7-11

What is life? Is it a handful of short stories or a game of cards? It is neither. Is it a bundle of sensations or thoughts? It is neither. Is it something made up of sobs, sniffs and smiles, with sniffs predominating? It is not. Is it progress from want to want or from enjoyment to enjoyment? It is neither. What is life, then? Life is Jesus Christ. St John again and again says, " He who has the Son has life and he who has not the Son of God has not life" (1 Jn 5:12). How? Jesus is life precisely because he is the Son of God, as proclaimed by God himself at his baptism: "You are my beloved Son; with you I am well pleased" (Mk 1:11). As the Son of God he is the source of every form of life. And hence, only those who live in Christ can be truly alive. To live in Christ is like being immersed in the fountain of life. Sometimes, green and fruitful trees are found standing on dry land, where there is not much rain. On careful examination we find that these trees are fresh and green, bearing fruit, because their hidden roots touch hidden streams of water running through the earth. So too, those who live in Christ, because they touch the fountain of life, they are full of peace, radiant with joy, leading fruitful life even amidst misery. Some persons in their folly use intoxicants, not only to forget their sorrow, but also to get a passive exhilaration. But the joy we find in Jesus is not like the pleasurable effect we might obtain from sources of stimulation whose effects are passing. The joy in Christ is real, for he is life.

(When Epiphany is celebrated on Sunday)

PRAYER GRANTED

Readings: 1 Jn 5:14-21; Jn 2:1-12

God always answers our prayer. The Lord never shuts his storehouse until we shut our mouths. God denies nothing to the one who knows how to ask. Mary asked her son Jesus to provide the wedding party with new wine, by simply exposing to him the embarrassing situation: "They have no wine" (Jn 2:3). Although Jesus expressed his unpreparedness to perform the miracle, Mary said to the servants, "Do whatever he tells you" (v.5). Here, Mary teaches us how to pray. In our prayer, there must be a realistic petition, confidence in the divine mercy, and unconditional submission to God's will. St John says that we must pray with the conviction that "we have obtained the requests made of him" (1 Jn 5:15). It means that the answer to our prayer, made according to God's will has been granted and completed in heaven as we pray, even though its showing forth on earth may not occur until long afterwards. It means this: Since our petition is made according to God's will, God takes over our will, "devours" it in his will and preserves it, and thus the infallibility of the divine promise of hearing the true prayer, becomes understandable. Therefore, after making a petition, we must treat God as if he has granted us our request. When a woman is married, she at once falls into a new attitude of wife and acts in accordance with the fact. So too, when we take God as our Father we must fall into the attitude of recognising him as our Father, and expect him to grant us what we have asked him.

MONDAY AFTER EPIPHANY / CHRISTMAS

TEST THE SPIRIT

Readings: 1 Jn 3:22-4:6; Mt 4:12-17,23-25

A teacher once asked a class of ten-year olds to write down a definition of religious faith. It was a quite a challenge for them. Nevertheless, one little boy wrote: "Faith is believing what you know is not true." If that is so, is faith a blind leap into the dark? For example, why do we believe that Jesus is God? St John says, "Every spirit which confesses that Jesus Christ has come into the flesh is of God" (1 Jn 4:2). Is he referring to blind faith? No. His own faith in Christ came from his personal contact with Christ and the grace of God. He was one of those "people who lived in darkness and had seen a great light" (Mt 4:16). Hence his faith was an enlightened and discerning faith. Our own faith has to be the same, not a blind one. That is why St John warns us, "Not every spirit is to be trusted" and asks us to "test the spirits to see whether they are of God" (1 Jn 4:1). Suppose there is big decision to be made: should one persuade one's still sprightly mother to put a badly senile father in a nursing home, so that she can be relieved of an almost unbearable burden? There may be a dozen reasons for and against. The family needs discernment of spirits in the presence of God. When the family approaches God in prayer, he makes them free. In that freedom they will be able to see more clearly what is good for the person in question and for the good of the whole family. They will cease to be selfish and the right course of action will emerge, because the Spirit of God who makes them children of God sets them free.

TUESDAY AFTER EPIPHANY / CHRISTMAS

ALL-EMBRACING LOVE

Readings: 1 Jn 4:7-10, Mk 6:34-44

"God loves us", wrote C.S. Lewis, "not because we are loveable, but because he is love; not because he needs to receive, but because he delights to give." Therefore, we are not surprised that Christ, God made flesh, "had compassion on the great crowds because they were like sheep without a shepherd" (Mk 6:34), and fed them for they were hungry, multiplying few loaves into thousands (cf. vv.41-2). St John, calling on us to love one another, adds, "Whoever fails to love, does not know God, because God is love" (1 Jn 4:8). We are urged to love all people since God loves everyone. Love is genuine only when it embraces all. We must endeavour to love him or her whom once we did not love, whom we have condemned, or who may have done us an injury. To love all human beings is difficult but it can be learned, if we closely consider the benefits of loving all people. One benefit surely is that it unites people. Modern technology may be useful for uniting people; however, without love, machines can easily separate people. Another benefit of love is that it makes the one who loves, very happy. If you hate even one person, all the joys will leave your heart. God wanted us to be happy, but happy in our belonging, and hence endowed us with a longing for love. Hence we will be happy only when we all love one another. We are like stones joined in an arch and are bound to collapse unless we support one another with love. To be in love with all people is the greatest good and hence the greatest happiness.

WEDNESDAY AFTER EPIPHANY / CHRISTMAS

LAW BREAKERS!

Readings: 1 Jn 4:11-18; Mk 6:45-52

A Christian was once crossing a high mountain pass in Tibet with his Tibetan guide. Suddenly they stumbled upon a man who had slipped from the path and was lying in the snow, but still alive. "Come, help me try to bring this unfortunate man to safety," said the Christian to his guide. But the guide said in fright, "If we try to carry the man, none of us will survive. So I am going away and if you want, come with me." Saying that, he set off down the path. But the Christian, alone, lifted the traveller on his back, slowly and painstakingly picked his way along the steep and slippery path. Soon it began to snow. Somehow he made it, with his heavy load, to the village. But at sunrise, he saw the frozen body of his guide lying on the ground; alone, the guide had succumbed to cold and wind. Love of self is the basic law of our fallen nature. The guide had succumbed to this law, but the Christian had broken that law by sacrificing his own comforts, to save someone else. In the process, he also saved himself. Jesus Christ could defy the law of nature and hence he could walk on the sea (Mk 6:48), which we cannot do. But Jesus expects us to defy some harmful laws of human nature such as selfishness. St John pleads: " Beloved, if God so loved us, we also ought to love one another" (1 Jn 4:11). It is easy and very human to care for a person, if that suits our own plans, or if it is convenient, or if the person in question is a relative. But if we love others as God loves us, we would be caring for anyone who is in need, as if that person is of our own family.

THURSDAY AFTER EPIPHANY / CHRISTMAS

THAT POOR FACE!

Readings: 1 Jn 4:19-5:4; Lk 4:14-22

If we do not love our neighbours, we do not love God. "He who does not love his brother whom he has seen can not love God whom he has not seen" (1 Jn 4:20). Who is the brother or sister John is talking about? They are the people whose drawn faces and restless, tearful eyes are caused by destitution, a dilapidated bed, foul air, hunger, sicknesses. They are the ones who are driven into the crucible of human suffering, by humiliating work conditions, unemployment, depression and war. Their miseries are often caused by other peoples' selfishness, conceit, cowardice, greed, and lust. The face of any person suffering from inhumanity of others, must haunt every Christian's conscience, for we are all partly to blame for the miseries of others. In order to drive home the point that our love of God must be translated into loving actions to alleviate sufferings of others, Jesus inaugurated his public ministry by proclaiming that he had been sent by his Father, "to preach the good news to the poor, to proclaim release to the captives, sight to the blind and to set at liberty those who are oppressed" (Lk 4:18). May the merciful Christ turn his divine light on us, so that, in his light, we can recognise in the afflicted, the faces we have cut, the mouths we have twisted, the eyes we have darkened, and the light we have extinguished, the effects of our own selfish indifference. May we always remember that selfishness is that detestable vice, the vice that one cannot forgive in others, and yet no one is entirely without it.

FRIDAY AFTER EPIPHANY / CHRISTMAS

WE CAN OVERCOME!

Readings: 1 Jn 5-13; Lk 5:12-16

God cannot create evil and so he is not responsible for disease, pain, and death. They are simply the natural result of human beings' disobedience to God. Pain and disease are the outward and visible fruits of the hidden and unseen disease of evil in human nature. Can we overcome the world of evil? Yes we can, by faith in Jesus Christ. St John asks, "Who is it that overcomes the world but he who believes that Jesus is the Son of God" (1 Jn 5:51)? To believe in Jesus Christ is to possess him, and to posses him is to possess "eternal life God has given him" (v. 12). And hence, to possess Christ's life is to overcome death, and to overcome death is to overcome the world of evil. Leprosy is one kind of evil. But the leper was cured of his disease when he believed in Jesus, saying, "Lord, if you will, you can make me clean" (Lk 5:13). But if we want our faith in Jesus to be powerful enough to overcome evil, it has to be practical. We have to give flesh and blood to the teachings of Jesus in our personal life. There are number of words in the Scriptures that hint just how practical our faith in Jesus must be. One word is "race". Christian life is compared to a race. This is an excellent image for it communicates both the exhilaration of running, and the realism of struggle. Another word is "builder". This indicates that our faith in Jesus has to urge us to be partners with God in building a kingdom on earth, as envisaged by Jesus Christ, a kingdom founded on truth, justice and love.

SATURDAY AFTER EPIPHANY / CHRISTMAS

THE REVEALER OF GOD

Readings: 1 Jn 5:14-22; Jn 3:22-30

Mortal eyes can see only those things that are mortal. For instance, you cannot see your own spirit; therefore, how can you behold its Creator?

When the spiritual eyes are opened, then surely you can see the one who is Spirit, and all spiritual realities as well. Who can open our spiritual eyes to see God? It is Jesus Christ. "We know that the Son of God has come and has given us understanding to know him who is true" (1 Jn 5:20). St John the Baptist confirmed that Jesus Christ was sent by God to reveal him as he is, when he said to his own disciples who complained about the baptism by Jesus, "No one can receive anything except what is given him from heaven" (Jn 3:27). It is Jesus who gives us not only the spiritual eyes to see God, but also a heart to experience God's presence. Take a piece of charcoal: however much you may wash it, its blackness will not disappear; but let the fire enter into it and its dark colour vanishes. So also, when we receive the fire of the Spirit of Christ, all the blackness of evil is driven away from our heart and thus we are able to experience God's presence. How fortunate are we who have been baptised by the fire of Christ to be able to recognise and experience the true living God! This gift of awareness of God is not to be hoarded and kept to ourselves. We are to share this gift with others. If people refuse to listen to us, we can still pray for them to the Father.

Lent

ASH WEDNESDAY / LENT

A JOYFUL RETURN

Readings: Joel 2:12-18; 2 Cor 5:20-6:2; Mt 6:1-6,16-18

Our desire for pure and perpetual joy is one thing, and the actual reality is another. It seldom happens to us that any joy comes so pure as not to be tempered by sorrow. Besides, when pure joy does come, it is very brief, for life batters at its sails. For many of us, life itself is an embodiment of contradictions: love and hatred, strength and weakness, humiliation and glory, truth and falsehood, direction and chaos, life and death. All these are weighing so heavily on us. Each of us, in some part of life, finds something upsetting that robs us of our joy. However, we believe that, God being the source of perfect joy, the more consistent we are in our closeness with God, the more permanent will be our joy. So Lent invites us to return to God and be reconciled with him in such a way that our relationship with him will remain intimate and lasting. God appeals to us during this Lent through Joel: "Return to me with all your heart" (Joel 2:12). St Paul reminds us that Lent is the "acceptable time… the day of salvation" (2 Cor 6:2). The ashes we use on Ash Wednesday remind us that if we have to rise to new life of pure joy, we have to acknowledge that our relationship with God has not been close enough, and hence the need to return to him with a broken heart. The good deeds such as prayer, fasting and almsgiving that our Lord mentions in the Gospel (Mt 6:1-18) are meant to make us pleasing to God; but they must be undertaken for the right reason. For example, what we save by fasting is to be offered to the hungry as almsgiving. These are Lenten opportunities. Just as the spring brings a cheer to the heart of those who look forward to a time of flowering and growth, so we are invited to approach the season of Lent with a hope of renewal and focus on the opportunities for deepening our relationship with God and thus set our feet firmly on the path to fuller joy.

CROSSES ARE WINGS

Readings: Deut 30:15-28; Lk 9:22-25

Turning our hearts to God is the first step on our journey to full life. But turning alone is not enough. We must choose God, preferring him to all other things, such as wealth, power, position, and the rest. Choosing is willing. Our will is ever free. It is like an engine in a car: it can't steer, but needs someone to direct it, to make it choose God. So, God urges us: "This day, I have set before you life and death... choose life, that you and your descendants may live" (Deut 30:19). When we choose God we choose life, the life God himself lives. Many people try all sorts of things but they are not satisfied. They chase after this or that, but remain unsatisfied. Why? Because they cannot be fully satisfied with things that change. What they really need is to possess God who alone is unchangeable, and therefore can satisfy our heart's yearnings. We ought to note, however, our efforts to return to God and choose him above all else will bring us face to face with difficulties, trials and sacrifices. But Jesus counsels, "If any man would come after me, let him deny himself and take up his cross daily and follow me" (Lk 9:23). Jesus is wise in his counsel because, difficulties and renunciations are necessary and beneficial to us; without them, progress towards God is impossible. In any case, no one in the world is exempt from their daily cross. In the words of Aristotle, "He who suffers no trial is either God or a beast." Our crosses are the means to countless blessings. Just as birds carry wings, yet the wings carry the bird, so the cross lifts up those who carry their cross and brings them safely to their destiny.

WHY FASTING?

Readings: Is 58:1-9; Mt 9:14-15

St Augustine wrote about fasting and mortification: "Don't believe that fasting suffices. Fasting punishes you, but it does not restore your brother!

Your fasting will be fruitful if you provide for the needs of another. How many poor people could be nourished by the meal you did not take today?" He was echoing the words of Isaiah who spoke in the name of God: "Is not this the fast that I choose... to share your bread with the hungry and bring the homeless poor into your house?" (Is 58:6-7). Our Lenten fasts should not become mere rituals. While our self-denial does some good to others, it must also help us to progress in our own spiritual life. Gandhi said, "A genuine fast cleanses body, mind and soul. It crucifies the flesh and to that extent sets the soul free." If fasting and prayer seem, at times, not to do us any spiritual good, it is not because they are pointless, but because the right spirit is not behind them. When Jesus said to John's disciples that his own disciples need not fast as long as he is with them, he was only emphasising the fact that where the Son of God is truly present, there is bound to be spiritual joy. He was not, therefore, denying the value of fasting and self-denial. That is why he added, "When the bridegroom is taken away from them, then they will fast" (Mt 9:15). As we know, Jesus demanded self-denial from his followers (Lk 9:23), and fasting is one form of self-denial by which one surrenders oneself to God. A complete fast is a complete and literal denial of self, but abstention from food and even water is the mere beginning, the least part of the self-surrender.

SATURDAY AFTER ASH WEDNESDAY / LENT

ALL-INCLUSIVE FELLOWSHIP

Readings: Is 58:9-14; Lk 5:27-32

We are human creatures in need of God. The pity is that we try to dress our need up in fancy clothing, and designate categories and rules, so as to camouflage our true needy reality. And yet God knows our needs, and seeks us out to help. He has promised that when we are in the dark, he can set "his light to rise in the darkness". He has promised that when we are lost as to our direction in life, he shall be like a watered garden, like a spring of water" (Is 58:11). But the Lord's help is tied up with our integrity in human relationships. That is why he told his people: no more oppression, physical or moral, of one's fellow people; but, sharing with those in need (v. 9). A caring love of this kind is the true way to be assured of God's light, his guidance and consolations. Jesus points out a particular area in our human relationships, very pertinent for us today. He does this, however, not by words but by action: he eats "with tax collectors and others" (Lk 5:29). Through this action he wanted to remind us that we need to develop a loving human fellowship which is all-inclusive, discriminating against none. And so we may ask ourselves: who are the kind of people whom we shun, or whom we hate or against whom we discriminate in our dealings with others? Do we use race or class or gender or colour of the skin to exclude people subtly from our company and fellowship? Let us not forget that happiness depends, not on what we can get, but what we can give. The question is: Do we give to strangers?

MONDAY – WEEK 1 / LENT

"I CAME TO YOUR HOUSE"

Readings: Lev 19:1-2,11-18; Mt 25:31-46

One day a pious old lady had a dream. In that dream, Jesus told her that he would visit her the next day. She cleaned the room, made it nice, put on the best dress, prepared a nice dinner and waited. Early in the morning somebody knocked at the door. Thinking it was Jesus, she hurried and opened the door. She saw an old man begging for some clothes; he was freezing. She politely said, "Do not disturb me today; I am waiting for Jesus." About noon, someone else came. To her disappointment, it was a poor man begging for some food. She also drove him away, saying she was waiting for Jesus. She waited and waited. Evening came and another knocked on the door. She hesitated but opened it. There stood a miserable man full of sores. She got angry with him and cried: "Don't dirty my house. Go away. I am waiting for Jesus." She waited all night for Jesus. But he did not come and so she went to sleep. Then she heard the voice of Jesus: " I came three times to your house but you did not receive me." And then she remembered, "As you did it not to one of the least of these, you did it not to me" (Mt. 25:45). God instructed his people through Moses, "You shall love your neighbour as yourself"(Lev 19:18).

But Jesus specified who our neighbour is: those who are in need. Just as a beautiful flower of varied hues gives out a sweet fragrance, just so is one who is full of charity and practices it. Our love and charity must be extended even to those who have hurt us. The tree does not ever withdraw its shade from the person who approaches it to cut it down. True charity never seeks a return; what return can we make to the cloud that lets its rain fall on us?

TUESDAY – WEEK 1 / LENT

OUR FATHER

Readings: Is 55:10-11; Mt 6:7-15

A poor self-image and poor God-image! These are the two major blocks which prevent many people from relating to God. Even those who think of God as their Father, keep him at arm's length because of some subconscious fear of him; and because they keep him at a distance, they never really experience his fatherly tenderness, compassion and mercy, revealed in the prayer taught by Jesus. He asked us to address God as "Our Father who art in heaven" (Mt 6:9), and present to him our needs; he only wanted us to begin the prayer with his own concerns: his name, his kingdom, his will, so that our prayer of petition does not become too self-centred. The "Our Father" is Jesus' prayer and so it is God's. Isaiah says about the Word of God: "As the rain and snow come down from heaven and return not thither but water the earth" (Is 55:10), so God's Word will not return to him unfulfilled. This means when we say the "Our Father", we are wielding a mighty power. We are assured that God will grant us our basic needs, he will forgive our sins as we forgive those of others and he will not test us beyond our ability to bear. In order that the "Our Father" may be really effective we, for our part, must trust that God is truly our Father. It is true that we are the adopted children of God. But this adoption is not a legal arrangement. Good foster parents can forge a relationship with their adopted children which is very similar to that enjoyed by natural partents; but they can never become their parents. With God and ourselves, it is different. We are truly his children.

SHUN PRIDE

Readings: Jon 3:1-10; Lk 11:29-32

Have your ever seen the so-called "blood rain"?: rain which is tinted a reddish colour, leaving a red stain on the ground. People would not be afraid of this blood-rain if they knew that the colour is due to the imprisonment in the drops of dust particles which have been carried along in the upper air from a desert, often for a long distance. So, too, if we know God deeper, we will not be afraid of his judgement, as we feel we have to return to him, leaving behind our wayward and wasted lives. One source open to us to help us know God as he truly is, is the study of Scriptures, and how God dealt with his people before the coming of Christ. The Ninevites had angered God by their disobedient lives, but when the whole people led by their king repented, after the warning of Jonah, God "repented of the evil which he had said he would do to them; and he did not do it" (Jon 3:10). The people of our Lord's time must have known from this that God is a merciful Father to those who repent, and not a dictator ready to condemn. And yet, when Jesus the Son of God, "greater than Jonah" (Lk 11:32) appealed to them to repent, and come back to God, many refused. It seems therefore that it was not their ignorance about God's fatherly tenderness, but their pride that blinded their eyes from seeing the love of God. God's love is like a bird's nest. When the green leaves decorate the trees, one cannot readily find the bird's nest; but when the winter strips the trees, anyone with half an eye can see it. Likewise, as long as we decorate our heart with the ugly leaves of pride, egoism, insolence and stubbornness, we will not be able to see God who is eagerly waiting for our return. May God strip us of our pride.

ASK, SEEK, KNOCK

Readings: Esther 4:17; Mt 7:7-12

Prayer has to be the key of the morning and the bolt of the evening. As Tagore wrote, "At sunrise, open and raise your heart like a blossoming flower and at sunset, bend your head and in silence complete the worship of the day." Both the readings of today speak of the prayer of petition. The prayer of Esther, "My Lord, hear my prayer, and have mercy upon your inheritance; turn our mourning into feasting" (Es 4:17), may have a more for didactic than historical purpose, but it is a beautiful glimpse of the conviction of the pious Jew that no matter how severe is our difficulty, in God alone is there lasting refuge. And Jesus, for his part, insists that we should "ask, seek and knock" (Lk 7:7), with firm trust in God's willingness to grant our petitions. Some ask: The Father knows all our needs. Then why pray for them? The purpose is to highlight human collaboration in the Father's plan for each of us. Our petitions are means through which co-responsibility is exercised. Our prayer influences the Father's will to the point of new act on his part. It is true that God is immutable. However, it is also true that in his relations with his children, the Father has freely decided to be receptive to our requests. The co-operation to which he invites us is not merely a facade. The Father wants our supplication to have the fullest possible efficacy. Therefore, all our perils are nothing so long as we have prayer. We could no more doubt the efficacy of prayer, than we could disbelieve in the law of gravitation.

A MATTER OF THE HEART

Readings: Ez 18:21-28; Mt 5:20-26

Lent calls us to conversion. The grace of God is more abundant and more freely available in this holy time. There is nothing like the joy which fills a person as when she or he is converted and forgiven by God. This joy is not to be identified with the thrill we get looking in the shop windows and in buying all that we can afford to buy. God's joy is deeper. But for God to forgive our wrongdoings, there are two things we need to do. The first is to own up our personal responsibility for the bad life we have been leading, without blaming others for it. The Jews of the Ezechiel's day used to quote a proverb justifying their disowning personal responsibility: "The fathers have eaten sour grapes, and the children's teeth are set on edge" (Ez 18:2). But God said through Ezechiel, "When a righteous man turns away from his righteousness and commits iniquity, he shall die for it" (Ez 18:26), thus hammering home the truth that ultimately each individual is responsible for their own actions. The second thing we need to do to obtain forgiveness from God is to do our best to set our heart right, rather than putting our external lifestyle in order. Jesus noted that killing another starts with the anger of the killer and anger is in the heart, and hence he warned that if one is "angry with his brother" (Mt 5:22), he will pay for it before God. It is a pity that some peoples' hearts are so shrunken we could say they are the spiritual equivalent of dried nuts. You can hear them rattle as they walk. Yet conversion is a matter of the heart and God forgives only repentant hearts. Forgiveness is our deepest need and highest achievement, because of the heavenly joy that leaps up in the forgiven heart.

SATURDAY – WEEK 1 / LENT

HUMAN PERFECTION

Readings: Deut 26:16-19; Mt 5:43-48

The Bible notes that after finishing his works on earth, "God saw it was good". But after creating the human being on the sixth day, God is not reported to have commented on the goodness of the human beings. Does this mean that the human person is not good? Possibly. But this is not the correct explanation. The Hebrew word translated as "good" in Genesis, is the word "toy", which is better translated as "incomplete". Therefore, we can conclude that human beings are born incomplete. But

God wants us to become complete. How? By observing his commandments which he gave us through Moses. So he insisted, "You shall be careful to do them with all your heart and with all your soul" (Deut 26:16). But Jesus went further. He revealed to us that the heavenly Father is not satisfied with making us complete beings, but he wants us to become perfect as he is. How? By imitating his divine manner of dealing with us. For example, God "makes his sun rise on the evil and on the good" (Mt 5:45). If we, then, love not only our friends and relatives but also strangers and our enemies, we are on the way to becoming perfect as God is. When Jesus said, "You, therefore must be perfect, as your heavenly Father is perfect" (v.48), he was not calling us to become little gods. It is not possible. God is perfect because he is not susceptible to evil; evil never has any appeal to him. But we are different. However, Jesus has asked us to keep God's perfection as our ideal. Those who aim at perfection and persevere, will come much closer to it than those who consider it unattainable.

MONDAY – WEEK 2 / LENT

WHO IS RESPONSIBLE?

Readings: Dan 9:4-10; Lk 6:36-38

Someone says, "Our world is consumed with consumerism"; another says, "Greed is the mark of the modern world"; another says, "The world is becoming increasingly materialistic"; still another says, "Violence dominates today's world more cruelly than ever before". In all these, people talk of the world as if it were somewhere up in the sky, without realising that it is people who make up the world or a nation. Daniel was different. Gripped by material tragedies, such as the destruction of Jerusalem and the temple, and the deportation of the people to Babylon, he squarely placed the blame for such woes on his own people and their disregard for the Covenant with their God. But he begged God to pardon them, saying "We have sinned, we have done wrong" (Dan 9:5). It is not too difficult to make such a confession our own, as we reflect on all the violence and crimes of our own century. Rightly we deplore wars, for the essence of war is violence. Rightly we deplore crimes, for every crime is a kind of disease. But Lent appeals to us to acknowledge our individual responsibility for the violence and crimes in our society. For example, each of us is responsible for violent crimes, in as much as we are not compassionate towards our fellows, as our heavenly Father is compassionate (Lk 6:36). In each of us there is a measure of greed and hatred, direct opposites of compassion and love. Once I saw a signboard on a Church door with these words: "There is so much good in the worst of us and so much bad in the best of us, that it is rather hard to tell which of us ought to reform the rest of us".

TUESDAY – WEEK 2 / LENT

THE WAY FORWARD

Readings: Is 1:10,16-20; Mt 23:1-12

No religion can be considered in abstraction from its soul; nothing is so fatal to religion as to darken its soul; and its soul is loving service. Nature teaches us to love self, but religion teaches us to love others, especially the needy. A people who do not care for those who suffer want, have lost the soul of their religion. Isaiah found the people of Judah in this condition. He describes a people who had failed to live out the implications of the Covenant with God, such as fair dealing and mutual assistance. And so he taught them: "Learn to do good, seek justice, correct oppression, defend the fatherless" (Is 1:17). Our Lord Jesus too describes a religion that had lost its soul. Although he appreciated the value of God's law, he repudiated those who had fallen in love with customs and conventions such as florid tassels and marks of honour, while neglecting loving service, the main point of the law. He accused them with harsh words such as these: "They bind heavy burdens, hard to bear, and lay them on men's shoulders, but they themselves will not move them with their finger" (Mt 23:4). A lamp does not burn without oil, so our religion cannot survive without loving service to others. The best religion is the most caring. If we feel we have lost the soul of our religion, God invites us like a friend: "Come, let us talk this over" (Is 1:18). It is like the welcome of a close friend when something has soured the friendship.

The Lord invites us, not so that we will wallow in our shame and regret, but because there is a way forward.

THE HUMBLE ARE WISE

Readings: Jer 18:18-20; Mt 20:17-28

Humility always walks hand in hand with adversity. That is why many people who want to be devout, do not want to be humble. Humility reveals the heavenly light, but it does so only through darkness. Humility is always grace, but grace bought with groans. Humility is not thinking meanly of oneself: it is not thinking of self at all. Humility is not a way of glory, but a road of surrender that leads to passion and death. Humility is drinking the cup handed to us by God and not knowing where that will lead us. Humility is service of others at the price of self-sacrifice. The most painful form of adversity many humble people suffer from is suffering through no fault of theirs. Jeremiah was one of these. He was telling God in prayer: "They have dug a pit for my life" (Jer 18:20). And who were 'they'? They were people to whom he was devoted and for whom he prayed in order to turn God's wrath away from them. Jesus was another example. He had done no harm to anyone. All that he had done was loving and caring. And yet, he warned his disciples on the way to Jerusalem that "They (the Pharisees) will condemn him to death" (Mt 20:18). Yet, the humility of Jeremiah and Jesus was not sheer passivity. Rather it was the proactive stance of one who knows himself to be loved by God. Jesus walks the road to passion and death because he chooses to go to Jerusalem. He drinks the cup handed him by the Father because he seeks to be true to God's call to him. The humble, like Jesus, are wise because when they accept adversity in their service to God's will or to their fellow people, they are sure they are secure in the love of God.

THURSDAY – WEEK 2 / LENT

"LIFE IS SHORT!" SO WHAT?

Readings: Jer 17:5-10; Lk 16:19-31

Some people have this for their motto: "Life is short, and so the sooner I begin to enjoy my health, the better!" It is a pity that people who seek happiness from the world's riches, don't realise that this world is like an onion. You peel off its skins in the hope of finding something inside it, but you are disappointed, since you find nothing but the last skin, for an onion is nothing but a collection of skins. The water of life, the true source of happiness cannot be found in man-made tanks or cracked cisterns. Those who seek it in such sources are like the person who lives "in the parched places of the wilderness" (Jer 17:6), ever dying of thirst. God being the only source of living water, only those who approach him will find satisfaction. The rich man in the Lord's parable had not realised this, and hence relied on riches, as it were, trying to obtain milk by milking the hoof of a cow. In his case, a worse thing had happened. He had not only distanced himself from God, but also from the poor Lazarus. With all his riches, he could not care a thing for this poor beggar. Hence the wealth on which he relied not only failed to give him happiness, but also it turned into a serpent, soft to touch but with a mortal bite. No wonder, then, when he died, he "was buried" (Lk 16:22) in torments; whereas Lazarus went to heaven. Therefore may we not rely for our happiness on the riches we accumulate, for they are like drops of water on a lotus, extremely unsteady; rather, may we rely on God. May we not forget that the rich man was condemned for eternity, not because he was rich, but because his wealth had made him indifferent to the plight of others.

GOD IS IN OUR DEFEATS

Readings: Jer 37:3-4,12-13,17-28; Mt 21:33-45,46

Life is not a straight-line pattern, moving us from success to success; rather it is often two steps forward and one step backward. Defeats are part of life's menu, and if we were wise, we would never wish to miss out on any of the courses. Defeats may serve us as well as victories. As the trunk of a great oak straining in the wind sends down deeper roots, so our defeats come to stretch out spaces in our hearts, for greater joy. We must, of course, take steps to improve the situation, when we suffer personal or professional defeats. But we must also believe that God is in our defeats. Because Joseph's brothers grew envious of him, first they planned to kill him, but later changed their minds; they sold Joseph to the Ismaelites "for twenty shekels of silver" (Gen 37:28). But what happened to Joseph? Heartlessly sold into slavery, he was providentially enabled by God to become a potentate in Egypt, and thus the saviour of the family of Jacob. Does this not show that God was in Joseph's defeat? It does. In the parable, the rebellious tenants rejected the prophets and Christ. In actual fact, like Joseph, Jesus too was betrayed for thirty pieces of silver. The enemies killed him. But then what happened to Jesus? He rose again. Thus, "the very stone which the builders rejected has become the head of the corner" (Mt 21:42). God seems to obtain his greatest victories from our apparent defeats. We believe that God who wants us to be victors, not victims, governs the world; hence we have only to do our duty wisely, and leave the rest to him.

THE TEST OF COURAGE

Readings: Mic 7:14-15,18-20; Lk 15:1-3,11-32

A man whose arm was broken on an accident came to a doctor and said, "Doctor, my arm is very painful. Take the pain away from me." The doctor told him that first of all the two broken bones must be set and knit together; then the swelling and pain would go away of themselves. In the same way, people who want peace and blessings of God, must first set right their relationship with God, broken by sin. This is called conversion, or returning to God our Father, trusting in his merciful forgiveness. Micah, calling his people to return to God, reminded them of God's incomparable mercy: "Who is a God like thee, pardoning iniquity and passing over transgression" (Mic 7:18). All of us have committed wrongs and have been living in broken relationship with God who is the source of true happiness. Some of us, like the younger son in the Lord's parable, have offended God by wasting away the world's resources God has given to all, by our greed and selfishness, leaving millions in hunger and poverty. The elder son, in his complaint to his father, manifested his pride in anger, resentment against his brother. Like him, we too at times observe all rituals, but underneath nourish anger, jealousy and resentment against others. Therefore, all of us have become victims of human sin; and Lent invites us to take moral courage and return to the Father to be reconciled with him and in him with our fellow human beings. Often the test of courage is not to die, but to live. The bravest thing in life is not to die like man, but to live like a child of God. Can we?

MONDAY – WEEK 3 / LENT

NARROW MINDS

Readings: 2 Kgs 5:1-15, Lk 4:24-30

St Thomas Aquinas warns us: "Beware of the man of one book!" He was referring to narrow-minded people. Narrow-minded people are like the narrow-necked bottles, the less they have in them, the more noise they make as their contents are poured out. The people of Israel had shown on many occasions how narrow-minded they could be. The cure of Naaman the Syrian brought him to recognise the God of Israel: "Behold, I know that there is no God in all the earth but in Israel" (2 Kgs 5:15). But this was something of an exception to the rule. Israel was not particularly interested in the conversion of the pagan world. The narrow-mindedness of Israel was seen at its clearest in Nazareth. The people were even displeased that Jesus should remind them of God's goodness to the Gentiles, and so "all in the synagogue were filled with wrath" (Lk 4:28) at the mere mention of it. What about us? As Catholics, do we think that we own God? Do we think that we own the whole truth and nothing but the truth? We must realise sooner than later that God is for all people and that his goodness is active also in people of other faiths and traditions, in very many mysterious ways. Only if we assume a broad-minded outlook, will we be able to work hand in hand with groups from other faiths, to ease the problems of humanity. We have to resist the temptation to get rid of whatever does not easily fit into our pettiness. A narrow-minded person is like an individual who knows only a corner of their living room, a place by the window, a strip of floor on which they walk up and down!

TUESDAY – WEEK 3 / LENT

SEVENTY-SEVEN TIMES

Readings: Dan 3:25,34-43; Mt 18:21-35

The custom of the world is to return good for good, but the custom of the child of God is to return good for evil. This is because we are children of a Father who does not "put us to shame but treats us in accordance with the greatness of his mercy" (Dan 3:42). What a world this would be, if God sat on a throne of justice only, and if no mercy were ever to be shown to us! In fact, every misery you and I miss is a new mercy! It is not surprising, then, that Jesus asks us to return good to those who injure us, by forgiving them "seventy-seven times" (Mt 18:22) which means "always". By forgiving such people we are not approving what they have done, but we refuse to judge them and to confine them forever in their frailty. When you forgive, it is a sign that you are strong because love always conquers in the end. By hating our enemies we only hurt ourselves. Hating people is like burning down your own house to get rid of a rat. The fire of hate compressed within our heart would soon burn fiercer and break into flames, consuming not only our own selves but also engulfing the world. Some say that the world will end in fire, others say in ice, but seeing the damage hate has done so far to races, nations and communities, we can also say that the world could end by hate. We hurt ourselves by contemplating revenge, because by doing so we keep our wounds open, which otherwise could heal.

WEDNESDAY – WEEK 3 / LENT

LOVE COMPLETES THE LAW

Readings: Deut 4:1. 5-9; Mt 5:17-19

Jesus regarded Christianity as a continuation of the religion of the Mosaic law. He could even repeat the current teachings of the rabbis that the law was eternal and that every detail in the law will endure. He agreed with Moses who told his people while giving the law: "Keep them and do them; for that will be your wisdom and your understanding in the sight of the peoples" (Deut 4:6). But what Jesus could not agree with Mosaic Judaism was the belief that mere external observance of the law assures a good relationship with God. So he spelt out his mission in these words: "Think not that I have come to abolish them but to fulfil them" (Mt 5:17). But how did he intend to complete the law? It was by showing that religion in its essence is a matter of the heart, that a man inwardly changed by the grace of God because he loves God and neighbour, becomes a law unto himself, being guided by the Spirit of God. Can we ever make black man white by pelting him with snowballs? Never. But we are trying to do a similar thing when we try to be saved by mere observance of the law. Law has a purpose: our heart is like a pool, and the law stirs the mud at the bottom of the pool, revealing how foul the waters are and compeling us to acknowledge the evil within. But it is not the observance of the law that can remove the evil. Only God's grace can do the cleansing. Those who observe the law from the motive of love are recipients of God's grace, and nothing can be done right without grace.

THURSDAY – WEEK 3 / LENT

BEING ON GUARD

Readings: Jer 7: 23-28; Lk 11:14-23

"Of all created things", wrote C.S. Lewis, "the most wicked is one who originally stood in the immediate presence of God: Satan." Many people say that believing in Satan is naïve and childish, but it is not. The Bible teaches that we are opposed by a living, intelligent, deceptive and cunning one, who can outlive the oldest Christian, outwork the busiest, outfight the strongest and outwit the wisest. The usual name by which Scripture calls Satan is "liar", for he can make human beings dance upon the brink of hell, as though they were on the verge of heaven. When Jesus warned: "He who is not with me is against me" (Lk 11:23), he implied that such a person is on the side of Satan. Once Satan has made inroads into the hearts of God-abiding people, he makes them self-righteous, and self-righteousness is the devil's masterpiece. Having fallen into the trap of Satan, the self-righteous refuse to listen to God, as the people of Israel did. They became so stubborn in their pride that God lamented: "I have persistently sent all my servants, the prophets, to them day after day; yet they did not listen to me" (Jer 7:5-26). I am told that in Africa there are three beasts that lie in wait for their prey: the hyena – it does not devour but attacks only the vital organs and quickly leaves after eating a few mouthfuls; the leopard – it too does not eat its prey, but desires only its blood; the lion – it completely devours its helpless victim, leaving not a single morsel behind. The lion is a perfect picture of Satan. Everyone of us must be on guard against Satan, for he is not limited to waiting outside at one door only.

FRIDAY – WEEK 3 / LENT

SERVING THE POOR

Readings: Hos 14:2-10; Mk 12:28-34

Jeanne Jugan was a loving 47-year old woman in France in 1839. One day she decided to welcome into her home an aged blind woman. Little did Jeanne realise that this act of love would inspire a worldwide community of sisters who would devote their lives to imitating what she did. Today, the "The Little Sisters of the Poor" share their home and their love with the elderly in 30 countries. Their practical everyday love has already reached a million people. The test of our love for God is the love we have for one another. "Love your neighbour as yourself" (Mk 12:31) was a commandment Jesus gave, not just to the Little Sisters of the Poor but to all his followers. When we see sisters begging at doorsteps in order to feed and clothe the needy in their care, we are ashamed of our own selfishness. When we don't love others in a practical way, we cease to love ourselves, we become our own enemy, or our own executioner, since God has created us such that our happiness depends on our making others happy. When nature decides to destroy a man in the struggle for life, it first cultivates his ego. If we are in the painful valley of selfishness, God is telling us as he said to Israel, "Return, O Israel, to the Lord your God, for you have stumbled because of your iniquity" (Hos 14:2). But it is not possible to love God unless we love our neighbour. If I really love God, my innate and persistent selfishness will have received its death blow.

SATURDAY – WEEK 3 / LENT

BEING HUMBLE

Readings: Hos 6:1-6: Lk 18:9-14

The best definition of humility is that a humble person thinks rightly of themselves; and right thinking about oneself is to acknowledge that all our gifts and talents, whether spiritual or otherwise, come from God. The more we have, the lower we ought to lie, and show it in esteeming others as high above us. The pharisee in the parable is not a model for humility, but for pride. For after boasting of his spiritual strengths, he ended up saying, "I am not like this tax collector" (Lk 18:11). We have to be very careful if we have received from God some special gifts because, when I am half an inch above the ground, I am that half-inch too high, and can backslide any time. Human nature is fickle. As God said when he grieved over Judah: "What shall I do with you Judah. Your love is like a morning cloud, like the dew that goes early away" (Hos 6:4). The pity with some Christians is that they feel proud simply because they are believers. In business, do we think it enough if we barely escape bankruptcy? No. Does a father say if his dear child who has been ill in bed for many years, that it is quite enough so long as the child is alive? No. How then can we remain satisfied and even feel proud, just because we are believers? Faith is only the first step in our climb up the hill of holiness. If you begin to slip on the side of a mountain of ice, the first slip may not be your downfall, for you can steady yourself. But when our feet begin to slide in our climb to holiness, the rate of the descent increases and the difficulty of arresting our downfall becomes greater.

MONDAY – WEEK 4 / LENT

THE SHADOW OF HIS HAND

Readings: Is 65:17-21; Jn 4:43-54

Fear of the future is a horrid thing, it prevents us from living for today. If we are sure we are in the journey of our faith, there is no need to fear, because we believe in God's promise that he is creating "new heavens and a new earth". (Is 65:17). When he said, "I create Jerusalem a rejoicing and her people a joy" (v.18), he was not referring to the city of Jerusalem alone but to the human city, the human race, as well. This means all the tomorrows of our lives have to take God into account, before they get to us. Therefore we can walk in our journey of faith with hope, as the official did in the Gospel narrative. When he appealed to Jesus to cure his son, Jesus said, "Your son will live" (Jn 4:49) and the man walked away in hope, and his son was cured when he was still on his way. Perhaps we are trapped in the shadowed chamber of sickness, the shadowed house of mourning, the shadowed life from which all life has gone. In such moments of darkness, let us believe that we are resting under the shadow of God's hand. As long as we do not lose hope in our journey of faith whatever the trials, we will realise that in God's plan for us, there is a service in the shadow that is not in the bright light. Some brand of corn never grows more rapidly than in the dark of a warm summer night. The stellar beauty is never seen at its best until the shadows of night slip over the sky. So too, let us believe that God is guiding us through the shadows of his hand. The way may be rough, but we believe that it is the right way to green pastures.

TUESDAY – WEEK 4 / LENT

THE WATER OF LIFE

Readings: Ez 47:1-10,12; Jn 5:1-16

Millions of Hindus covered with sacred ash plunge into the river Ganges in Northern India on a particular day, during the 15-week long Kumba Mela or pitcher festival, held every 12 years, in the city of Hardwar. They believe that the freezing water from the Himalayas will wash away their sins, and help them achieve freedom from the cycle of death and rebirth. What the Hindus do is the expression of the longing of every human heart, to be washed of its guilt. As Christians we long for people to recognise that the divine power not only to wash away guilt but also to make us into wholesome healthy individuals is to be found in Jesus Christ. The angel who appeared to Ezechiel pointed to a flowing river and said: "Everything will live where the river goes" (Ez 47:10). It was a prophecy about Christ, who will come to the world as God's living water. That is why the man who was invalid for 38 years, and could not manage to get into the pool of Bethesda in Jerusalem, the water of which was believed to have the power of healing, was cured without the help of that water, at the mere command of Jesus: "Rise, take up your pallet, and walk" (Jn 5:8). When we approach Christ for healing, he will give it to us; but the water we receive from him must flow, through us, to others. In Palestine, the fresh sweet water of the river Jordan is flowing all the time into the Dead Sea, but that Sea still remains dead because it is not sending out streams. So too, though the living water of Jesus is flowing into all Christian churches, some of them remain dead, because they are not giving out any water to others.

WEDNESDAY – WEEK 4 / LENT

"I WILL NEVER FORGET YOU"

Readings: Is 49:8-15; Jn 5:17-30

On many occasions, God seems to be not on time. We pray and ask for something, but nothing happens. We ask to be healed, and we remain sick. We pray for more money to pay bills, and nothing comes. We pray for deliverance from our short temper, but we are still getting angry at the least annoyance. Too often God seems to be not on time. Does God have his own time which is different from ours? Indeed he has. He demonstrated it in his dealings with Israel: "In the time of my favour, I have answered you, in a day of salvation I have helped you" (Is 49:8). How can a God who protested, "Even if a woman forgets her suckling child I will not forget you" (v.15), fail to come to our aid? The assertion of Jesus that "Whatever the Father does, that the Son does likewise" (Jn 5:19), and his death on the cross for the redemption of humankind, reveal that through his Son's death, God demonstrated his own motherly love for us all. And so, after praying to him in desperate need, we can confidently expect, that God's love will move him to come to our help, at the right time. He does not promise help for us before help is needed. He does not remove obstacles out of our way before we actually confront them. We are not to panic at the mere sight of adversity. We are not to expect God to make the way plain, miles and miles before it gets really rough. We have to get into the waters of trials and into the floods of tribulations, before we can claim his promise. And his promise to help is always there.

THURSDAY – WEEK 4 / LENT

THE UNPREDICTABLE GOD

Readings: Ex 32:7-14; Jn 5:31-47

God is unpredictable: we ask for health that we might do greater things; but he gives infirmity, that we might do better things. We ask for riches that we might be happy, but he gives poverty, that we might be wise. Why can't we predict God's ways? It is because we only know *that* God is, but not *what* God is. A man born blind knows that there is such a thing as fire, for he feels its warmth; but what it is, he does not know. We are in his situation. Therefore, concerning God, humble silence is the best form of eloquence. The Jews in the time of Moses were not humble, and hence would not stand an unpredictable God. So they made a golden calf (Ex 32:8), as a symbol of Yahweh's power, so that they could harness that power, and domesticate God by a visible image. The Jews of Jesus' time were not different. Jesus listed four witnesses – John the Baptist, the Scriptures, God himself, and the works of God he did – to testify that God had sent him (Jn 5:36). And yet they refused to believe in him, because they did not want an unpredictable God who spoke through a carpenter from Nazareth. We cannot expect God to come into our own lives in a predictable way. God can come close to the woman whose husband has suddenly left her for another woman; to a couple with a sick infant; to a man trying to kick drugs; to a teenager struggling with depression, or to a man who has lost his job. To expect God to come in the way we would like, is trying to fit God into a diagram. May we not try to *imagine* God, lest we have only an imaginary God.

FRIDAY – WEEK 4 / LENT

A CROSS-LESS CHRIST?

Readings: Wis 2:1,12-22; Jn 7:1-2,10,25-30

Take away the cross of Christ from the Scripture, and it is a dark book.
The faithful Jew described in the first reading took the risk every person
of faith takes. His virtuous life and upright speech, only provoked his
enemies to say, "Let us lie in wait for the righteous man" (Wis 2:12).
Jesus taught in the name of God about the Truth, the Way and the Life,
and for that his enemies " sought to kill him" (Jn 7:1). Thus, a cross-less
Christ would be no more than a Christ-less cross. Pope Paul VI wrote in
Evangelii Nuntiandi: "For the Church it is a question, not only of
preaching the Gospel, but also affecting and as it were upsetting, through
the power of the Gospel, humankind's criteria of judgement, determining
values, points of interest, lines of thought, sources of inspiration and
models of life, which are in contrast with the Word of God and the plan
of salvation." The Christian ministry for establishing justice and peace
in the world, is tethered to the cross. And so bishop Oscar Romero was
shot dead while celebrating the eucharist for championing the rights of
the poor. And so the Rev. Martin Luther King was assassinated, for
pleading for equal rights. In every country there are Christians who have
suffered death, the ultimate price of standing up for what is right and
just. Perhaps we have seen such people who suffer for their faith in our
own neighbourhood, and we might ourselves be among them.

SATURDAY – WEEK 4 / LENT

CHRIST DIVINE!

Readings: Wis 2:1,12-22; Jn 7:1-2,10.25-30

Despite the acid rain of modern man's scepticism, the Christian message
is still intact. This is in itself quite remarkable, when you consider that

more intellectual energy has been expended in trying to debunk Christianity than on almost anything else in this century. Some people will interpret each new discovery as a fatal blow to Christianity, whether it be evolutionary theory, quantum mechanics, the selfish gene or cloning. Yet, Christianity is still alive and vibrant. One basic reason for the indestructibility of this religion is that its founder is the Son of God, sent by God as the Saviour of the world. Many of those who listened to Jesus said, "This is the Christ" (Jn 7:40). Even the soldiers who came to arrest him were overawed by his divine presence. The timid Nicodemus, too, urged that Jesus be given a trial. Yet the pharisees and sadducees, moved by fear and hatred, were planning to kill him. As the enemies of Jeremiah said, "Let us cut him off from the land of the living" (Jer 11:19), the enemies of Jesus had decided to eliminate him and finally killed him. But then Christ still lives because, as St Ambrose said, "As the print of the seal on the wax is the express image of the seal itself, so Christ is the express image – the perfect representation – of God." That is why his religion thrives being in the centre of the world religions. The Christian message has stood the test of time despite all the venom and hatred poured upon it. On the basis of this evidence alone, we can believe that Christ is divine; we can entrust our life to him.

MONDAY – WEEK 5 / LENT

JUDGING OTHERS

Readings: Dan 13:1-9,15-17,19-30,33,62; Jn 8:1-11

In our dealings with others, sometimes we have to judge people's character, so that we can have a smooth relationship with them. But our judgement of them must have two qualities: one is fairness. We must avoid judging anyone rashly. By the rashness with which we judge others, we can literally torment them. For example, if they are devout, we accuse them of hypocrisy; if they are not, of impiety. If they are humble, we look on their humility as weakness. If they are generous, we look on it as pride. Even doubtful accusations leave a stain behind them; but what of outright accusation, as in the case of Susanna? She was falsely accused of adultery. She was saved only by God's intervention through a boy called Daniel who called her detractors "fools" (Dan 13:48) for condemning an innocent woman. Rashness often succeeds, but still more often it fails, thank God! The second quality that our judgement should have is kindness. Some pharisees brought an adulterous woman to Jesus. They were ready to stone her to death according to the law (Jn 8:5). But Jesus was kind to her. He did not condemn her, but let her go with the advice to change her life. Kindness makes the moment more pleasant for both the giver and receiver. It is the civilising touch that takes the brutish rush out of everyday living. Our kindness to each other is also a reminder of God's kindness to us. God did not have to give us his Son, but he did. The little rhyme by someone says it all: "Kindness is a little thing, dropped in the heart's deepest well — The good, the joy that it may bring, time alone can tell."

TUESDAY – WEEK 5 / LENT

THE CROSS OF CHRIST

Readings: Num 21:4-9; Jn 8:21-30

It is a terrible thing to hear a father or a mother say, "Out of my sight! You are no child of mine." Similar words were uttered by Christ to the unbelieving pharisees: "You will die in your sins, unless you believe that I am he" (Jn 8:24). His words sound like the so-called fire and brimstone sermons of days gone by, which may not be welcome today. But it is good for us to remember that it would be a terrible thing for any of us to hear from God, "Out of my sight! You are no child of mine." None of us need fear such an outright rejection by God, provided we look up to the crucified Christ in faith. When the Israelites in the desert were punished for their sins by means of deadly serpents, they were saved by looking up to the "bronze serpent" (Num 21:9) lifted up by Moses. Likewise, we can always turn to Christ and be forgiven and healed. The heart of Christ dying on the cross became like a reservoir in the midst of mountains. On Calvary, all of humanity was joined together in Christ nailed to the cross. All the tributary streams of human iniquity ran down and gathered into his heart as into a vast lake, shoreless and eternal, in order to be washed out. If I do not believe in the forgiving power of Christ's death, I ought never go to see believers die, for at the point of death they trust in nothing else except in the power of the crucified Christ. Take away the cleansing blood of Jesus from Christianity, and what is left to the guilty? Deny the vicarious death of Christ on behalf of all humanity, you have denied all that is precious in the Gospel. We cannot understand Christ until we understand his cross.

WEDNESDAY – WEEK 5 / LENT

FREEDOM

Readings: Dan 3:14-20,91-92,95; Jn 8:31-42

It is always the best policy to speak the truth unless, of course, one is an exceptionally good liar. Truth is the best because it frees a person. But every so-called truth frees us; a thing is not necessarily true because a man dies for it; we need also beware of half-truth, since it may be the wrong half. What frees us is the truth Jesus revealed. Jesus asserted, "If you continue in my word, you will know the truth, and the truth will make you free" (Jn 8:31-32). For example, he revealed that God is our Father and all human beings are God's children. Just imagine, if just this one truth were to take home in every human heart, how free the world would become! For example, the goods of creation would not be plundered by the selfish few, but would be shared among all. There would be no talk of the First, the Second and the Third world, but only of one world. Once we refuse to accept our common origin, we are trapped in a cycle of violence, crime, war and unhappiness, all of which confirm that we are not free. If we accept this truth, we will share the goods of creation with one another and be free from being harmed by one another. But the truth of Christ is demanding. Some people like Nebuchadnezzar have always bowed down before more convenient truths, before less demanding gods of their own making. In his case it was an imaginary statue that enshrined his truth and he threw into a "burning fiery furnace" (Dan 3:15) those who refused to worship his less demanding truths.

However, it does not hurt the Truth not to be believed: it only hurts you and me, if we don't believe it.

THURSDAY – WEEK 5 / LENT

DEATH-LESS LIFE

Readings: Gen 17:3-9; Jn 8:51-59

Our heart's desire can be satisfied only by God, for it is he who has created the heart and the desire in it. Because God has created us in his own likeness, each of us has something of the divine nature and hence we long for fellowship with the Divine. Like is drawn to like by the laws of being. It follows that when we are rooted in the Eternal Being, we shall be satisfied both here on earth and in the eternal life to come; and in this sense, we will never die. The amazing thing is that Christ claimed to be this Eternal Being in flesh; and all the evidence in his life, teachings, works and events after his death show that he was right. And hence his words, "If any one keeps my word, he will never see death" (Jn 8:51) must be true. If we listen to his word and keep it, we will never see death. But do we listen to the words of Christ and keep them? Abraham listened to God. He listened to the difficult commands to leave home and move to a strange land and sacrifice his only son. And God rewarded his obedience by making an "everlasting covenant" (Gen 17:7) with him, to make him the father of many nations. And Jesus came in fulfilment of this covenant. Hence we can confidently listen to Christ's words and keep them, in the hope that we will never see death, as he has promised. Therefore, may we not hesitate to obey the words of Christ. He will never lead us where his grace cannot keep us. Besides, as George Eliot put it, "How will you find good? It is not a thing of choices; it is a river which flows from the foot of the invisible throne and flows by the path of obedience."

DETRACTORS

Readings: Jer 20:10-13; Jn 10:31-42

There is a nest of hornets. If we disturb the hornets we will probably get stung terribly, and get nothing for our pains, for even their honey may not be worth a search. It is like this when we lose patience with our detractors and begin to retaliate. We easily get turned aside from the grandeur of our life's work, by pursuing our grievances against detractors, until our life gets into one little petty whirl of warfare. But there are two better ways to face our detractors. One is: legitimate defence. Jesus had said he was doing the works of his Father, but his detractors called this "blasphemy" (Jn 10:33), and were ready to stone him. Jesus only defended himself by saying, "I have shown you many good works, works from the Father; for which of these do you stone me?" (v.32). The second useful thing we can do in the face of calumny is: complain to God. Jeremiah's detractors poured abuse on him, but he went to God and complained, "O Lord, terror is on every side... you try the righteous... To you I have committed my cause" (Jer 20:10-12). God does not frown on our prayer of complaint. He will in the right time come to clear our name. Of course, nothing tests our patience more than some evil thing said about us. But this is the file that soon proves whether we are electroplate or solid gold. It is possible to be patient when we are reviled, if we keep in mind that our detractors may also at times do us a favour. Our friends tell us what they like in us, but enemies tell us what they don't like in us; thus they rub off our artificial varnish, and make us see our natural complexion.

UNIVERSAL SAVIOUR

Readings: Ez 37:21-28; Jn 11:45-56

Jesus Christ is the one sent by God as the Saviour of the whole human race. Any faith and grace that may be outside of Christianity, draw their saving power substantially from the death and resurrection of Jesus. The grace of Christ is the cause and the substance of salvation for everyone, whether they are inside or outside the Church of Christ. "The religion of the Incarnation", wrote Pope Paul II, "is the religion of the world's redemption through the sacrifice of Christ, wherein lies victory over evil, our sin and death." The promise of Christ as the universal saviour coming in the line of David was already implicit in Ezechiel's prophecy: "My servant David shall be king over them; and they shall all have one shepherd" (Ez 37:24). When Caiphas said that it was good that one man should die for the whole nation, the universality of Christ as the Saviour of all was also implicit in his prophecy. According to St John he was prophesying that "Jesus should die for the nation, and not for the nation only, but to gather into one the children of God who are scattered abroad" (Jn 11:52). Saved! How sweet the word sounds to the one who sees his vessel going down but who discovers that a lifeboat is near and will rescue him from the sinking ship! But to be rescued from sin and death by Christ is greater salvation still, and hence demands a louder joy. We will sing it in life and whisper it in death and chant it throughout eternity: saved by the Lord!

MONDAY – HOLY WEEK / LENT

FIRE WITH FIRE?

Readings: Is 42:1-7; Jn 12:1-11

In many countries Christians or Catholics are a minority among people of other religious traditions. As a minority, we often experience opposition, threats and ridicules from others, when we claim our legitimate rights to profess, practise and propagate our faith. How are we to react to such opposition? Shall we fight fire with fire? Or, shall we adopt a pacifist position? Pacifism has a simple attraction. But it raises a question: is it right for me not to oppose someone who will destroy not only me, but others who may not be able to stand up for themselves? While using force can appear immoral, pacifism too can be immoral, in that I am passively collaborating in suffering that is caused to others. This is a dilemma. But this dilemma has a solution in Christ. He was violently attacked in word and deed by his enemies. However, "he will not cry or lift up his voice," but "he will not fail till he has established justice in the earth" (Is 42: 2-4). In the face of unjust violent attacks, Jesus defended his position, but with respect and courtesy. When Mary anointed his feet with costly ointment, Judas criticised her for wasting money, and in that criticism he had implicitly included his Master. But Jesus' reaction was one of gentle defence: "Let her alone... The poor you always have with you, but you do not always have me"(Jn 12:6-8). We too, when attacked for what we profess, can defend our stand and give an account of our faith, but with gentleness. Fighting fire with fire cannot be reconciled with Christianity, for which force is always not only the last resort, but a conditional resort.

TUESDAY – HOLY WEEK / LENT

IN GOD IS OUR STRENGTH

Readings: Is 49:1-6; Jn 13:21-33,36-38

While in England I have watched all manner of royal parades and processions for weddings and coronations. I have seen there much splendour and opulence. I have seen every branch of police force, royal guards, cavalry being paraded, gun salutes and planes flying past. Behind the crimson carpets and flashing jewels, I have seen a massive show of strength, military and otherwise. This is a show of triumph and victory. Jesus too was triumphant and victorious in his resurrection, but he taught us to be humble by riding on a donkey, when he entered Jerusalem as king. If we are humble, we will always be conscious of our human frailty and hence our need for strength and support from God. As the suffering servant of God, all through his passion, Jesus could repeat the prophecy: "My God has become my strength" (Is 49:5). Peter in today's Gospel reveals no such humility. He was a man who was cocksure of his own strength to follow the Lord even to death. But Jesus warned him: "The cock will not crow, till you have denied me three times" (Jn 13:38). And Peter did disown him. We should therefore be humble. Our daily temptations alone are enough to keep us humble. How subtle, how persuasive, how tender, how sensuous are temptations! When I leave my house, temptation is waiting to jump on me in my most unguarded moment. I read a newspaper, and there it is hidden in the words of a harmless story. And so we need to be watchful lest we stumble. But humility is not morbid timidity. It is to make a proper assessment of oneself. It is a joyful and childlike dependence on God.

WEDNESDAY – HOLY WEEK / LENT

NON-VIOLENCE

Readings: Is 50:4-9; Mt 26:14-25

Basic human nature is non-violent. Examine different mammals, for example, animals such as tigers or lions. They very much depend on others lives for their basic survival, and so they have long teeth and long nails. But look at peaceful animals such as deer. They are completely herbivorous and so their teeth and nails are gentle. Likewise, we human beings belong to the gentle category. Our teeth and nails are very gentle. And so we have a non-violent nature. We are expected to live and behave non-violently according to our nature. Jesus gave an example of a non-violent conduct. According to the prophecy of Isaiah, "I gave my back to the smiters" (Is 50:6), Jesus was non-violent all through his passion and crucifixion. "When it was evening, he sat at table with the twelve disciples" (Mt 26:20). He was eating with those who would soon betray him, Judas by kissing him, and others, except John, by running away when he was arrested. This is how he handled opposition, violence and betrayal. Many of his great followers imitated his non-violent approach in their struggle for freedom and justice. Martin Luther King said, "To our most bitter opponents we say: we shall match your capacity to inflict suffering by our capacity to endure suffering." Non-violence is not just accepting violence to oneself. It is something more positive. The true expression of non-violence is compassion. "Non-violence," said Gandhi, "is an active force of the highest order. It is a soul force or the power of Godhead within us. Even an infinitesimal fraction of it, when it becomes active in us, can work wonders."

THURSDAY – HOLY WEEK / LENT

"FIND THE NEEDY"

Readings: Ex 12:1-8,11-14; 1 Cor 11:23-26, Jn 13:1-15

A man told me that one of the most popular aquarium fish is the shark. He explained: if you catch a small shark and confine it, it will stay a size proportionate to the aquarium. Sharks can be six inches long yet fully matured. But if you turn them loose in the ocean, they grow into their normal length of eight feet. Likewise, if we get out of our own selfish preoccupation and reach out in loving service to others, we can develop our human and divine potential to the full. If, however, we live all for ourselves, without any care and concern for others, we will end up remaining six-inch Christians, who swim around in a little puddle. In order to instil into us the importance of loving service to others, Jesus washed the feet of his disciples and said, "If I then, your Lord and Teacher, have washed your feet, you also ought to wash one another's feet" (Jn 13:14). If we love Christ for what he has done for us on Calvary, if we have learnt to see him in others, especially the needy, it will be possible for us to love and serve them, as Christ has commanded us. As Mother Teresa said, "We have to find the needy." What she meant was that we cannot be content with some kind of abstract notion of mercy and service. We can't say, "I love humanity; it is only people I can't stand." She meant to say that it is in people, in individuals, that we will discover Christ as we serve them. Maybe, sometimes, we won't discover Christ in people we serve, behind the dirty hands, the wrinkled face, the matted hair. But those who love God and want to serve him, will serve any person who is in need. They serve when they are tired and when it is inconvenient and repulsive. There are no violins playing softly in the background when they serve others. Yet, in the name of love they are able to bear it all.

THE OUTSTRETCHED ARMS

Readings: Is 52:13-53;12; Heb 4:14-16,5:7-9; Jn 18:1-19:42

Once I saw on the pulpit of a church an outstretched arm, carved in wood, the hand of which held a cross. It is holding forth of the cross of Christ to the world – the only thing that can restore it and bring it to the fullness of life in God. "Surely he has borne our griefs and carried our sorrows… wounded for our transgressions… upon him was the chastisement that made us whole" (Is 53:4-5). By his death on the cross, he not only brought us back and sent us on a return journey to God, he also taught us that we should carry our own daily cross until we reach our final home. There is the daily cross of habit. We may have returned or resolutely turned to God from the past false or unpromising ways, because we realised that the attitudes and values we held before do not lead us to full life. Yet we may continue to be attracted by the same values and attitudes. That is a cross. There is the cross involved in serving others in need. A friend of mine confronted two teenage burglars one evening, when he saw them trying to force the kitchen window of his neighbour's house. The burglar turned and stabbed him. Then there is the cross, even persecution, we have to face when trying to live for the values of the Gospel, when we refuse to live a life that is not upright, that does not seek justice for every one especially for the poorest of the poor. Yet, in all our sufferings, justified or unjustified, let us look upon Christ dying on the cross. What brought Jesus to the cross ultimately was not the Jews and the Romans, but God's love and purpose for humanity.

WHY GOD, WHY?

No Liturgical Text Today

Why does the God of love allow me to suffer, even on a massive scale? He is supposed to be a Father. How can a Father not respond to his hurting child? Such questions can knock even the strongest believers down and reduce their faith to rubble. There are no easy answers to suffering, but some searching questions can usefully be asked while we suffer. Why do I suddenly demand relief from God for what I have brought upon myself by my sins? Am I not screaming, only because now I am faring poorly, while I remain placid when others suffer? Am I not quite satisfied with the course of the world, as long as it favours me? Why am I so enamoured of this world with its meagre luxuries? Am I not full of childish impatience when I can't wait for the day when the eternal patient God will reckon with all of world's history? Is it possible for me as a creature to comprehend God's ways and judgements? Why do I think myself so important, when I hold God's glory and God's will to be so unimportant? Am I sure that the evils I cry against are really evils when measured by the ultimate stands of God? The answers to such questions might lessen the bitterness we feel against God. For one thing, God has acted in our world to reverse the effects of man's original fall, but of course he has not done it in the way we could expect. And he has a right to choose his way, for he is our Maker. So he came down to live with us as man. He experienced the whole range of human suffering from the womb to the tomb. God is not a distant and distinterested God, who views our pains with indifference. He knows what it feels like to live for a lifetime, in a fallen world.

Easter

A FACT OF HISTORY

Readings: Acts 2:14,22-33; Mt 28:8-15

On Easter Monday, the young boys of the Hungarian villages go from house to house, and wherever young girls live, they come up to the door, recite a blessing and splash the girls with water. The girls in turn invite them in and every one feasts on Easter specialities and the girls give the boys some of their carefully painted eggs to take home. This is Easter joy. It is right and proper that we celebrate the days of Easter with joy. But the intensity of our Easter joy will be in the measure of our conviction that Jesus really rose from the dead. It is our belief that Jesus rose from the dead. We have historical evidence though not proof, to support our faith. Two of these pieces of evidence are the prophecy about the resurrection and the eye witnesses who saw the resurrection of Christ. St Peter in his address to people, placed the resurrection against the background of David's prophecy: "You will not abandon my soul, nor let your Holy One see corruption" (Acts 2:27). And citing himself as an eye witness to the risen Christ, Peter added, "This Jesus God raised up, and of that we all are witnesses" (v.32). Because of such historical evidence, the chief priests'cover-up story, that "Christ's disciples came by night and stole him away while we were asleep" (Mt 28:13), could not stand the test of time. The resurrection is a fact better attested than any event recorded in history. The resurrection of Jesus as a historical fact is so central to Christianity that the Gospels do not explain the resurrection, but the resurrection explains the Gospels.

HE IS ALIVE!

Readings: Acts 2:36-41; Jn 20:11-18

A certain queen once sitting for her portrait commanded that it be painted without shadows. "Without the shadows!" said the astonished artist. "I fear Your Majesty knows not of the law of light and beauty. There can be no good portrait without shading." Nor there can be any true Christian life without stormy trials and sorrows. In our journey of faith, at times we have to pass through a period of utter loss of direction, of utter despair, and sorrow. In such moments, we are like Mary Magdala who came to the tomb where they had buried the body of her beloved Master but found only an empty tomb, and hence stood "weeping outside" (Jn 20:11), in grief and astonishment. But the risen Jesus soon called out her name. If only we could trust in the presence of the risen Christ by our side, we will never lose hope, however grave might be the situation, however much we are afflicted at a particular time. Afflictions are often the blackfolds in which God sets the jewels of his grace so that they may better shine. Any fervent Christian can attest to the fact that our faith never looks so grand in summer weather, as it does in winter. Faith, like love, is often like a glow-worm: it shines brightly only in the dark. Our faith in the presence of the risen Christ always by our side must be strong. If not, we must repent and believe he is alive. When Peter on the day of Pentecost told the crowd "you must repent" (Acts 2:38), he was calling not only to feel sorrow for having killed Jesus, but also to accept that Jesus is alive.

EASTER WEDNESDAY / EASTER

SO, WHAT?

Readings: Acts 3:1-10; Lk 24:13-35

As the two disciples were on their way to Emmaus, downcast and disappointed, Jesus himself joined them walking; "but their eyes were kept from recognising him" (Lk 24:16). So, what? That something that prevented them from recognising Christ could be the fact that they were looking for what they wanted, not for what Christ was presenting to them. Don't we all, in meditation, in our hopes and aspirations, tell God at least subconsciously, how the Divine Self should appear to us, how the Divine Person should solve our problems, how the all-powerful God should fit into our lives? After the resurrection of Jesus, using Christ's risen power, Peter at the Temple cured a crippled man by saying, "In the name of Jesus Christ of Nazareth, walk" (Acts 3:6). So, what? So, we too, can claim on the power of the risen Christ. How? One way is Jesus' Prayer: Sit down alone and in silence. Lower your head, shut your eyes, breathe out gently and imagine yourself looking into your heart. Carry your thoughts from your head to your heart. As you breathe out, say "Lord Jesus Christ, have mercy on me." Say it moving your lips gently, or simply say it in your mind. Try to put all other thoughts aside. Be calm, be patient, and repeat the process very frequently. You will experience a great relief in your heart, as if a big stone has been lifted up, and you will enjoy an unspeakable peace within you.

EASTER THURSDAY / EASTER

THE SPLENDOUR OF THE SPRING

Readings: Acts 3:11-26; Lk 24:35-48

What glorious spectacle we witness each year as nature awakens from her winter slumber! What transformation in fields and forests, as the pall of ice and snow is blown aside by Spring's warm winds, and buds appear on trees and bushes! If our gaze could but penetrate nature's workshops and see the tremendous activity in every sector: how tiny roots are bursting with life-giving sap, ready at a moment's notice to break forth and form the thick, soft carpet of leaves and flowers, upon which Spring will make her triumphant entry into the land! However, we must not remain on the plane of nature; for us, nature is a holy symbol. It is a picture book given by God to his children in which they may see another world, the world of supernatural life within us, which can become alive, with all its splendour, because Christ is risen. The only condition is that we repent and return to God. The risen Christ said to his disciples, "repentance and forgiveness of sins should be preached in his name to all nations" (Lk 24:47). Accordingly, St Peter said to the people gathered at the Portico of Solomon, "Repent therefore, and turn again" (Acts 3:19).

But repentance alone is not enough. The sin must be forgiven by the grace of God. If I hurl a stone at a man and he dies and I repent, such repentance may prevent me from repeating the folly in the future, but the harm that has been done cannot be undone. God alone can forgive me, and give an opportunity to the dead to make up in the next life for the loss sustained by him in this life.

EASTER FRIDAY / EASTER

IT IS THE LORD!

Readings: Acts 4:1-12; Jn 21:1-4

Emerson, the great essayist and poet, once remarked, "Our chief want in life is someone who can make us do what we can." What he meant was that we, as human beings, are constructed in such a way that we need somebody or something outside of ourselves to inspire us and to fire us to live up to our potential. Christians find that somebody in the risen Christ. And so, when questioned by what power the crippled man was cured, Peter and John replied that it was "by the name of Jesus Christ of Nazareth... whom God raised from the dead" (Acts 4:10). We marvel, not that Christ himself performed miracles, but rather that he performed so few, for he is God's everything for man's total need. The highest sin and the deepest despair cannot baffle the power of Jesus. One early morning, after Jesus had risen, Peter and other disciples were at sea fishing, but could not catch any even for their breakfast, and so were downcast in spirit. But surprisingly, the risen Christ stood on the shore, and on his instruction, they cast the net again and caught 153 fishes (Jn 21:11). Like the disciples, we too, at times, seem to be "at sea", frustrated by our useless efforts, angry with our own failures. But suddenly, Jesus gives us a sign of his presence; perhaps a shock of some kind. And "the beloved disciple" in us realises that it is the Lord. May we never give up our faith in the invisible presence of the risen Christ, however dark might be our situation. Faith does not operate in the realm of the possible.

There is no glory for God in that which is humanly possible. Faith begins where man's power ends.

PROCLAIM THE GOSPEL!

Readings: Acts 4:13-21; Mk 16:9-15

The majority of Catholics, these days, are not strongly inclined towards evangelisation. One reason may be that the Catholic Church is highly institutional, sacramental and hierarchical in its structures. Another reason could be that many Catholics of our day seem never to have encountered the risen Christ. They know something about him, from the teachings of the Church, but they lack direct personal familiarity with Christ. Whatever may be the reason, we cannot forget the command the risen Lord gave to his Church: "Go into all the world and preach the Gospel to the whole creation" (Mk 16:15). When Peter and John were threatened by Sanehedrin with dire consequences if they continued to proclaim the Gospel, they retorted, "We cannot but speak of what we have seen and heard" (Acts 4:20). So, the need to proclaim the Gospel to all is indeed great. Pope John Paul II has been stressing also the need for new evangelisation, which includes evangelisation of those who are already baptised. When speaking of the dangers of political and social ideologies that point to a false salvation in purely temporal terms, he said, "What will free us from the signs of death? Experience in the world today increasingly shows that ideologies are unable to defeat the evil that keeps peoples enslaved. Christ is the only one who can free us from the evil. It makes the task that the Church is facing more urgent: to rekindle in the heart of the baptised the grace they received."

EVANGELISING SAINT

Readings: Acts 4:23-31; Jn 3:1-8

A woman had a strange dream. An angel took her to a church to worship.
The organist played, but no music came from the organ. The choir sang,
the singers' mouths opened and closed, but no sound came from their lips.
The congregation prayed, their lips moved, but no sound could be heard.
The woman said to the angel, "Why don't I hear anything?" The angel
said, "There is nothing to hear." The implication was that the Holy Spirit
was not working in any of them. We Christians, instructed by the Master
to proclaim the good news to every creature, must be first born in the
Spirit. This is what Jesus reminded Nicodemus of when he said, "Unless
one is born of water and the Spirit, he cannot enter the kingdom of God"
(Jn 3:5). The first step we have to take in our work of evangelising the
world is to make sure that we ourselves live in the Spirit. The Spirit-
filled life is not a special deluxe edition of Christianity. It is part and
parcel of the total plan of God for humanity. The Spirit is the principal
agent of evangelisation, and it is the Spirit who quickens in our world the
seeds of the kingdom of God to come. Our work of evangelisation will face
opposition and threats. And again, it is the Spirit who provides us with
courage, as it did for the early Christians, who filled with the Spirit they
"spoke the word of God with boldness" (Acts 4:31). Hence, one might as
well try to catch sunbeams with a fishhook, as to lay hold of God's strength,
unassisted by the Holy Spirit. We could not even pray were it not for the
Holy Spirit. The work of the Holy Spirit is as needful as that of Christ.

BORN FROM ABOVE

Readings: Acts 4:32-37; Jn 3:7-15

An Indian friend, a Hindu, committed his life to homeless and suffering
people even into his old age, partly because he himself had suffered a lot

due to divisions among peoples. He was living in Punjab in 1947, during its division into India and Pakistan, and witnessed the carnage as the people panicked in their attempts to rush to safe areas. Thousands of people were slaughtered and displaced. Terence Kushal turned his cottage into a refugee centre, where he never spared himself in providing physical and spiritual support to desperate people, often at great personal risk. He later worked in Nigeria during the civil war, and when he was over 80, he went back to India to work with Tibetan refugees. Terence dedicated his life to building up understanding and respect between people of different faiths and cultures, while he himself lived in a single room. The Holy Spirit who, like the wind, "blows where it wills" (Jn 3:8), was definitely moving Terence. We Christians by baptism are people already "born from above" (v.7) and claim to have the indwelling Spirit. Futhermore, we have the inspiring example of unity among early Christians: "The company of those who believed were one of heart and soul" (Acts 4:32) and were living a life in which they shared everything in common. Therefore the world expects Christians to be at the forefront in working to build up the world into a united and sharing family, a family in which the glaring gap between rich and poor will disappear and in which all will care for each other as brothers and sisters, discriminating against none on the basis of faith, culture, caste, or colour.

WEDNESDAY – WEEK 2 / EASTER

IS THERE ANYTHING PURELY SECULAR?

Readings: Acts 5:17-26; Jn 3:16-21

There is a necessary connection between faith and action. For example, I cannot obey unless I believe; I cannot believe unless I obey. Observe the Word of God in today's readings. The angel who brought the apostles out of prison instructed them: "Go and stand in the temple and speak to the people all the words of this life" (Acts 5:20). But will people receive the new life in Christ just by believing that he is the giver of new life? No. To Nicodemus Jesus said, "He who does what is true comes to the light, that it may be clearly seen that his deeds have been wrought in God" (Jn 3:21). What it means is that practice is the incarnation of faith.

This fact is well illustrated in some strands of Christian cultures. Many of the early Celtic crosses, for example, have scenes from the Bible on one side, and scenes from everyday life on the other. The early Celtic Christians prayed to God at every time of the day and even at night, and they did not separate prayer from their other activities, but prayed and sang on every occasion. Nothing was secular. The people prayed with the understanding that Christ and Mary were joining with their works: cooking, farming, and with life in general. African Christians are another example. They are people of community, poor, and yet generous in their welcome of strangers, hard working but humorous, struggling for a future. A group of Kenyans who visited Britain tried to sum up their Christian faith, and finally after much discussion, said that they are "People in pain, who still dance!" Yes. Faith and life can never be separated.

THURSDAY – WEEK 2 / EASTER

"BE MY WITNESSES"

Readings: Acts 5:27-33; Jn 3:31-36

Jesus never said, "You shall be my preachers." He said, "You shall be my witnesses". It is quite possible to be a great preacher, without being a witness for Christ. It is also possible to be a great and living witness for Christ without being a preacher. John the Baptist and the Apostles were two of the most outstanding witnesses for Christ through speech and living. Unafraid of losing his own importance as a prophet in the eyes of his disciples, John persuaded them to go and follow Christ, saying, "He who comes from above is above all" (Jn 3:31). That is a witness through both speech and life. Brought before the Sanhedrin in order to be questioned and threatened, the Apostles, unafraid of the dire consequences, said to the high priest, "We are witnesses to these things and so is the Holy Spirit" (Acts 5:32). Theirs, too, was a witness through speech and living. Some of us can be witnesses through speaking; but all of us can be witnesses through living. We do not have physical experience with Jesus as the Apostles had, but we can have even now the spiritual experience of the risen power of Jesus, through the reception of the sacraments. It would have been a great thing if Jesus had written the Gospel himself, but he did not write a single word. Nor did he ask his disciples to write about him. He did not tell them, "I am going to dictate, take down notes." Why? Because he relied on his spiritual presence in our hearts so that we can imbibe his spirit and become life witnesses for him. Therefore, all of us baptised in the power of the Spirit of Jesus and growing in his Spirit through the reception of the sacraments, can truly be witnesses for Christ, through our living.

FRIDAY – WEEK 2 / EASTER

AGELESS CHRISTIANITY

Readings: Acts 5:34-42; Jn 6:1-15

It is quite possible that some day there might evolve a world religion, but Christianity would still stand alone, because it is of divine origin. Christianity did not originate in a lie and that is why it is still thriving, in the face of persecutions and threats, both from within and without. When the sanehdrin were planning to stop the apostles preaching, by putting them to death, Gamaliel said, "Let them alone; for if this plan or this undertaking is of men, it will fail, but if it is of God, you will not be able to overthrow them" (Acts 5:38). And that is what has happened. If one would ask how Jesus Christ keeps his religion still alive and growing, the answer is simple: As he had promised, he lives in his believers through baptism and through feeding them with his own body and blood in the eucharist. The miracle of the multiplication of loaves (Jn 6:13), was partly in view of his intention to institute the holy eucharist. Once when I was walking in a forest I saw a tree covered with insects. I did not at first see that they were insects. They were sitting on the leaves and I thought they were leaves, until I looked carefully and saw that they were not leaves, but insects. In colour, shape, and everything they were just like the leaves of the tree. A man living in the forest told me that these insects were born on that tree, they eat the tree and the tree is everything to them, and so they are exactly like the leaves of the tree. We who eat the flesh and drink the blood of Christ in the eucharist, live in him and he in us, and we become like

Christ. Thus, Christ continues to live as the cornerstone of Christianity through his followers, and that is the secret of the indestructibility of Christianity.

SATURDAY – WEEK 2 / EASTER

TOGETHER, TOWARDS TOMORROW

Readings: Acts 6:1-7; Jn 6:16-21

Look at a building. Individually, each of its parts, is not of much use. But when fitted together, the whole is greater than the sum of the parts. Which part of the building would we like to get rid of: the wood, the plaster, or the glass? We need all of them. Similarly, we all need to be in the Church, playing our particular role, using our individual talents. As the early Christian community expanded, responsibilities had to be shared. And so "seven men of good repute" (Acts 6:3), were selected to take on the practical concerns of pastoral care, while the apostles dedicated themselves to prayer and preaching. Our active participation in building the kingdom of God on earth depends on the needs a particular church is experiencing. In Africa, for example, the church is vibrant with lot of vocations. But in so many African countries there is also the challenge of poverty and the prevalence of disease. In Europe and the West, though there is an overall increase in lay participation in church, there is a strong attack on religion from secularist forces. Whatever the particular need of a church might be, all its members have to join with the Church in its mission. There will be times of storms and upheavals as we journey together as a Church, but we need not be afraid, for we are convinced of the risen Christ's presence in his Church. After the disciples travelled three or four miles on the calm waters, the sea became rough. But Jesus walked on the waters assuring them: "Do not be afraid" (Jn 6:20). There is nothing to fear if we trust in Jesus. The past we need not fear, for it is forgiven. The present we need not fear, for it is provided for. The future we need not fear, for it is secured by the living power of Jesus.

MORAL MIRACLES

Readings: Acts 6:8-15; Jn 6:22-29

When the word "bridge" is heard, we immediately picture two sides that are connected. The main idea in the word is joining together. It takes a lot of time and strength to build a bridge, but only a few seconds to destroy it. It took years to build a bridge across the Danube, connecting the area where the Orthodox lived with that of the Catholics. Yet a single bomb during the war demolished it. But we should not be impressed only by a physical miracle such as a bridge across a huge river. It takes a moral miracle, too, to bridge two fighting communities and to help them to live in the peace of Christ, without mutual discrimination. It is such moral miracles that our world needs urgently today. Stephen was one of the seven deacons in the early Christian community. His job was to remove the discrimination that prevailed in the early Church against Hellenistic widows in the distribution of food. He did succeed. It was a moral miracle that he performed, besides other physical miracles. "Full of grace and power" (Acts 6:8) he worked these great signs. Jesus chiding the crowd for following him merely for perishable bread, told them to look for " the food that endures to eternal life" (Jn 6:27). That food is his peace, a peace that enables people to live together in harmony. Many people ask: if the Lord truly bequeathed to us his peace, why is there still so much hatred and violence in the world? The answer to this question is another question: what have we done with the Lord's gift of peace? Perhaps we have preferred the kind of peace that the world gives, a peace that consists in the silence of the oppressed and in the humiliation of those whose rights are trampled underfoot.

TUESDAY – WEEK 3 / EASTER

THE BREAD OF LIFE

Readings: Acts 7:51-8:1; Jn 6:30-35

Standing on the bank of a huge lake in the rainy season, I threw into the water a succession of little pieces of bread, and soon small fishes came in shoals, until there seemed to be more fish than water. They came to feed, and needed no music. Similarly, after Jesus fed with miraculous bread more than five thousand hungry people in the desert, they followed him in crowds. But Jesus told them that they should not seek after the bread that will not have lasting use, but seek after the true bread from heaven, and added "I am the bread of life" (Jn 6:35). What he meant was that if we take him as our food and drink, or, to give one interpretation of thse words, if we adopt his life-style as our own, we will imbibe his Spirit. The result will be that not only we will change for the better, but also we will be able to change our world into a better world. Stephen had made Christ the bread and butter of his life, and hence was full of the Spirit. That is why he was able to forgive his executioners (Acts 7:60). Like him, if we were to make Christ our bread of life, we could bring love and forgiveness into this world where there is so much hatred. Once I came across a very dirty village. There was such a bad smell that it nearly made me vomit. After a few days, I passed the same village again and saw a wonderful change. There was dirt as before, but a wonderful flower was growing in the midst of the dirt and the sweet scent of that flower overcame the bad smell of the dirt. Christians who have made Jesus Christ the bread of their lives, are like flowers in a world where there is so much selfishness, greed and indifference.

WEDNESDAY – WEEK 3 / EASTER

IS IT FAIR?

Readings: Acts 8:1-8; Jn 6:35-40

According to the statistics published in 1994 by Walter B. Night, approximately 9 percent of the world's population is English-speaking;

91 percent, non-English speaking. Yet, 90 percent of the world's Christians are to be found among the 9 percent who are English speaking and only 10 percent among the non-English speaking. Fully 94 percent of the ordained preachers minister to the 9 percent, and only 6 percent to the 91 percent. Is it fair? Is it fair to Jesus who claims that it is Father's will that "everyone who sees the Son and believes in him should have eternal life" (Jn 6:40)? Is it fair to the Christians who believe that Christ is the "Bread of Life" (v.35)? Is it fair to the millions who are still in the dark concerning Jesus Christ? Is it fair to our Christian ancestors who have left us an inspiring example of missionary zeal: "Those who were scattered went about preaching the word" (Acts 8:4). The following is the inspiring record of a modern Christian family: "John Scudder and his wife were missionaries to Ceylon and India. Of their ten children, who grew to adult life, one died while preparing for the Christian ministry and nine became foreign missionaries, five being medical missionaries. In 1919, the year marking the centenary of Scudder's influence in India, three great-grandchildren sailed for that land. Thirty-one descendants have worked in India, while seven others are missionaries elsewhere." There is no need for everyone to go to foreign lands to witness. Lay apostles can witness to Christ where they are: at home, a coffee house, in the market place, at the road side, in a plane or a train.

THURSDAY – WEEK 3 / EASTER

DIVINE PULL

Readings: Acts 8:26-40; Jn 6:44-51

God's creative presence is everywhere in nature. Early in the morning there is silence in my room. I switch on the radio and I hear beautiful music. How? The room is always filled with the waves that carry the radio and television signals. Since God's creative energy is everywhere, pressing the buttons on the radio brings these frequencies to life. On a higher level, there is also the supernatural power of God influencing all creation, especially human beings. It is drawing all people to the fullness of truth in Jesus Christ. Jesus rightly claims, "No one can come to me unless the Father draws him" (Jn 6:44). A liar may tell lies himself, but he does not like other people to tell him lies. Why? The reason is that God the Father, by his mysterious presence in human hearts, is drawing all to the full truth in his Son Jesus Christ. But we need to remember that God only draws, the actual coming to Christ has to be the work of the individual. We are not like bees. Bees make their hives and gather honey from flowers by instinct. But human beings have to seek after truth consciously. One means available to us which enables us to come to full truth, is the Holy Scripture. An Ethiopian was reading the Scriptures as he was on his way to Jerusalem as a pilgrim (Acts 8:28). But alas! he needed help to understand the Word of God and Philip came to his rescue. He explained the passage and the Ethiopian accepted Christ and was baptised. Those of us who know about Christ are expected to come to the aid of those who are seeking after him. In this way, each of us can be a missionary. It is a pity that too many Christians seem to be missionaries by proxy, but not in person.

FRIDAY – WEEK 3 / EASTER

"IT IS ME!"

Readings: Acts 9:1-20; Jn 6:52-59

As all the rivers run into the sea, so all the streams of the Church's sufferings run into Christ. If the clouds are full of rain, they empty themselves on the earth. And if the Christian's heart is full of trials, it empties itself into the breast of Christ. You know why? The Church is the Body of Christ and all the baptised are members of the Body. When Saul was on his way to kill Christians, he was struck down and heard Jesus say, "Saul, Saul, why do you persecute me" (Acts 9:4)? We cannot water down Christ's identification of himself with his Church. Stupendous is our privilege to be called the Body of Christ; but equally stupendous ought to be our responsibility to one another. If we truly appreciate the presence of Christ in every member, we all will do our part to make the Church into a community that cares, that heals, that comforts, that consoles, that shares, and that knows no divisions of culture or class or colour. Because Christ lives in the baptised, the Church cannot be a static institution. The risen Christ needs men annd womenn to make him present in the flesh. It is obvious that, in spite of our baptism in Christ, we are still weak and sinful human members of Christ's body. That is why Jesus has provided us with the eucharist. Since he asserted, "My flesh is food indeed and my blood is drink indeed" (Jn 6:55), we receive the whole Christ in holy communion. This is how Jesus wanted to nourish our baptised selves in order that we may truly live and act in the Church as the members of his risen Body. By offering us his Body and Blood, Jesus offers us the most intimate communion possible both with himself and with one another.

SATURDAY – WEEK 3 / EASTER

INTOLERABLE LANGUAGE?

Readings: Acts 9:31-42; Jn 6:60-69

When we invite friends for a meal, we do much more than offer them food for their bodies. We offer friendship, fellowship, good conversation, closeness, and intimacy. When we say, "Help yourself... take some more... don't be shy... have another glass," we offer our guests not only our food and our drink, but also ourselves. A spiritual bond grows, and we become food and drink for one another. The same thing happens, but in the most complete way, when Jesus gives himself to us in the eucharist as food and drink. When we worthily receive the eucharist, we become to our neighbours their food and drink; we become their brothers and sisters. Just imagine: if you and me were to become food and drink to our neighbours through the risen power of Jesus in the eucharist, we would be performing a moral miracle. This miracle will be more stupendous in its efficacy than the healing miracle of Peter (Acts 9:34), and his miracle of raising one from the dead (v.40). Why? Because our moral miracle will sow the seed of love and service which will work in the world as an antiseptic to the hatred, selfishness, greed, division, and discrimination that are ravaging our world. It was because of the tremendous spiritual power that he was investing in the eucharist that

Jesus was insisting that in the eucharist he was truly offering his own Body and Blood as food and drink. Many who heard it said, "This is a hard saying" (Jn 6:60) and went away. But Jesus did not pacify them. He even was ready to see his close disciples desert him on this account. The reason was that the eucharist was so critical to his Church's mission in the world.

MONDAY – WEEK 4 / EASTER

GATE TO RECOVERY

Readings: Acts 11:1-18; Jn 10:1-10

The world lies before us like a land of dreams: so various, so beautiful, so new! In science, it is a miracle; in technology, it is wonderful; in its vast expanse of space and planets, it is inscrutable; and in its abundant resources for life and joy, it is magical. But all is not well with this world. It is a world of oppression and injustice. The vast majority of people of the world suffer deprivation. Economically they are exploited, socially they are discriminated against, and politically they are rendered powerless. Is there any hope for our world? There is. It lies in Christ who says, "I am the door" (Jn 10:7). He is the gate to abundant life. "I came", he asserts, "that they may have life and have it abundantly" (v.10). What he means is that those who accept him as the giver of abundant life and adopt his lifestyle, will receive power to reverse the downward trend of our chaotic world. Jesus is the gate to abundant life for all human beings, not just for Christians. When he was in Jaffa, Peter witnessed some non-Jews receiving the Holy Spirit and together with him all people glorified God saying, "To the Gentiles also God has granted repentance unto life" (Acts 11:18). In order to overcome the problems of today, we must have a life that is more abundant than our own poor nature. Therefore, the world has to take the power of Jesus Christ if it wants to succeed in overcoming the forces of darkness that are suffocating it. We may knock at a thousand gates, we may cry and pray and groan and agonise and sweat even drops of blood, but there is only one gate to full recovery and that is Jesus Christ.

CHRISTIANS

Readings: Acts 11:19-26; Jn 10:22-30

Out of all our Saviour's names, there is not one which rings with such sweet music as the blessed name: 'Christ'. I suppose the reason of this is that it has given us the name by which we are known: Christians. Followers of Christ were first called "Christians" in Antioch (Acts 11:26). Helped by the Scripture, we can describe Christians by four names. Christians are "saints", on account of their holiness. Holiness is to be the driving ambition of Christians. Holiness is their everyday business. To be holy, they have to live in this world as in a boat. A boat is useful in the water, but not when the water is in the boat. Similarly, we must live in the world but not the world in us. Christians are "believers", on account of their faith in Christ. They believe in what Jesus claimed to be: "I and the Father are one" (Jn 10:30). Therefore, to know what God is, one has to study Christ. They believe that Christ was God not because he was virgin-born, but that he was virgin-born because he was God. Christians are "disciples" on account of their knowledge of their Master. True Christians are not satisfied with knowing Christ's teachings, rather they are attached to the person of Christ. What the sun is to the day, what the moon is to the night, what the dew is to the flower, such is Christ to the Christians. The first stage in their Christian journey may start "without Christ", but in the second stage they are "in Christ", and in the third stage "with Christ". Christians are "brethren", on account of their love for one another. Imitating their Master's own love, they never ask, "How much must I do?" but "How much can I do?" That is the kind of love they have for others.

GUIDED BY THE SPIRIT

Readings: Acts 12:24-13:5; Jn 12:44-50

A sparrow was lying on its back, holding its legs towards the sky. A woman who saw it asked the sparrow, "Why are you lying like this?" The sparrow replied, "We are told that the sky is going to fall today." The woman laughed uproariously and said to the sparrow, "Do you think that your toothpick legs can hold up the sky?" "No", said the sparrow, "but I must do what I can." We all want our parish to shine as the light of Christ in the world. But that is possible only if each of its members does his or her part to make it so. Any parish has many needs, and these needs require that the parish community meet to discuss and decide upon certain actions, such as liturgy, evangelisation, social action, and the rest. But we need to remember that only the Holy Spirit can guide us to a group consensus. Saul and Barnabas were chosen to be sent to Seleucia on mission by the consensus of the group led by the Spirit (Acts 13:3). How does the Holy Spirit speak to us? The Spirit reveals to us God's will through the words of Jesus, since he said, "I have not spoken of my own authority, the Father who sent me has himself given me commandment what to say and what to speak" (Jn 12:49). The Spirit speaks to us in prayer. He speaks to us through circumstances that confirm what we have heard in prayer. He speaks to us when we converse on a subject with our fellow Christians, and reveals to us the right course of action through our past experiences. Engineers understand engineers, and brokers understand brokers, and students understand students. Why? Because they all have the same spirit. Similarly, we must live our life in the Holy Spirit, so that we can understand him when he speaks.

THURSDAY – WEEK 4 / EASTER

BREATH-TAKING GESTURE

Readings: Acts 13:13-25; Jn 13:16-20

A poor artist in France made a fine figure of clay. When he was going to sleep at night, it occurred to him that it might be spoilt by the damp and all his work go for nothing. So he covered it with his warm bedding, with the result that the poor artist froze to death, but the figure which is still in Paris, survived. When there are people in the world to give their lives for inanimate things and as many who spend all their savings on animals like pet dogs, how much more is it our duty to serve our fellow human beings, created in the image of God but who are dying for want of the basic necessities of life. Jesus, after washing the feet of his Disciples, a breath-taking gesture of service, told them to do the same to one another, reminding them, "A servant is not greater than his master" (Jn 13:16). Is my service to my neighbour of any value, when God has promised to provide for all the needs of his children? Yes. God requires human help that he may take care of his creatures. For instance, the removal of the stone from the grave of Lazarus was work human beings could do, and it was not necessary for God to put forth his power to do that. But when the people had rolled away the stone, God gave life to the dead Lazarus, a feat beyond the power and the skill of man. One invaluable service we all can do to others is to bring the knowledge of Christ to them, as Paul did to his listeners, convincing them that Jesus was the saviour of the world (Acts 13:23). Once I saw an ant going up to a small grain, but running away as soon as it touched it. I thought that perhaps it left the grain thinking it to be bitter or spoilt. But I saw it later bringing many more ants along with it. Then I realised that it had gone to give the news to its fellows and to call them. We have tasted the risen life of Jesus. How eager are we to bring others to him?

ROOM FOR ALL

Readings: Acts 13:26-33; Jn 14:1-6

John Bunyan of Pilgrim's Progress wrote: "Let death come when it will; it can do the Christian no harm, for it will be but a passage. It is a passage out of a prison into a palace; out of a sea of troubles, into a haven of rest; out of a crowd of enemies, into an innumerable company of loving and faithful friends; out of shame, reproach and contempt, into exceedingly great joy." Bunyan could write such defiant words, because he believed in the revelation of Christ about heaven, the eternal life waiting for all humans. Jesus told us about heaven sometimes in figurative language such as, "In my Father's house are many rooms" (Jn 14:2). St Paul speaking in Antioch to a mixed crowd of Jews and Gentiles said, "We bring you the good news that... God promised to the fathers" (Acts 13:32): if they believed in the risen Christ, they would inherit a place in heaven. How do we convince the non-Christian world that heaven is for them too? The best we can do it is through the presence of heaven within us. When Jesus said, "I will come again and will take you to myself" (Jn 14:3), he was referring to his presence in the believer by the power of his Spirit. If heaven is where Jesus is, then Christians can give to the world a strong witness to the existence of heaven by living their lives united to the Spirit of Christ here on earth. It is therefore necessary for us first to experience heaven here and now, through our life of union with Christ. Besides, if we do not get acquainted with heaven already now, we won't be spending our earthly life as a journey to heaven.

A CHALLENGE

Readings: Acts 13:44-52; Jn 14:7-14

If I read the Bible from beginning to end, and still can't see that Christ is both wholly human and wholly divine, then I can look all over the sky at high noon on a cloudless day, and not see the sun. Jesus repeatedly asserted:

"I am in the Father and the Father in me" (Jn 14:11), and supported his claim by referring to the prophecies and to his mighty works. God becoming human in Jesus Christ is the starting point of Christianity. Here it is not simply the case of man seeking God, but of God who comes in Person to speak to man of himself and show him the path by which He may be reached. This is our faith, and it has been baptised in blood; swords have been drawn to slay its confessors; it has been sealed by the martyrs. But there is question: if we claim that we have been baptised in Christ and hence God dwells in us through the power his Spirit, how do we give witness to it in our secular life? Can the fact that we are in touch with God himself through the Spirit of Christ in us be seen by others in our lifestyle? Is our actual life such that the Lord's command, "I have set you to be a light for the Gentiles" (Acts 13:47) has come true in our life? One of the objections by non-Christians against our claim that Christianity is unique is that Christians do not manifest any extraordinary quality of life, that they have to their credit nearly all the sins of the non-Christians, and hence they have no monopoly of holiness, but they are just ordinary people making an extraordinary claim. This criticism is hard to meet because there is truth in it. What should we do, then? We are faced with a challenge!

MONDAY – WEEK 5 / EASTER

RELIGION IN ESSENCE

Readings: Acts 14:5-18; Jn 14:21-26

As the needle of the compass is attracted towards the magnetic north, so the heart of a human being responds to the attraction of God, its Creator, and turns towards him in worship. You will hardly find any human beings who do not have some kind of instinct to worship. If atheistic thinkers or scientists, filled with a materialistic outlook, do not worship God, they often worship great men or heroes or some ideal, which they have exalted into a Power. Even illiterate people are found worshipping some spirit. But the question is: why do people want to worship? Many people worship some spirit, because they fear it will bring on them some harm. There are others who worship some kind of god, if they think they have obtained from it some material favours. St Paul found such people in

Lycaonia. When people witnessed his cure of a crippled man, they shouted, "The gods have come down to us in the likeness of men" (Acts 14:11). But Jesus Christ gave a radical twist to the meaning of religious worship. For him the goal of religion is that a human being enters into union with God. And so he said, "If a man loves me, he will keep my word, and my Father will love him, and we will come to him and make our home with him" (Jn 14:23). What Jesus is saying is that the essence of true religion consists not in worshipping God out of fear or to obtain some material favours, but in doing God's will as revealed in his Son Jesus Christ, and enjoying an inner union with God, a union which will be a foretaste of heavenly bliss, where our union with God will be complete. Thus, the only religion which is of any use is that which brings us back into harmony with the divine will, and thus into the orbit of perfect fellowship with God.

TUESDAY – WEEK 5 / EASTER

PEACE OF CHRIST

Readings: Acts 14:19-28; Jn 14:27-31

Sadhu Sundar Sing, a holy man who converted to Christianity and lived from 1889 to 1929, was once travelling in Sweden where he met a man. That man himself had travelled much and Sadhu asked him what he had sought in his travels. He received this answer: "I was in search of a country where one can live in comfort and joy, a country without illness and sorrow, without heat and cold, but I have not found it." Then Sadhu told him about the peace he had found, not in a country, but in Christ. Then he said, "I travel to witness to this peace." On his way to his passion and death, Jesus said to his disciples, "Peace I leave with you; my peace I give to you; not as the world gives do I give to you" (Jn 14:27). The peace of Christ is something positive. His peace is unity born of tranquillity and harmony. With his peace, nations can be truly at peace with one another, a family can live together in harmony, and a person can be at peace with himself and with his neighbours. His peace does not mean absence of hostility or persecution from others. On the contrary, his peace gives the person who suffers unjustly, inner strength, even inner joy. To such a person, troubles are outside him or her, not within them. For example, St Paul was stoned almost to death in Derbe for preaching Christ, and yet he was not broken. Instead, on his return to his place, he encouraged others saying, "Through many tribulations, we must enter the kingdom of God" (Acts 14:22). This is the kind of untroubled courage one possesses through the gift of Peace from Christ. Indeed, Jesus Christ is able to give us his Peace, even when our lives are going to pieces.

WEDNESDAY – WEEK 5 / EASTER

NEW ARRIVALS

Readings: Acts 15:1-6; Jn 15:1-8

A woman was travelling along a mountain track, carrying her child in her arms, when the child, catching sight of a pretty flower, lept vigorously out of its mother's arms and fell headlong down the mountain side, struck its head upon a rock and died on the spot. It is perfectly clear that a child finds safety and sustenance in its mother's arms. Using a similar allegory, Jesus has told us, " I am the vine, you are the branches. He who abides in me, and I in him, he it is that bears much fruit" (Jn 15:5). This means that the success of our individual and communal efforts to advance the reign of God on earth depend on our being united to Christ, the source of life. Take for example, our parish life. Some newly baptised, but belonging to a different culture with different customs and habits from ours, come to join the parish community. What is our reaction going to be? Rejection? In this reaction, differences are not tolerated. Swallowing up? In this reaction, differences are accepted, provided they can be absorbed by the dominant group. Toleration? In this reaction, differences are allowed to exist as in a salad, but interaction is not encouraged. None of these reactions are fitting for a true Christian community if the members are united to Christ as vine and branches. If they are truly united to Christ, their reaction to the new arrivals would be to see them as a source of enrichment, in which differences are talked over with charity. This is what happened in the early Christian community. When the Gentile Christians joined the Jewish Christians, some demanded that the former be circumcised (Acts 15:1). But this problem was amicably solved by discussion among the leaders of the different cultural groups.

THURSDAY – WEEK 5 / EASTER

DOING THINGS TOGETHER

Readings: Acts 15:7-21; Jn 15:9-11

There are some ants called "bridge makers" who show wonderful intelligence. In order to ford a river, they link themselves together into a continuous chain. One end of this chain allows itself to serve as a living bridge, and over that bridge the rest of the company crosses safely. Then all those who previously went over, unite their strength to those who first arrive, and pull the living bridge on to the new side of the gulf. This is a beautiful example of co-operation. As a parish community, can we cooperate like this? In order to enlist the co-operation of all, however, we have to foster a sense of equality among all members. On the arrival of Gentile Christians in the Jewish Christian community, there grew some dislike among the Jews. But St Peter reminded them: "God made no distinction between us and them" (Acts 15:9). In fact, Jesus commanded his disciples not only to treat each other as equals, but to be servants to each other and added: "If you keep my commandment, you will abide in my love... that your joy may be full" (Jn 15:10-11). One concrete sign of equality among members of a group is doing things together. We often think that service is doing things for others. That sometimes need be. But service takes on its true character when we do things with others. We find it easier to do things for others. We can then be our quick and efficient self. We can then be available or withdraw when it suits us. Such service may make us feel good, but it frequently disempowers the other person. A slow job done together is better than a fast job done alone. When service is seen as a form of companionship, there will be a special joy that is not found when doing things alone.

FRIDAY – WEEK 5 / EASTER

"WE ARE SORRY"

Readings: Acts 15:22-31; Jn 15:12-17

A parish church is a community of God's people, but being human, every community is liable to suffer from inner conflicts. Dissentions can develop within a choir if certain singers appear to be unfairly favoured. Organists and ministers can be involved in long-standing and bitter strife about the choice of music for the church. Conflicts about status can arise when enthusiastic members of church councils dispute over decision-making and leadership roles. Gossip concerning relationships between church members may provoke quarrels and enmity. How do we resolve such conflicts? By love and humility. Jesus said, "This I command you, to love one another" (Jn 15:17). If we love others, we will not make them suffer pretending ourselves to be blameles and they the sole cause of the conflict. Rather, we will humbly acknowledge the dark side in our own character and be prepared to say, "I am sorry" for our part in the conflict. When hurt feelings were prevalent among the Gentile Christians in Antioch, caused by harsh words uttered by some Jewish Christians, the Apostles sent a letter to the Gentile group, in which they stated after greeting them: "We have heard that some persons from us have troubled you with words, although we gave them no instruction" (Acts 15:23-24). In short the leaders were telling the hurt Gentiles: "You are our brothers and sisters; we love you; we are sorry if our people have disturbed you." It is no use sweeping conflicts under the church carpet. We must rather allow the conflicts to challenge us in a constructive way, and resolve the conflict with love and humility.

SATURDAY – WEEK 5 / EASTER

"I AM NO LOSER"

Readings: Acts 16:1-10; Jn 15:18-21

Man's deadly enemies are not only big animals like tigers, wolves and snakes. Small germs which can only be seen through the microscope can also be deadly, when they enter into us through food, water, or air. Similarly, we Christians have to face in this life big and small persecutors, simply because we live for Christ. Jesus warned, "If the world hates you, know that it has hated me... If they persecuted me they will persecute you" (Jn 15:18-20). When a person goes to a foreign country, the people there consider him a stranger and the dogs bark at the sight of him. As Christians we too are strangers in this world, living in the world but not of the world. So persecutions are to be expected. Persecutions are good for us, because the shock of suffering opens up within us the hidden springs of living water, just as after a shock of earthquake, springs of sweet water sometimes emerge from desert places. Persecutions are good also for the Church as a whole. Never did the Church so much prosper as when she was baptised in blood. How do we react to persecution? St Paul is a model. He suffered from the whippings, stone-throwing, imprisonment and abuse of all sorts directed at him by his enemies. Yet, he and his companion refused to give up their mission, and kept moving from place to place, to preach and to found churches (Acts 16:6). If we live for God, no persecution can shake us. When our goods are taken away, we will say, "I am no loser; I gave my goods to God long ago." When we are put in prison, we will say, "I am no loser; I gave up my freedom to God long ago." If we are threatened with death, we will say, "I am no loser; for I gave my life to God long ago."

MONDAY – WEEK 6 / EASTER

WOMEN APOSTLES

Readings: Acts 16:11-15; Jn 15:26-16:4

I once heard a lecture on the theme, "Men are from Mars, women are from Venus." The speaker was trying to explain how and why women are different from men. Whether the difference is biological or cultural is irrelevant: we know that the differences exist. But if there is one thing in the New Testament which calls us to give special credit to women, it is for their fervour in continuing the mission of Christ. Before his ascension, Jesus said to his disciples, "You also are witnesses" (Jn 15:7). And from the dawn of Christianity to this day, women have been in the forefront of witnessing to Christ. Beginning with Mary and Elizabeth who rejoiced in the birth of the Saviour, Luke in his Gospel speaks of groups of women following Jesus everywhere, meeting him on his way of the cross, and standing at the foot of the cross. They were the first ones to visit the tomb and were the ones who carried news of the resurrection to other disciples. And again in the Acts, Luke speaks of groups of women coming to help the Apostles in their missionary works. One of them was Lydia, a devout person, who after being baptised invited Paul and his companion to come and stay in her house. "And she prevailed" upon them (Acts 16:15). Even in our own time, in most churches, it is women who fill the churches on Sunday, and hundreds of congregations of sisters and thousands of women groups throughout the world are engaged in prayer and service. Suddenly, however, women are under represented in the authorised ministry of today's Church. Many churches still see the role of evangelist as exclusively male. We would like to see more women called to and affirmed in their zeal for the reign of Christ.

TUESDAY – WEEK 6 / EASTER

SECURITY

Readings: Acts 16:22-34; Jn 16:5-11

Nothing is as good as being secure; and so an English proverb says: "It is a folly to bolt the door with a boiled carrot." But where should we place our life's security? It is in our nearness to God, not in our distance from danger. And yet, on national and international levels, peoples build structures, economic, political, social, upon which they rely for their security. But at different times, these structures prove fragile. On a more personal level, each of us build our own security in fixed daily routines and procedures, hoping that we are safe with them. But when friends prove unfaithful, when job is lost, when earthquake shakes our home or when we have a brush with death, we realise how vulnerable we are. The jailer who was guarding Paul and Silas thought everything was safe, as long as the prisoners were locked up. But the miraculous release of them made him look incompetent, and so he looked for a deeper source of security and found it in the baptism of the Spirit (Acts 16:33). Jesus said to his Disciples, "If I go, I will send the Counsellor to you" (Jn 16:7). Our crises break apart whatever fragile security we may have. But the Holy Spirit promised by Jesus enters into the fissures lying within us that are caused by the crises; and with his entrance, we are transformed and we begin to see that it is in God alone that our true security lies. The net under a circus performer keeps him from falling on the ground and breaking his neck. But it also serves another purpose. Because he knows that there is a net below, he dares to perform very dangerous acrobatics boldly. What a net is to a circus performer, God is to our life performance.

WEDNESDAY – WEEK 6 / EASTER

ADAPTATION

Readings: Acts 17:15,22-18:1; Jn 16:12-15

In a dance hall when people dance, they dance to the tune that is played. That is adaptation. "Adapt or perish," wrote H.G. Wells, "now as ever, is Nature's inexorable imperative." We all have to pass on our Christian faith to others at various levels. Parents to children, teachers to students, clergy to the faithful and so on. But in teaching faith to others, we have to take people where they are and adapt to their level. St Paul did that. When he preached to the Jews of his time, he presumed that they had an understanding of God, from the revelation given to their fathers. But when he went to Athens, he started with the basics that there is but one God, "the Lord of heaven and earth" (Acts 17:24). Jesus too adapted, and that is why he was patient and slow in instructing his Disciples, so that at the end of his life he declared to them, "I have yet many things to say to you, but you can not bear them now" (Jn 16:12). So, we too have to adapt our message and method of passing our faith on to others. For example, we have to spoon-feed the children with rudiments of faith, little by little. The method has to be relevant to them. If we want to know where 5-7 year-olds are today, we need to watch TV programmes for children. It is a very hi-tech, glitzzy, multimedia pop-oriented approach, with items lasting for no more than three or four minutes. Similar methods are required when we teach the faith to children. Adaptation calls for patience. We live in a success-oriented society in which the "sales of the year" is rewarded with fine holidays and expensive banquets. But in evangelising we are called to be faithful rather than successful. It is a fool's game to try to measure our success. The Holy Spirit alone brings the increase; we only sow the seeds.

THURSDAY – WEEK 6 / EASTER

SORROW INTO JOY

Readings: Acts 18:1-8, Jn 16:16-20

"To walk out of God's will is to walk into nowhere." wrote C.S. Lewis. Equally, to walk into God's will is to walk into joy. To have the bright aspirations of a young life forever blasted, to bear a daily burden never congenial and to see no relief, to be pinched by destitution, to be fettered by some incurable physical disability, to be stripped bare of loved ones until I stand alone to meet the shocks of life, and to be able to say with Jesus in such a school of suffering, "Shall I not drink the cup which the Father has given me?" is the highest form of obedience, for it is the crowning point of faith. Such a faith deserves pure joy which the world can not give, but only God can. In fact, Jesus promised this joy to those who suffer for walking by God's will. He told his disciples: "You will be sorrowful, but your sorrow will turn into joy" (Jn 16:20). St Paul experienced sorrow and joy in his missionary endeavours. In Corinth, the Jews insulted him for preaching Christ, but in Gentile territory, to his great joy, many came forward to be baptised (Acts 18:8). A 13 year-old girl had just died of leukaemia. While going through her belongings, her parents found a poem written several months previously. A portion of it reads as follows: "O God, I am free! Valleys are green and the sun shines through the storm and tempest. Your hand came through and I grasped it. O God, you brought me life. You came through the dark; a faint spark; but it lit my soul; my fire is burning Lord; no one can put it out. My God, I am free!" Our Lord's promise that if we live by the Father's will, he will turn our sorrow into joy, will really come true. We can try it.

FRIDAY – WEEK 6 / EASTER

THORNS IN ROSES

Readings: Acts 18:9-18; Jn 16:20-23

The pearl-oyster in the sea has to endure a great deal of trouble, because anything that gets into it, such as a small fish or a grain of sand, becomes a source of irritation to it; and this irritation results in the creation of beautiful pearls. It is through pain and irritation that beautiful pearls come into being. Similarly, through pains and sufferings we grow into spiritually mature Christians. It is not God's will that we run away from sufferings. Jesus linked sufferings to our following of him. He encouraged us to accept sufferings, for they will not only be forgotten later, but will prove very worthwhile. So, after saying, "You will be sorrowful, but your sorrow will turn into joy" (Jn 16:21), he gave the example of a woman who gave birth to a child (Jn 16:21). The allusion is particularly apt because the pain of childbirth lead to a new life, and the sufferings of a Christian lead to spiritual flowering and to eternal life in the end. St Paul had his share of sufferings. When he was in Corinth preaching for 18 months, "the Jews made a united attack upon Paul and brought him before the tribunal" (Acts 18:12). However, he accepted these trials in union with Christ, and his loving submission to suffering led to glory for him, as it did for Christ. As long as we are in this world as followers of Jesus Christ, we have joys and sorrows. The bee not only gathers honey; to serve a particular purpose, it also carries a sting. It is not without reason that beautiful fragrant roses are accompanied by thorns. In the same way, it is necessary for us to go through experiences of suffering , for the fulfilment of a final and eternal purpose.

SATURDAY – WEEK 6 / EASTER

PRIVATE PRAYER

Readings: Acts 18:23-28; Jn 16:23-28

Sometimes people ask: "Since God is fully aware of our needs and knows how to supply them in the best way, why should we pray to him about them?" This question arises from an imperfect understanding of what prayer is. Prayer to God is not an act of begging. Prayer is an effort to lay hold of God himself. When we have found him and have entered into communion with him, then the whole of life with all that makes life perfect is ours, since God is the source of life. This is why, after telling his disciples, "Ask and you will receive", Jesus added, "that your joy may be full" (Jn 16:24). We cannot alter the will of God, but a person of prayer can discover the will of God with regard to themselves. To such persons, God makes himself manifest in the hidden chamber of the heart and holds converse with them, and when his gracious purposes are shown to be for their good, then the doubts and difficulties of which they complain pass away for ever. We need to be men and women of this kind of prayer, for other reasons too. This world is like a widespread ocean, in which human beings could sink. But look at marine mammals. They carry on their lives in the deepest water, because they occasionally come to the surface and take in a certain amount of air, which enables them to live in the depths. We, too, have to come out of this world for frequent private prayer, so that we can breathe in the Spirit of God. Although whales, dolpins, and seals spend their whole life in the saltwater of the sea, they do not themselves become salty, because they have life in them. So, too, if we have within us the life of God through frequent prayer, can we live in this morally defective world untainted.

MONDAY – WEEK 7 / EASTER

PEACE UNDER PRESSURE

Readings: Acts 19:1-8; Jn 16:29-33

A Christian takes his or her daily trials and reads them in a different way to that which might be expected. Trials come and say, "Your hope is dry." The Christian replies: "My hope is not dry; while I may be undergoing a trial, I have a ground for hope." Tribulation comes and says, "Your God has forsaken you." The Christian replies, " My God has not forsaken me; for the Lord has said, 'You shall have tribulation;' and I have it." Such a stance taken by Christians in the face of trials clearly speaks not only of their courage to bear any trials, but also of the peace they enjoy when they are being tried. This is because of Christ who said, "Be of good cheer, I have overcome the world" (Jn 16:33). The "world" Jesus has conquered is not, of course, the world of nature, God's creation. It is the world of sin and all the evils of sickness and death consequent upon it. And he shows his victory by imparting his Spirit, the source of inner peace, to his followers who are undergoing trials for his sake. An example of Jesus conquering the world is the visible manifestation of the Spirit who came upon some disciples in Ephesus "when Paul had laid his hands upon them" (Acts 19:6). The following poem written by an unknown Christian speaks for all true followers of Christ: "I have been through the valley of weeping, the valley of sorrow and pain; but the Lord of all comfort was with me at hand to uphold and sustain. As the earth needs the clouds and the sunshine, our souls need both sorrow and joy; so he places us often in the furnace, the dross from the gold to destroy; so we will follow wherever he leads, let the path be dreary or bright; for we have proof that our Lord can give comfort, our Lord can give songs in the night."

DEFINING ETERNAL LIFE

Readings: Acts 20:17-27; Jn 17:1-11

Sometime ago, in Kasi, North India, I saw a man lying on a bed of spikes. I went to him and asked: "What aim have you in wounding and torturing your body in this way?" He replied: "I mortify my flesh and worship God in this way; I confess that the pricks of these spikes are not so bad as the pain I get from my evil desires. My aim is to crush the desires of self that I may gain eternal life". I asked: "How long have you been doing this and how far have you succeeded in your object?" He replied, "I began eighteen months ago, but I have not yet gained my object". Then I told him what Jesus said, "This is eternal life, that they know thee the only true God, and Jesus Christ whom thou has sent" (Jn 17:3). St Paul laboured all his later life and gave his life to pass on this "gospel of the grace of God" (Acts 20:24) to others, both Jews and Gentiles. But we need to note that eternal life is not just to know God and Jesus Christ. "Knowing" in Scripture really means "becoming united" with the one whom we claim to know. Therefore, to obtain eternal life after death and peace of heart in this life which is a foretaste of the eternal life we have to know not only about Christ, but we must know Christ, that is, become united to him, personally experiencing him. Life is not measured by length but by depth. And a life in depth is possible only in union with Christ. Life is only lived wisely to the extent that it is spent in preparation for the eternal life that follows. And one who lives away from Christ, is getting farther and farther away from eternal life, for he is eternal life. Our earthly life ought to be our childhood of immortal life.

WOLVES ARE AROUND

Readings: Acts 20:28-38; Jn 17:11-19

A honeybee goes to a flower to gather honey. While engaged in this delightful task, it is sometimes stung by a spider. This sting makes it numb and the bee falls an easy prey to the spider. Likewise, a Christian community can be attacked by the Evil One while engaged in doing good and useful work. Knowing that he was about to go to his Father leaving his disciples on their own, Jesus asked his Father "to keep them from the evil one" (Jn 17:15). St Paul calls the Evil One and his army "wolves". Before he left his flock in Ephesus, he warned them: "I know that after my departure fierce wolves will come in among you, not sparing the flock" (Acts 20:29). Suppose we ask: In what ways could the Evil One invade our Christian Community of today, both on the local and universal level and cause people to drop out of churches? The intrusions of the Evil One can be of many kinds: theological errors, twisting of the Gospel truths, the deterioration of Catholic family life, the diminishing loyalty to a specific parish, impersonalism of the large parish, or suspicion and quarrelling that can destroy a community's sense of the Lord's presence in it. There is a way to guard ourselves against such attacks of the Evil One. In snowy countries, nature clothes animals and birds in white, so that they are of one colour with the surrounding environment and thus are safe from attacks. When the environment is different, the animals are clothed in a different way. Similarly, to be safe from all attacks and dangers from the Evil One, Christians must live so close to the Lord that they are like him, and thus remain protected from the intrusions of the Evil One.

THURSDAY – WEEK 7 / EASTER

TAKE COURAGE

Readings: Acts 22:30-23:6-11; Jn 17:20-26

A Christian is one in whom Christ lives. When St Paul wrote, "I live, no longer I, but Christ lives in me" and "Let this mind be in you, which was also in Christ Jesus", he was referring to the presence of Christ in us. This is what Jesus prayed for to his Father before his death saying, "that the love with which thou hast loved me may be in them, and I in them" (Jn 17:26). This is why, however harsh a situation may be for us, we can count on the support of Christ who lives in us. St Paul experienced this support. In Jerusalem he was arrested for proclaiming Jesus Christ and was put in prison. He must have been disheartened as he awaited the next turn of events. But Jesus appeared to him and said, "Take courage" (Acts 23:11), and promised him his help in Rome as in Jerusalem. At every turn in our Christian journey we can find something that will disturb us, disappoint us, dishearten us. In those moments, we must look at the temperature of our faith in Christ and see whether it is well up. This faith can change any situation. No matter how dark it is, a quick lifting of the heart to Christ who is with us can alter the situation or our attitude towards it. The measure of faith we have in the inner presence of Jesus, is the measure of our light in darkness and strength in trials. Have you been to the top of Alps? If not, try it once, if you can. You will notice the rain falling under you, but not one drop ever falls on you. Likewise, those who are in touch with the indwelling Spirit of Christ may find themselves in the midst of troubles, yet will not be shaken by them. Those who have Christ for their protection have an inner strength that is never depressed by adversity.

FRIDAY – WEEK 7 / EASTER

SHEPHERDS FOR CHRIST

Readings: Acts 25:13-21; Jn 21:15-19

In his dialogue with Peter by the Sea of Tiberias and at breakfast, Jesus deals with the most vital point. The question is not, "Simon, son of John, do you know me?" though that would not have been an unreasonable question, since Peter had said, "I do not know the man" (Mt 26:74). He might have asked, "Simon, do you know the deep mysteries of God?" But the Lord did not examine Peter with regard to his mental endowments nor on any of the many possible spiritual qualifications, but only on this one: "Simon, do you love me?" (Jn 21:15). Does this not plainly show us that the chief endowment of a pastor is to love Christ supremely? When Peter said, "Yes, Lord, you know that I love you" (v.15), you half thought that the Lord would answer, "Ah, Peter, and I love you!". In fact, he did say this in different words. Jesus in effect said, "I love you so that I trust you with that which I purchased with my heart's blood. The dearest thing I have in all the world is my flock. I make you the shepherd of my flock. I gave everything for them, even my life. Now, Simon, take care of them for me." Peter did take care of them unto his death on the cross. St Paul with equal love for his Master, took care of his flock for whom he underwent untold hardships, including two years' imprisonment in Caesarea (Acts 25:14) and martyrdom in Rome. All faithful shepherds of Christ have since been taking care of their flocks, some even dying for them in our own time. The flock also has a duty to look up to its pastor as a representative of Christ, the Good Shepherd, and pray for them, since they are as human and weak as their flocks are.

IT IS OUR TURN

Readings: Acts 28:16-20,30-31; Jn 21:20-25

Has any of us known a secret Christian? No. Because, if it had been a secret, how come you or me know it? There can be no secret Christian. If you are a husband, you will never be content until you have told your wife and family about Jesus Christ. And if you are a parent, I am sure you will be eager to make the Gospel known to your children. It is a great and holy fire that will burn and not smoulder. The story about Jesus Christ will be told until the end of time by his witnesses. St Paul, though a prisoner in Rome for two years before his execution, "welcomed all who came to him, preaching the kingdom of God and teaching about the Lord Jesus Christ" (Acts 28:30-31). John the Evangelist ends his Gospel saying that, "This is the disciple who is bearing witness to these things, and who has written these things; and we know that his testimony is true" (Jn 21:24). It is now our turn to witness to Christ in our own time, for we too live the same risen life as the first Christians did, and we live by the same Spirit of Jesus. We have kept the memoirs and letters of the Apostles as an eternal reminder of that early and fresh faith, which spread like wildfire throughout the known world. We too are carriers of that fire. It is a great privilege to bear witness to the living Christ, a privilege not given even to angels in heaven because they cannot bear witness to Christ's saving power. They have no experience of salvation because they were never sinners, but we who were once sinners, have been saved by Jesus, and therefore we have the exalted privilege of witnessing to Christ the Saviour, both in word and deed.

Solemnities, Feasts and Obligatory Memorials

JANUARY 1 * SOLEMNITY

MARY, MOTHER OF GOD

The celebration of this feast was enjoined by Pope Pius XI. The Council of Ephesus insisted that the holy fathers were right in calling the Holy Virgin Theotokos (God-Bearer). Thus the precise title, "Mother of God" goes back at least to the third or fourth century because Mary had an important role to play in the Incarnation of the Second Person of the Holy Trinity. Mary's role as the Mother of God places her in a unique position in God's redemptive plan. The tradition reaches to our day. The Second Vatican Council's Dogmatic Constitution on the Church says: "The Blessed Virgin was eternally predestined in conjunction with the incarnation of the divine Word, to be the Mother of God. By decree of divine providence, she served on earth as the loving mother of the divine Redeemer, an associate of unique nobility and the Lord's humble handmaid." The arch in the Basilica of St Mary Major decorated with mosaics, restored in modern times by Pope Pius XII, remains as a striking moment of the proclamation of Our Lady's incomparable honour as the Mother of God.

On this day, all of us are called to pray for the unity of the Christian churches. May she, who is loved and venerated with such ardent piety by the separated Christians of the East, not suffer them to wander and be unhappily led further away from the unity of the Church, and therefore from her Son.

JANUARY 2 * MEMORIAL

BASIL THE GREAT (330-379) AND GREGORY NAZIANZEN (330-390)
Bishops and Doctors

These two men born in 330AD were lifelong friends. They were both learned, with great intelligence, and powerful speakers. Both became monks in a monastery and devoted their lives to silence, reflection, study and writing. Both became bishops, positions of great responsibility in the Church. Both fought against heresies such as Arianism, which denied the divinity of Christ. Both loved and served the poor. Basil, especially, urged Christians to care for the poor, homeless and the hungry. Both suffered in their service for faith and God's people many hardships both within and without the Church. Together they give witness to the power of the spiritual life.

It is not the political force that will save the world, but spirituality. "One truth stands firm" wrote Albert Schweitzer, "All that happens in world history rests on something spiritual. If the spiritual is strong, it creates world history. If it is weak, it suffers world history." It is not science and technology that will satisfy the human spirit, but spirituality. A person has spirituality if he or she has faith in God, has experience of God within, has a rich inner life of peace. Spirituality expresses itself in meditation and communion with God, in humility and service, in responsibility and courage for life. Basil the Great and Gregory Nazianzen were exemplary spiritual men.

There are countries in the world today where the majority are Christians who have enjoyed down the ages the blessings of Christian spirituality. But they seem to be losing interest in spiritual life, being Christians only in name. At one time the ostrich could fly, but because it stopped using its wings, it became unable to fly. So, too, if we become more and more indifferent to spiritual life handed down by our forefathers we might lose it altogether.

JANUARY 17 * MEMORIAL

ANTHONY
Abbot (251-356)

One day Anthony went into the church and heard the following Gospel passage: "If you would be perfect, go, sell what you possess and give to the poor, and you will have treasure in heaven; and come, follow me" (Mt 19:21). Anthony went out immediately and gave to the villagers the possessions he had inherited from his parents, which consisted of some three hundred fertile acres of land, keeping only a little for his sister.

Then he devoted himself to the ascetic life not far from his home, living in recollection, practising self-denial and prayer.

But no saint is antisocial, and Anthony drew many people to himself for spiritual healing and guidance. At 54, he founded a sort of monastery of scattered cells. Because this open-hearted man was very attractive, many people were drawn to join him and his ascetic way of life. At 60, during Roman persecution, he fearlessly exposed himself to danger while giving moral and material support to those in prison. Not only saints like Anthony, but all of us are called to Christian asceticism: to deny ourselves, to deny our selfishness so that others may flourish. Of course, this takes the form of hard work and daily prayer.

JANUARY 21 * MEMORIAL

AGNES
Virgin and Martyr (d. 258?)

Agnes was very young (12 or 13) when she was martyred in the last half of the third century, either by beheading, burning or strangling. Many young men wanted to marry her since she was very beautiful. One of those whom she refused to marry reported her to the authorities as being a Christian. She was arrested and confined to a house of prostitution. It is said that a man who looked upon her lustfully lost his eyesight but got it back through her prayer. She was later condemned, executed and buried near Rome in a catacomb. What strikes us is her maturity of judgement in spite of her extreme youth, her firmness of decision in spite of her feminine attractiveness, her dauntless courage in spite of the cruelty of her torturers.

In the words of St Ambrose: "This is a virgin's birthday; let us follow the example of her chastity. It is a martyr's birthday; let us offer sacrifices; it is the birthday of holy Agnes: let men be filled with wonder, little ones with hope, married women with awe, and the unmarried with emulation. It seems to me that this child holy beyond her years, and courageous beyond human nature, received the name Agnes [Greek: pure], not as an earthly designation but as a revelation from God of what she was to be."

JANUARY 24 * MEMORIAL

FRANCIS DE SALES
Bishop and Doctor (1567-1622)

Francis was born in Savoy. He was destined by his father to be a lawyer, but Francis wished to enter the priesthood. His father strongly opposed his wish, but after some persuasion he finally consented. Francis was ordained and eventually became the bishop of Geneva, then a centre for the heretical Calvinists.

His great work for which he is justly famous, is the *Introduction to the Devout Life*. In this book he explains how everyone can live a holy life precisely in the place and the circumstances of his or her own life. It is a vindication of the value of the laity and of the lay vocation. Holiness is not the possession or the preserve of "religious" people. Our paths to God may differ, but it is the same journey and the same destination that is given to us all. He wrote: "It is an error, or a heresy, to say devotion is incompatible with the life of a soldier, a tradesman, a prince, or a married woman… It has happened that many have lost perfection in the desert who had preserved it in the world."

One of the great teachings to come from the Second Vatican Council was the one concerning "the universal call to holiness." Conscious of the Church's image as a male-dominated, priestly society with a subservient laity, the Council fathers put on record for the following generations to absorb the teaching that every person in the world is called by God to be holy.

JANUARY 25 * FEAST

CONVERSION OF PAUL
Apostle

Paul was born at Tarsus in Cilicia about the year 10AD, of a Jewish family of the tribe of Benjamin. He was a Roman citizen. As a young man he was educated in Jerusalem by Gamaliel who gave him a thorough grounding in the religious doctrine of the school of the Pharisees. He became a bitter persecutor of the infant Church and played some part in St Stephen's martyrdom. On that famous road to Damascus Paul met his match when he met his Lord. In response to his famous question, "Who are you, Lord?" the answer came: "I am Jesus and you are persecuting me." Paul was shaken to his foundations. He travelled a little in Arabia, and then returned to the community in Damascus to become a follower of Christ.

From then on, his only work was to preserve everyone perfect in Christ. It was with single-minded determination that he preached Christ as the one universal Saviour. This Saviour he served passionately and selflessly. He knew what work he had been given to do and he let nothing stop him doing it, be it hard work, exhaustion, suffering, poverty, danger of death. Far from letting these things weaken his love for Christ, he welcomed them, since they helped him to grow into the image of his suffering and crucified Saviour. Unless it is for Christ, he saw that all the zeal of his dynamic personality was being wasted, like the strength of a boxer swinging wildly. How devoted are we to the person of Christ and how deeply are we caught up with his Good News?

JANUARY 26 * MEMORIAL

TIMOTHY AND TITUS
Bishops

Timothy had a Greek father and a Jewish mother named Eunice. It was his grandmother, Lois, who first became Christian. Timothy was a convert of Paul around the year 47AD, and later joined him in his apostolic work. He was with Paul at the founding of the Church in Corinth. During the 15 years he worked with Paul, he became one of his most faithful and trusted friends. He was sent on difficult missions by Paul, often in the face of great disturbance in local churches which Paul had founded. Timothy was with Paul in Rome during the latter's house arrest. Later Timothy himself was in prison.

Titus has the distinction of being a close friend and disciple of Paul as well as a fellow missionary. He was Greek, apparently from Antioch. Titus is seen as a peacemaker, administrator, and a great friend. When Paul was having trouble with the community at Corinth, Titus was the bearer of Paul's severe letter and was successful in smoothing things out. We need not be like Paul; but we can be like Timothy and Titus, helpers and co-workers in the works of evangelisation.

<hr>

JANUARY 28 * MEMORIAL

<hr>

THOMAS AQUINAS
Priest and Doctor (1225-1274)

Thomas Aquinas was born at Roccasecca, Italy. When Thomas was five years old, his parents entrusted him to the care of some Benedictines. At the age of 15, he went to study at the University of Naples, where he was attracted to the life of the Dominicans and received the habit of the Order at 19. Later he continued his studies under St Albert the Great. Thomas was called "the dumb ox" since he was a quiet man. St Albert prophesied about Thomas: "This dumb ox will one day fill the world with his bellowings." From 1259 to 1268, he lectured in Italy. His written works run into many volumes. He died at the age of 49 and was canonised in 1323 and declared a doctor of the Church in 1567.

The clear, penetrating and tranquil mind of St Thomas and his deeply contemplative spirit of prayer are abundantly clear from his writings. He tried to bring about a synthesis between dogma, philosophy and all other subjects: not, either philosophy or theology, but both philosophy and theology: not, either faith or reason, but both faith and reason. St Thomas teaches us to think correctly. Correct thinking is important. Otherwise we will be piling up knowledge as we pile up stones. Simply by piling up stones, we will not have a building but merely a heap of stones.

JOHN BOSCO
Priest (1815-1888)

John Bosco experienced great poverty in his childhood, and it was a struggle for him to get an education and to follow his vocation to become a priest. That struggle left an indelible mark on his character and determined the thrust of his adult years. He would devote himself to helping poor boys in his native Turin to grow up with a firm foundation of affectionate care and a good education. For this purpose he founded two religious congregations, the Salesians and the Helpers of Mary, to care for boys and girls and to give them a good start in life.

John Bosco educated the whole person – body and soul together. He believed that Christ's love and our faith in that love should pervade everything we do – work, study, play. For John Bosco, being a Christian was a full-time effort, not a once-a-week, Mass-on-Sunday experience. It is searching and finding God and Jesus in everything we do, letting their love lead us. Yet John realised the importance of job-training and the self-worth and pride that comes with talent and ability. So he trained his students in the trade crafts, too.

G.K. Chesterton wrote: "Every education teaches a philosophy, if not by dogma then by suggestion, by implication, by atmosphere. Every part of that education has a connection with every other part. If it does not all combine to convey some general view of life, it is not education at all."

PRESENTATION OF THE LORD

At the end of the fourth century, a woman named Egeria made a pilgrimage to Jerusalem. Her journal, discovered in 1887, gives an unprecedented glimpse of liturgical life there. Among the celebrations she describes is the Epiphany (6 January), the observance of Christ's birth, and the procession in honour of his Presentation in the Temple, 40 days later: February 15. The observance spread throughout the Western Church in the fifth and sixth centuries.

When the infant Jesus was brought into the Temple in January by his parents to be presented to the Lord, he was just a face in the crowd. Thousands of people thronged in the Temple precincts every day, and regularly children were presented there. Nobody knew the child, Jesus, and nobody had the least suspicion of the good that he would do; nobody except the old man Simeon, and the prophetess Anna. They were on the lookout for such a child. They looked for the comforting of Israel, and for the salvation of the Gentiles. When a young couple came cradling a child, their hearts leapt for joy and they held the child realising that it was the light of the world.

Today there is the ceremony of the blessing of the candle and procession. The lighted candle represents Christ. The procession symbolises our journey to the heavenly Jerusalem. We must always have this light of Christ. This light will disperse the darkness of our mind. It will enlighten our mind. It will make us see things in their true reality.

FEBRUARY 5 * MEMORIAL

AGATHA
Virgin and Martyr (d. 251?)

The island of Sicily is famous for its active volcano, mount Etna and for the Mafia criminal organisation. Both are violent forces in their own right. Sicily is also famous for a young girl called Agatha who became the unfortunate victim of violence during the persecutions of Christians in the reign of the emperor Decius. This young girl suffered three trials: firstly, a Roman senator, Quintianus, a man she did not love, tried to woo her. Secondly, after she had spurned the senator's advances, she was put in the charge of a woman, who, it was hoped, would corrupt her. This too Agatha withstood. Finally, she was tortured and put to death.

The same kinds of trials come to people of our own day: exploitation of people for financial and sexual gain, corruption of people for the same purposes, and physical and mental cruelty and violence.

Sadly, these things are common currency in our world. We will probably have to cope with them in some form or other, even if only in so far as they are presented to us in the media day after day. It is a great temptation in violent times to be violent oneself, in corrupt times, to be corrupt oneself, in dishonest times to be dishonest oneself. But the Gospel urges us to persevere in being and doing good.

<hr>

FEBRUARY 6 * MEMORIAL

<hr>

PAUL MIKI AND COMPANIONS
Martyrs (d. 1597)

In 1597 Nagasaki witnessed an explosion of violence when the persecution of Christians began. Paul Miki and twenty-five companions were subject to terrible tortures and finally crucified in imitation of Christ their Lord. On the day of his death, Paul Miki addressed the onlookers: " I am both a Japanese and a Jesuit. The only reason for my being killed is that I have taught the doctrine of Christ. I thank God that it is for this reason I die."

In what he said is the powerful truth that God is the Father of us all, and Jesus is the Lord of all. The Gospel is not meant to wear only European clothes. It is for every nation and peoples and culture. It is not right to deny people traditions, or to suppress their ways. Sadly, this has not always been the case. The Gospel when truly preached embraces people as they are. Its greatest teaching is to love our enemies, and to forgive them. With such a teaching, the Gospel is surely large enough to accept people's different ways and traditions. On the 9th of August 2000 nearly thirty-thousand people gathered in Nagasaki to remember the victims of 1945 and to call for a total ban on nuclear weapons. May we join them in spirit and in the spirit of Paul Miki. May we walk in the path of universal brotherhood.

SCHOLASTICA
Virgin (480-542?)

Scholastica and her brother, St Benedict, lived in Monte Cassino, Italy, spending their lives in the love of God and in great affection for each other. When Scholastica's days in this world were ending, she arranged to meet her brother one last time, and spent a long and happy day talking with him. She must have known that her days were numbered for she pleaded with Benedict to stay overnight, and with the aid of a thunderstorm she got her wish. Three days later she died. Her body was brought to the monastery for burial, and when Benedict died he was buried beside his beloved sister.

This story of family love contrasts sharply with the bitter loss of life that occurred during the Second World War when in 1943 a great battle was fought between German forces and the Allies, in which the entire town of Cassino was destroyed together with the beautiful monastery of Benedict, which was later rebuilt. How many loving families were destroyed during the war! If we do not learn from history, we shall be doomed to repeat it. Today, everything in Cassino tells us to value life and to welcome all that lives.

CYRIL AND METHODIUS
Monks (d. 884)

Saints Cyril and Methodius were brothers, natives of Thessalonica, Greece. Cyril was the younger brother, born in 827, but entered the service of the Church first, and also died before Methodius. Cyril died in Rome after his visit to Pope Adrian II. Methodius died 16 years after his brother.

Both were missionaries in Moravia which was situated between Byzantium and Germany. To bring the words of the Gospel to the Slav people they set themselves the great task of translating the Bible into the

Slav language. To facilitate their task, they invented an alphabet to express in written form the language of the Slav people.

To this day many people have a narrow-minded suspicion of foreigners, and need no excuse to insult and attack them. People of a different country, culture and language are often the target of violence, frustration, and hatred, simply because they are different. One way to draw different people together is through their own language. When we speak in their language, strangers become friends and we will welcome them into our group, and thus we can promote worldwide friendship.

FEBRUARY 22 * FEAST

CHAIR OF PETER
Apostle

Today we celebrate the Chair of St Peter. Chair means office. We, then, celebrate Peter's office. Today we call to mind Peter's pre-eminent position in the Church. Today we praise God for having given us the Apostle Peter as the teacher and guide of our Christian faith, and for having made him the centre of unity. In the New Testament, Peter appears as the first of the Apostles. Peter was given authority to rule as a representative of the Master. The metaphor "of binding and loosing" means to exclude someone from the community and to re-admit, also to impose an obligation and to release from it, to declare something lawful or prohibit something. Christ gave him the care of the whole flock. Among the Apostles, Peter was to be the first witness to Christ's resurrection. In the Acts of the Apostles, Peter appears as the head of the young Church, conscious of his responsibility and full of the power of the Holy Spirit.

Down the ages, the Popes have been Peter's successors playing his role. The Pope is the symbol of the unity of the Church throughout the world, and it is his call and duty to be an effective principle of unity for everyone. In the history of the Church, this unity has been broken, and for many people the Pope is a stumbling block to unity. Yet Jesus gave clear instructions to his Disciples that his Church should have leaders, and that among them one should be foremost as the centre of unity for all.

POLYCARP
Bishop and Martyr (d. 156)

There are very few Fathers about whom we are so well informed as we are about St Polycarp. He was born about the year 69AD and was a disciple of St John the Apostle before becoming the Bishop of Smyrna. He had known St Ignatius of Antioch. St Irenaeus of Lyons was one of his disciples. He was burned to death in Smyrna about the year 155. He was an old man, 86 years old, when he suffered martyrdom. He welcomed with charming good humour those servants charged with execution.

Every act of violence demonstrates our lack of understanding of ourselves as God's children. It was for such ignorance that Jesus asked forgiveness for his persecutors from his cross. Whenever tensions run high, wherever feelings have been hurt, people can be tempted to do terrible things. Cruelty and killing can become addictive. And when people are caught up in a crowd or culture of violence, then this cruelty can very easily engulf us. Hence we have to stand firm in the life of the Spirit so that we don't add to the violent atmosphere in the world. "Stand fast," wrote Polycarp, "in the conduct of faith and follow the example of the Lord, as lovers of brotherhood, loving each other, united in faith."

PERPETUA AND FELICITY
Martyrs (d. 203?)

Perpetua, belonging to an upper-class family, was born in 181AD. She was a married woman aged 22, with a young son whom she was nursing at the time she was martyred. Felicity was a slave. Both Perpetua and Felicity were martyred with others in Carthage in the year 203 for their faith in Christ.

Perpetua's mother was a Christian and her father a pagan. He continually pleaded with her to deny her faith. She refused and was put in jail at 22. Perpetua wrote: "When my father in his affection for me was trying to turn me from my purpose by arguments and thus weaken my faith, I said to him: 'Do you see this vessel-waterpot or whatever it may be? Can it be called by any other name than what it is?' 'No,' he replied. 'So also I cannot call myself by any other name than what I am – a Christian.'" What kind of sacrifices are we making to be steadfast in our Christian faith?

MARCH 19 * SOLEMNITY

JOSEPH
Husband of Mary

Joseph was the husband of Mary. Since marriage is the highest degree of association and friendship, involving by its very nature a communion of goods, it follows that God, by giving Joseph to the Virgin, did not give him to her only as a companion for life, a witness of her virginity and protector of her honour; he also gave him to Mary in order that he might share, through the marriage pact, in her own sublime greatness.

Joseph was the adoptive father of Jesus. He had certainly an influence on the psychological and emotional development of the child. Joseph prepared Jesus for adult life. Among other things which Joseph naturally taught Jesus was his own trade. Education of a child is the most grave obligation and the primary right of his parents. Joseph certainly must have fulfilled this obligation and right towards the child Jesus.

If Joseph was the protector of the physical and historical Christ, he must also be the protector of the Mystical Body of Christ, for we all form one body with Christ. He is the patron of the universal church. In a special way, he is the patron of workers, of families, of the poor, of the dying, of the sick, and of interior life. So let us go to Joseph in all our needs, remembering the famous words of St Teresa of Avila: "I do not remember ever having asked anything of St Joseph that he did not grant me."

MARCH 25 * SOLEMNITY

ANNUNCIATION OF THE LORD

We often hear announcements, such as the announcement of a new President of a country, of a new Prime Minister, of a new Bishop, of a birthday, a feast day and so on. Today we celebrate the announcement of the Incarnation of Jesus Christ, the coming of God into the world in human form. It is the greatest of all announcements. The feast of the Annunciation is one of the most important and best remembered mysteries of our faith. In fact, we re-live it when we recite the "Angelus" three times a day.

The day of the Annunciation is the day of Mary's vocation. God invited her to be the mother of his beloved Son. She accepted it, saying: "Let it be done to me according to your word." (Lk 1:38) From all eternity, God had destined her not only to be the mother of Jesus, but also to be closely related to him in the creation and redemption of the world. We can say this since God's decrees of creation and redemption are joined in the decree of Incarnation. Thus Mary has an important role to play in God's plan.

Our Lady's vocation is a unique vocation. Yet it has its analogies in the life of the Church. Christian life is a vocation. Religious or priestly vocation resembles in a special way our Lady's vocation. Hence, meditating on what happened at the Annunciation, we think about our own vocation. A vocation always marks a sort of turning point on the path of our relationship with the living God. A vocation opens us to a new perspective, a new meaning and dimension. It calls for a choice and a mature decision.

APRIL 7 * MEMORIAL

JOHN BAPTIST DE LA SALLE
Priest (1651-1719)

As a young seventeenth-century Frenchman, John had everything going for him: scholarly bent, good looks, noble family background, money, refined upbringing. At the early age of 11, he received the tonsure and started preparation for the priesthood, to which he was ordained at 27. He seemed assured then of a life of dignified ease and a high position in the Church. But God had other plans for him.

He became involved in education after meeting a layman, Adrian Nyel who was opening a school for poor boys. Thereafter, John became the driving force in some revolutionary developments in education. Founding the Institute of the Brothers of the Christian Schools, he introduced classroom teaching instead of individual instruction and he also permitted the use of the vernacular instead of Latin.

The words of St Paul to Timothy are particularly apt: "What you have heard from me before many witnesses entrust to faithful men who will be able to teach others also" (2 Tim 2:2). The work of John Baptist spread all over the world effecting Christ's teaching: "Anyone who welcomes a little child in my name, welcomes me." At a time when we are becoming more and more conscious of the tragedy of children being neglected or abused, today will be a good day to beg the Lord to bless all those entrusted with the care of the young and especially the de la Salle Brothers.

APRIL 11 * MEMORIAL

STANISLAUS
Bishop and Martyr (1030-1079)

Stanislaus was born in Poland about the year 1030. He became a priest and later the Bishop of Cracow. He fearlessly rebuked King Boleslav and was murdered by him in 1079. He is the patron of Poland. A later Bishop of Cracow, who was to become Pope John Paul II, also experienced an attempt on his life in 1981 because he, too, was perceived as an enemy of the state.

As Christians, we have battles to fight. This is not an invitation to be hostile to anyone, but a warning to us about the hostilities we must face. We are neither to seek warfare nor to shrink from it. The test is sure to come and we must be ready for it. Our weapons are a love of the truth, faith in the Gospel, trust in God and a pure conscience.

As bishop, Stanislaus made a point of visiting the priests of his diocese every year. This was an act of great solidarity. Solidarity was the name of the movement which transformed Poland in the 1980s. It is a very Christian concept when understood in the context of the body of Christ. The faith in Poland today is the faith handed down through the centuries. This reminds us that we are called to look after each other's spiritual welfare and help one another in the battles of life.

APRIL 25 * FEAST

MARK
Evangelist

Mark's Gospel is an action-packed thriller, telling the story of the life and death of Jesus. He pictures Jesus as a gentle and humble man who suffers greatly on his way to the wonder of the resurrection. It is this great suspense that characterises Mark's tale, the great struggle between the forces of evil and the goodness of the Son of Man. In his account of Jesus' arrest and trial, as Jesus is led away from Gethsemane, all his friends run away. Then Mark says: "A young man who followed him had nothing on but a linen cloth. They caught hold of him, but he left the cloth in their hands and ran away naked." This could very well be Mark's personal appearance in the dramatic hours of Jesus' sufferings, just as Alfred Hitchcock makes a personal appearance in his thrillers. The frightened young man later became a disciple of Paul on his missionary journeys, a companion to his cousin Barnabas, and finally a disciple of Peter in Rome. It is the fruit of all this experience that is poured into the writing of his Gospel.

Mark fulfilled in his life what every Christian is called to do: to proclaim to all people the Good News that is the source of salvation. In particular, Mark's way was by writing. Others may proclaim the Good News by music, drama, poetry or by teaching children around a family table.

APRIL 29 * MEMORIAL

CATHERINE OF SIENA
Virgin and Doctor (1347-1380)

Catherine was born in Siena, Italy, in 1347. She was the 24th child of her parents. Catherine grew up an intelligent, cheerful and very religious-minded person. It is reported that at the age of 7, following a vision of Christ, she vowed her virginity to God. Her mother wanted her to marry but when she refused, she was persecuted. But her father gave her a room for herself for prayer and penance. She became a tertiary of the Dominican Order.

She was an ascetic, a mystic for whom the supernatural penetrated every moment and every action of her life; yet she was very active in the service of God and neighbour. She nursed the sick, especially victims of the plague and those suffering from the most distressing diseases. She ministered to condemned prisoners and gave spiritual counsel to a great many people who sought her guidance.

At a time when women are more and more taking their rightful place in society and in the Church, we may be tempted to imagine that the only way to sainthood for women in the past was in a homely and subservient role. Catherine of Siena certainly lays that myth to rest. She was an extraordinarily determined woman who could even challenge the Pope when she thought it was necessary. In her peace-making apostolate, Catherine saw that the only way to resolve conflict, caused by the darkness of sin, was to let the light of God shine on the situation. She would do whatever it took to achieve that, even if it meant proverbially knocking people's heads together.

MAY 2 * MEMORIAL

ATHANASIUS
Bishop and Doctor (c. 295-379)

Athanasius lived a tumultuous but dedicated life of service to the Church. He was a great champion of the faith against the widespread heresy called

Arianism, which denied the divinity of Christ. The vigour of his writings earned him the title of Doctor of the Church. Born of a Christian family in Alexandria, Egypt, and given a classical education, he entered the priesthood, became secretary to Alexander, the Bishop of Alexandria and eventually was named bishop himself. As secretary to the bishop of Alexandria, he attended the Council of Nicea in 325, which produced the Creed, still professed at Sunday Mass. In his fight against heresies, he made enemies even within the Church and was exiled five times for the defence of the doctrine of Christ's divinity. The words of the Gospel, "If they persecute you in one town, take refuge in the next", must often have rung in his ears.

Integrity always stands out as a beacon when intrigue and duplicity are at work. Athanasius was a man of deep integrity, which was built on a spiritual life of intense prayer. Among his close friends and confidants were some of the early monks, including Anthony, whose life he wrote, and it was Athanasius who introduced to the Western Church its first understanding of the monastic way of life. As we celebrate his feast we might ask his prayers that we may live with integrity, supported by good spiritual leaders and advisers.

MAY 3 * FEAST

PHILIP AND JAMES
Apostles

James was the son of Alphaeus whom Jesus chose to be one of the 12 pillars of his Church. Philip came from the same town as Peter and Andrew, Bethsaida, Galilee. Jesus called him directly, whereupon he sought out Nathanael and told him about Jesus. The yearning to know more about the afterlife is a strong instinct of our nature. When Jesus described himself as God's Son, the apostle Philip pressed him to tell more. "Let us see the mysterious Father you talk about. That would satisfy us," is the tenor of what he said.

Living in this world, it is not possible for us to see God as he is. But the amazing thing is that we can see God in the face and form of Jesus Christ. If we concentrate our gaze on Jesus, who lived among us in the days of Philip and James, and who lives among us in the Church today, then we can see God. It was this conviction that made Philip and James into faithful apostles of the Lord. Philip's preaching ministry is recorded in the Acts of the Apostles while James, who was known to be the leader of the Church in Jerusalem, bringing many of his fellow Jews into the faith, was martyred in the Holy City in 62AD. These men lived in the company of Jesus, heard him, saw him die and were witnesses to his resurrection. Through them we come to know God, even in this life, in Jesus, the Son of God.

MAY 14 * FEAST

MATTHIAS
Apostle

On October 16th, 1978, a plume of white smoke rose from St Peter's in Rome announcing the election of the Polish cardinal, Karol Wojtyla, as the new Pope, John Paul II. The election was carried out by the secret ballot of the cardinals of the Church. Before electing the new Pope, the cardinals spent a long time in prayer, reflection and discussion before each session of secret voting. In electing the Pope, prayer and politics combined. So it was with the election of Mathias. The Apostles were guided by the Spirit to fill the post left empty by the betrayal of Judas. They assembled the Church, one hundred and twenty disciples, and held discussions. Then they put forward the names of two men considered worthy to join the company of the Apostles. They left the final decision to the Lord and resolved the election by drawing lots. The lot fell to Matthias.

The primary task of the newly-elected apostle was to be a witness to the resurrection of Jesus. There is no greater work for him to do. All the other tasks of the Church can be shared out among the entire community, from teaching to the caring of the poor, from community prayer to arranging missions. But the foundation of it all is the witness to the truth of the resurrection, and this experience was given, first and foremost, to the Apostles. We ourselves are today's witnesses to the Lord. The Lord makes himself known to us, and chooses us. Let us take up our mission.

PHILIP NERI
Priest (1515-1595)

Philip Neri was born in Florence. He lived his life in Rome and he is described as a true Renaissance man. The city of Florence witnessed the rebirth of Renaissance's classical ideas in literature, art and architecture. This period was dominated by Leonardo da Vinci and Michelangelo.

One of the many gifts Philip possessed was the art of conversation. It is an art to meet and talk with people in mutual harmony, thus promoting affection, honesty and generosity with one another and this leads us in the ways of understanding and compassion. Living in an age of instant entertainment, we are perpetually distracted; hence it is good to be reminded that our deepest joy and happiness is to be found in genuine personal relationships. Living in a world that is always in a rush, it is important that we learn to take our time to be with one another.

Philip took great interest in nursing the sick, helping the poor and visiting those in prison. After becoming a priest, he founded the Oratory, where people gathered for prayer, spiritual reading and singing. Philip's own prayer life was especially devoted to the Blessed Sacrament. To be conscious of the presence of God leads to a deep respect for the presence of every human being. Like Philip, may we become not less but more human through our striving for holiness.

VISITATION

The Visitation of the Blessed Virgin Mary to Elizabeth was an ordinary event. It is not like events such as the Immaculate Conception or the Assumption. But through an ordinary event, extraordinary things happened. First of all, Elizabeth was filled with the Holy Spirit; secondly, she exclaimed the words, "Blessed are you among women, and blessed is the fruit of your womb" which form part of the "Hail Mary". Thirdly, John the Baptist was also filled with the Holy Spirit. Fourthly, Mary uttered the hymn, "the Magnificat" which forms part of the liturgy of the hours in the evening prayer of the Church. Thus through ordinary events, extraordinary things can happen. This is true also in our own lives. Through our ordinary actions, we can bring grace, peace and help to others.

One of the invocations in Mary's litany is "Ark of the Covenant." Like the Ark of the Covenant of old, Mary brings God's presence into the lives of other people. As David danced before the Ark, John the Baptist leapt for joy. As the Ark helped to unite 12 tribes of Israel by being placed in David's capital, so Mary has the power to unite all Christians in her Son. At times, devotion to Mary may have occasioned some divisiveness, but we can hope that authentic devotion will lead all to Christ and therefore to one another.

MAY (Friday after Corpus Christi) * SOLEMNITY

SACRED HEART

Devotion to the Sacred Heart is as old as Christianity. The early Fathers of the Church saw in the blood and water issuing from the crucified side of Christ the fulfilment of his promise to give the world living water, the fountain from which the Spirit flows upon the Church. Medieval piety placed less emphasis on Jesus' heart as the source of grace and moved toward more personal devotion. Towards the end of the seventeenth century, St Margaret Mary Alacoque received visions of the Lord exposing his heart and urging public devotion. These apparitions gave impetus to the devotion and shape to its purpose: to offer reparation for human ingratitude, especially indifference to the Blessed Sacrament. Popular devotions include the nine First Fridays and the enthronement of an image of the Sacred Heart in homes as a sign that love is the Christian way of life. Whoever does not love does not know God, because God is love.

JUSTIN
Martyr (d. 165)

Justin was a philosopher in the Roman world of the second century; he took part in many disputations on matters of truth and public life. He conducted a school in Rome and wrote many books on Christian faith and philosophy. Justin was born of a pagan family in Samaria, and philosophy became his life's work. He became a Christian at the age of thirty, visited Ephesus and finally settled in Rome. It was when he was living and working in Rome that a persecution of Christians broke out. His refusal to sacrifice to idols was regarded as treason to the state and together with five others, he was condemned to death and executed.

We are all prone to error, especially in reference to the deep questions concerning life and existence, and hence we should be willing to correct and check our natural thinking in the light of religious truth. Thus we will be able to say with learned saints like Justin: I believe in order to understand in order to believe. Justin wrote: "Philosophy is the knowledge of that which exists, and a clear understanding of the truth; and happiness is the reward of such knowledge and understanding."

CHARLES LWANGA AND COMPANIONS
Martyrs (d. 1886)

Uganda, a beautiful East African Country, lies across the Equator, but it has a very temperate climate. Lake Victoria is partly in Uganda and the river Nile flows right through the country. Yet, this beautiful place has seen some terrible times. In the 1970s, during the reign of Idi Amin, there were mass arrests, massacres and other atrocities, which only ended with the exile of Amin in 1979. Almost 100 years earlier, the country was ruled by an equally wicked tyrant, King Mwanga. He had a hatred of religion and a perverse sexual nature, and he began a vicious persecution of those who would not yield to his desires.

One of 22 Ugandan martyrs, Charles Lwanga is the patron of youth and Catholic action in most of tropical Africa. He protected his fellow pages, aged 13 to 30, from the homosexual demands of the King, and encouraged and instructed them in the Catholic faith during their imprisonment for refusing the ruler's demands. For his own unwillingness to submit to the immoral acts and his efforts to safeguard the faith of his friends, Charles was burned to death on June 3, 1886, on Mwanga's orders.

Like Charles Lwanga, we are all called to be witnesses to the Christian faith by the example of our own lives. We are all called upon to spread the word of God by word and deed. We live as Christ lived, if we remain courageous and unshakeable in our faith during times of great moral and physical temptation.

JUNE 5 * MEMORIAL

BONIFACE
Bishop and Martyr (672?-754)

Boniface was born in England about the year 673. He entered the Benedictine monastery at Nursling, was ordained a priest and became director of its monastic school. However, he left England in 716 and went to Germany as a missionary where he became the apostle of Germany. During a visit to Rome, he was consecrated bishop by Pope Gregory 1I. He travelled throughout Germany and established dioceses and set up monasteries. He was martyred in 754.

In his life, Boniface dedicated himself to contemplation and action. His days in England stress the life of prayer and contemplation. His years in Germany are full of journeying and exertion. The life of silence and meditation is the inspiration for the life of action in the world. Calling us all to devote to good works he says: "The Church is like a great vessel on the sea of the world. We are in a way steerers of this ship. The direction the ship takes in a way depends on us. Steering the ship consists in our preaching all that God has decreed by word and example, to great and small alike, to rich and poor, in season and out of season."

BARNABAS
Apostle

Originally named Joseph, Barnabas was a native of Cyprus. When he met the Apostles in Jerusalem, he was converted to the Faith. Barnabas not only gave up his property and brought the money and laid it at the Apostles' feet, but also dedicated himself to the spread of the Gospel. He was sent by the Church in Jerusalem to check out the new converts in Antioch and to encourage the new Christians. He went in search of Paul and brought him back to Antioch to work there together. A year later they set out together on the first missionary journey to Asia Minor. Barnabas was the mediator when Paul made the awkward journey to Jerusalem to meet the apostles for the very first time. Clearly Barnabas smoothed the way for people to be able to get on with one another. There was a time when Paul and Barnabas fell out, but later they agreed to disagree. Barnabas spent the end of his life in Cyprus

Often we will not be the best judges of our own situations. There will be times when we will need a Barnabas, a go-between, who can be dispassionate and who can lead us into the ways of peace. The role of peacemaker is especially blessed by the Lord. It is he who makes all things possible.

ANTHONY OF PADUA
Priest and Doctor (1195-1231)

Anthony was born in Portugal. He joined the Franciscans after his ordination. The Gospel call to leave everything to follow Christ was the rule of Anthony's life. Like all saints, he is a perfect example of turning one's life completely over to Christ. God did with Anthony as God pleased, and what pleased God was a life of spiritual power and brilliance that still attracts admiration today. He whom popular devotion has nominated as finder of lost objects, found himself by losing himself totally to the providence of God.

Anthony also teaches us how to speak to others. He wanted to go to Africa to preach the Gospel. Instead, he was sent to France and Italy and enjoyed a great preaching career. At that time, Europe was affected by the teachings of the Cathars who thought that all material things are evil. Anthony preached about the goodness of all creation and he communicated his message in a warm and affectionate style. Thomas Aquinas was later to say that the truth must breathe love. Anthony was a great exponent of this approach. In our dealings with each other, even the truth can be used coldly, cruelly exposing not only the faults of others, but also revealing our own lack of care and concern for their welfare. Anthony tells us how our body language and our spiritual attitudes are all conveyed to others when we speak. Whenever we speak we are not simply imparting information; we are communicating affection or indifference or even hostility.

JUNE 21 * MEMORIAL

ALOYSIUS GONSAGA
Religious (1568-1591)

The experience of sickness brings us close to the crossing place between this world and the next, and our thoughts in sickness more readily turn to the Lord and his promises. The Grotto in Lourdes is such a crossing place, where earth and heaven meet. The HCPT (Handicapped Children's Pilgrimage Trust) is an organisation that takes sick children to Lourdes. It began when a doctor made a trip to Lourdes and took four of his sick young patients with him. They enjoyed the trip so much that the doctor decided that they had hit upon a winning formula: not only do we need medical attention and care when we are sick, but our spirits thrive when we are uplifted and inspired, through faith and prayer. Aloysius is an example.

Aloysius was born in Lombardy and was brought up piously by his mother. He entered the Society of Jesus at the age of 17 and he died at 23, having succumbed to the plague while nursing the sick. His spiritual sensitivity was heightened by his contact with the dying and by his own illness. Writing to his mother he told her not to worry because he would be soon in the "land of the living". He regarded the imminent loss of his life in this world as but a momentary setback, which would be immediately restored to him in the resurrection.

Aloysius, born to a princely family, was exposed to a society of glamour, wealth and sex. But he fasted, scourged himself, sought solitude and prayer and avoided looking at women. He seems an unlikely patron of youth of today when asceticism is confined to training camps of football teams and boxers, and sexual permissiveness has little left to permit. Can an overweight and air-conditioned society deprive itself of anything? It will when it discovers a reason, as Aloysius did.

JUNE 24 * SOLEMNITY

BIRTH OF JOHN THE BAPTIST

The greatness of John can be seen in the announcement of his birth and the event itself, similar to the same occurrences in the life of Jesus. John attracted countless people to the banks of the Jordan and some people thought he was the Messiah. But he constantly deferred to Jesus, even to the point of sending away some of his followers to become the first disciples of Jesus.

John the Baptist spoke up for those who were suffering. He pointed out the faults, especially of those in power, those who were in a position to improve and alter things. So genuine was the man that people went to him in crowds. When they listened they were cut to the heart. They went down into the Jordan to be cleansed of their sins and to renew their lives in this world. The Lord himself joined them and was baptised. John called the people to justice as the basic foundation for good and peaceful world. The voices of many modern day followers of John the Baptist call out today. News reporters and aid workers continue the work of the Baptist, calling us to turn our hearts in compassion towards each other.

JUNE 28 * MEMORIAL

IRENAEUS
Bishop and Martyr (130?-c200)

Irenaeus was born in Smyrna, Asia Minor. He was a disciple of Polycarp who in turn was a disciple of St John, the Apostle. He migrated to France and became a priest at Lyons and later became bishop of the same city. Tradition has it that he was martyred about the year 200. He was a theologian, a powerful defender of the faith against those who said our Lord's body was not real, that he was not a true person and that all matter was bad. Famous are his words: "God's glory is the living men and full life for men is in the vision of God."

A group of Christians in Asia Minor had been excommunicated by Pope Victor III because of their refusal to accept the western Church's date for celebrating Easter. Irenaeus, the lover of peace, as his name indicates, interceded with the Pope to lift the ban, indicating that this was not an essential matter and that these people were merely following an old tradition. The Pope responded favourably and the rift was healed. Like Irenaeus, may we bring peace and understanding where there is discord and disunity.

JUNE 29 * SOLEMNITY

PETER AND PAUL
Apostles

Peter and Paul were very self-assured men. Peter was strong-minded and straightforward. But he only realised who he was when a servant girl at a fireside revealed to him his human weakness through a simple question. He denied the Lord and broke down in tears. It really hurts when we discover that we are not what we think we are. Paul knew exactly what he was and what he believed. He was a man of strong faith, until he was struck blind on his way to Damascus and found Christ. The shattering crisis brought Peter and Paul into a new life of Christ. They now placed their confidence not in themselves but in the Lord. Through crushing experiences, the Lord restored these men to full health and strength. Our strong front is usually a protection against some inner fear, but the Lord reminds us that there is no need to fear.

Both Peter and Paul were executed in Rome about the year 67AD, that is, about 35 years after Jesus' death and resurrection. According to an ancient tradition, Peter was crucified while Paul was beheaded. Peter was buried in a common burial ground but soon his tomb became a place where Christians flocked to pray, and right on that tomb now stands St Peter's Basilica. There is another beautiful church in Rome called the church of St Paul. It is built on the spot on which, according to tradition, Paul was beheaded. May the Lord change us, transform us, so that, like Peter and Paul we may also bear witness to Christ in our lives.

THOMAS
Apostle

Today we celebrate the feast of St Thomas, the Apostle. According to the tradition he went to India, established Christian communities especially in Kerala and then went to Tamilnadu and was martyred in Madras. In the Gospels we owe to St John whatever we know about the Apostle Thomas. On the first Easter day, the family and friends of Jesus must have been engulfed in tears of joy at the sight of the risen Lord. But Thomas was not there. When he was told about the risen Lord, he refused to believe, for no one comes back from the dead.

Thomas refusing to believe represents many human beings in their honest views and feelings about life and death. But Thomas' response was an act of providence. Thomas' doubt is to our advantage. When Jesus appeared again and talked to Thomas, he touched him and he believed in the risen Christ, exclaiming: "My Lord and my God!" In this short phrase, Thomas expressed the great mystery of faith, that the resurrection is true and that Jesus is Lord. Just as Thomas surrendered himself totally and completely to the Lord, we also should. This total and complete surrender should of course mean that we accept whatever plan God has for our life.

JULY 11 * MEMORIAL

BENEDICT
Abbot (c480-543)

Benedict was born into a wealthy family in Norcia in Italy, and as a young man went to Rome to complete his education. What he found there was decadence and corruption, and Benedict fled to the hills. His reaction was extreme. From the tumult of city life he ran away to become a solitary and a hermit: fearful of the temptations of the flesh, his remedy was to roll around in nettles.

Benedict's first attempts at forming monastic community life were extreme and severe, and hence his fellow monks tried to get rid of him. It resulted in his coming to Cassino, where he built his famous monastery and instituted a more moderate rule. Prayer, reading and manual labour were the basis of his new approach to monastic life. Regarding manual labour he was like Gandhi. Gandhi and his wife were developing a community life-style in an "ashram", but disagreed over whose task it was to clean out the toilets. Gandhi insisted that there was nothing demeaning in this and that all work in the service of one anther is noble and worthy. Centuries earlier, Benedict had discovered something similar.

Benedict learned to be close to God, close to the earth and close to his fellow human beings. But he learned them in a hard way, as we all do. His gift to the world is his monastic Rule and so he is regarded as the father of monasticism in the West. Full of wisdom and moderation, Benedict came to realise that a person only becomes a person in the company of others.

BONAVENTURE
Bishop and Doctor (1221-1274)

Bonaventure was born in Bagnoregio, a town in central Italy. He became a Franciscan at the age of 25. A brilliant pupil, he was sent to Paris where he studied alongside Thomas Aquinas. They received their doctorates together. Pope Gregory X made him Cardinal Archbishop of Albano and asked him to use his gifts of spirit and administration to prepare for the Second Council of Lyons, which he did. The Church officially recognised the saintliness of this man in 1482 and his gifts of intellect and wisdom were honoured when he was declared "Doctor" in 1587.

   In his own lifetime he was best known for his gentle courtesy, compassion and accessibility. An unknown chronicler provides his impression of the Franciscan cardinal: "A man of eminent learning and eloquence, and of outstanding holiness, he was known for his kindness, approachableness, gentleness and compassion. Full of virtue, he was beloved of God and man. At his funeral Mass that same day, many were in tears, for the Lord had granted him this grace, that whoever came to know him was forthwith drawn to a deep love of him."

MARY MAGDALENE

Mary Magdalene had been one of Jesus' closest friends. Rescued by him from the many troubles of her own life – seven demons were cast out of her – she accompanied the Lord on his round of preaching, and when all was lost, and all had run away, she remained steadfast by the cross with Mary, Jesus' mother.

   The Easter garden in Jerusalem was a very sad and somber place when Mary Magdalene came to visit the tomb of her Lord. She brought with her spices to anoint his body, bringing to a fitting end the chapter of Calvary's cruelty. But on entering the tomb she found the tomb empty. This was a double blow. Sorrow broke her heart. Now alone in the garden, she cried out her questions to anyone who would hear. And someone did. The voice was the Lord's. Thus she became the first witness to his Resurrection. Why not Peter or John? Perhaps it had something to do with the heart that perseveres, long after the head has given up hope. Like Mary Magdalene, may we also be faithful to the bitter end and beyond the bitter end, for beyond it is the beginning of new life.

JULY 25 * FEAST

JAMES
Apostle

With his brother John, he was tempted to call down fire and brimstone on a Samaritan village that was inhospitable to Jesus. At the Transfiguration of Jesus he saw the glory of human destiny in Jesus. In Gethsemane he saw the terror of fear that can grip the soul. He saw the bloodshed of Calvary and then the incredible triumph of the Resurrection. How did he die? During the persecution of Herod Agrippa, James fell beneath the sword. A legend tells us that when James was arrested in Jerusalem and condemned to death, his accuser repented at the last minute, and they were executed together.

With his brother John, James sought glory in Jesus' kingdom and wanted a special place in the kingdom. In his enthusiasm for the glory, James was very quick to say that he could drink the cup and accept the same baptism as the Lord. But Jesus gently told him that the Lord's kingdom is a spiritual one. To occupy high places in his kingdom one must drink the bitter cup of self-sacrifice in the service of others. He said to him that true glory resides in persevering goodness, in being faithful to all that is good and true and loving, when all around you is breaking into violence. Let us therefore seek not the vanities of this world, but the true glory that Jesus promised to James.

JULY 26 * MEMORIAL

JOACHIM AND ANNE
Parents of Mary

The Church of the second century was losing the record and reminiscences of the first century and had a great desire to hold on to them. A "Gospel of James" appeared, giving an account of the life of our Lady and of her parents, the grandparents of Jesus. Based on the Old Testament story of Samuel and his mother, Hannah, even the name of Mary's mother Anne may well be a literary invention. The Gospel of James, therefore, is not a work of factual history. Rather it is a testimony of honour and reverence paid to the older generation, a work of love of those certainly historical people, the mother and father of Mary. In the Middle Ages, the increased cult of Mary brought with it an increase of devotion and interest in her parents, Joachim and Anne.

The strong character of Mary in making decisions, her continuous practice of prayer, her devotion to the laws of her faith, her steadiness in moments of crisis, and her devotion to her relatives – all indicate a close-knit, loving family that looked forward to the next generation even while retaining the best of the past. Joachim and Anne, whether these are their real names or not, represent that entire quiet series of generations who faithfully perform their duties, practise their faith and establish an atmosphere for the coming of the Messiah, but remain obscure.

JULY 29 * MEMORIAL

MARTHA

Martha, the patron saint of lay sisters and of housewives, knew very well how galling it can be, doing all the manual labour while others pursue more intellectual endeavours. When Jesus was a guest in her house, and when Martha was busy preparing a meal to welcome him properly, she was not impressed by her sister Mary sitting idle. Yet in truth, her sister was not idle or doing nothing. Mary was paying attention to the Lord and listening to him. Both of these practices, preparing a meal and paying attention to people, are part of the practice of hospitality, and so Jesus was well cared for in that house.

But because Martha was not sitting at the feet of the Lord to listen to him as Mary did, we need not conclude that she was an un-recollected activist. The Evangelist is only emphasising what our Lord had said on many occasions about the primacy of the spiritual: "Man shall not live by bread alone" (Lk 4:4); "Seek first the kingdom of God and his righteousness " (Mt 6:33); "Blessed are those who hunger and thirst for righteousness"(Mt 5:6). Martha's great glory is her simple and strong statement of faith: "Yes, Lord, I believe that you are the Christ, the Son of God" (Jn 11:27). We are called to imitate Martha in her faith and active service to others, especially by acts of hospitality.

JULY 31 * MEMORIAL

IGNATIUS OF LOYOLA
Priest (1491-1556)

The founder of the Jesuits was on his way to military fame and fortune when a cannonball shattered his leg. Because there were no books of romance on hand during his convalescence, he whiled away the time reading books on the life of Christ and the lives of the saints. And so a long and painful turning to Christ began. Having seen in a vision the Mother of God, he made a pilgrimage to her shrine at Montserrat (near Barcelona). He remained there almost a year, praying and doing penances. He suffered harrowing trials of scruples. At length his peace of mind returned. It was during this period of conversion that he wrote his spiritual masterpiece: *The Spiritual Exercises.*

Ignatius was all on fire for the greater glory of God and it was to give concrete expression to this zeal that he founded the Society of Jesus. He kindled the hearts of his followers with this fire. He reformed the Church from within, by a life of holiness, of service, of prayer and penance. This is attested to above all by the 41 saints and 142 Blesseds the Society has given to the Church – of every age and of every category, almost as if to indicate that in every moment and in every stage of formation — from porter's lodge to university chair — perfection and mission can be lived fully with the grace of God. Speaking of Ignatius Loyola, Pope Paul II said: "It was his firm conviction that an apostle, every apostle, must maintain intimate union with God in order to allow himself to be guided by the divine hand of God."

AUGUST 1 * MEMORIAL

ALPHONSUS LIGUORI
Bishop and Doctor (1696 -1787)

Albino Luciani was elected in the summer of 1978 as Pope John Paul 1. His warmth heartened our world and his gentleness was felt by all: for a short time only, since he died a month after his election. He revealed that his inspiration for all his life was Alphonsus Liguori, the founder of the Redemptorists. He used to tell his priests in the Diocese of Venice that they should model their lives on the example of St Alphonsus Liguori.

In his life, Alphonsus suffered a lot. His greatest sorrow came towards the end of his life when he could not get the Rule for the Order he founded recognised because of the connivance of a highly placed Redemptorist official. It was only after his death that this problem was solved. At 71, he was afflicted with rheumatic pains which left an incurable bending of his neck. He suffered a final 18 months of "dark night" – scruples, fears and temptations against every article of faith, but with God's grace he overcame them all.

Liguori lived until the age of 91 and filled his life with energy and action as a lawyer, priest, missionary, musician, artist, writer, scholar, preacher, confessor, bishop, founder, and Doctor of the Church. Beneath all these talents and achievements, one could detect a simple man with a simple philosophy of life: God loves us passionately in Christ, therefore, let us love God passionately and translate this love by our service to humankind.

AUGUST 4 * MEMORIAL

JOHN VIANNEY
Priest (1786-1859)

John Vianney was an unpromising candidate for priesthood. He was a farmer's son with no early education, a tender of sheep, a conscript soldier, a slow and unsuccessful seminarian. He scraped through to his ordination to priesthood only on a reputation of holiness. He was an assistant priest for two years before he was sent to Ars. Although this parish was a backward place, he flourished there for the rest of his life, for nearly forty years. In his parish, he campaigned against drinking, and dancing; but later he mellowed because he became slowly sympathetic towards human frailty.

This understanding of the frailty of human nature came to him as he listened to thousands of penitents who poured out their troubles to him in the confessional. The number of people visiting Ars to talk to Vianney was as many as 300 a day, 1000 a week, and 20000 a year. No university could have given Vianney the knowledge and wisdom he gained from listening to human stories as they confessed their sins. He could read their hearts and could set them back on the right track. Each of us should find a similar spiritual counsellor for ourselves.

Many people look forward to retirement, to taking it easy and doing the things they always wanted to do, but never had the time. But Vianney had no thought of retirement. As his fame spread, more hours were spent serving God's people. He became priest with a spiritual vision, and who but a man with a vision like him could keep going with ever increasing strength!

AUGUST 6 * FEAST

TRANSFIGURATION OF THE LORD

The transfiguration of the Lord on Mount Tabor prepared the Apostles for the cross on Calvary in the perspective of the Resurrection. He revealed to them his glory to strengthen them against the scandal of the cross. The transfiguration of the Lord tells us of our own transfiguration. After our death Christ will raise our mortal bodies and make them like his own in glory.

The Apostle Peter was one of the three who witnessed the transfiguration of the Lord. And so he was able to encourage those who suffer for Christ in words such as these: "We saw Jesus in glory on the mountain. We heard God's voice to identify him as his son. Hold on to this faith. It will be a light, a lamp to guide you through dark days." Peter confirmed his promise by shedding his own blood for Christ. Our knowledge of Christ's transfiguration and the experience of our own "little transfigurations" on earth, must not turn us into daydream believers. Rather, like Peter, we must get fully involved in our daily lives as God has charted an earthly course for each of us.

AUGUST 8 * MEMORIAL

DOMINIC
Priest (1170-1221)

Dominic Guzman was a Spanish priest. As canon of Osma cathedral, he suddenly burst into missionary activity. He was then 34; he travelled to Southern France to preach to the people of Albi and to convert them from their heretical belief that all material things are evil. He did not engage in a bloody crusade against this heresy, but sought learning and scholarship to promote the Gospel and preserve the people from many follies of religion. He had enormous influence in founding the University of Toulouse.

He founded the Order of Preachers. They were first called "Black Friars" and later Dominicans. They were known for their simplicity and scholarship and devoted their lives to missionary preaching, as they have done to this day. People of today, relying on science and technology, can easily dismiss religion as pure fantasy. But the preaching of Dominic and his followers stressed that the study and contemplation of the Gospel is worthy of the full attention of humankind, a thing worth giving one's life to. The wisdom that Dominic contemplated and has passed on to us is this: to come to know Jesus Christ and in him the beauty of all things is the most precious treasure one should seek to obtain.

AUGUST 10 * FEAST

LAWRENCE
Deacon and Martyr (d. 258?)

The esteem in which the Church held Lawrence is seen in the fact that today's celebration ranks as a feast. He is one of those whose martyrdom made a lasting impression on the early church. In the days before photography, the most powerful way to preserve the presence and the memory of loved ones was to recall their stories. In the community of the Church this recollection is done in written and spoken words, especially in liturgical prayers. Accordingly, the name of Lawrence is mentioned in the Roman Canon or Eucharistic prayer. Lawrence was a Roman deacon under Pope Sixtus II. Four days after this Pope was put to death, Lawrence and four clerics suffered martyrdom during the persecution of Emperor Valerian. On the spot where Lawrence was buried, a church was built later, the Basilica of St Lawrence. He is often depicted holding a purse, since alms-giving was his great responsibility as a deacon, and he was renowned for his kindness and generosity to people. His life of service and martyrdom teaches us that only by service comes greatness. The people whom the world remembers with love are those who served others. Of course, a life of selfless service can only result from an unshakeable faith, for which St Lawrence shed his blood.

AUGUST 11 * MEMORIAL

CLARE
Virgin (1194-1253)

Clare, coming from a well-to-do Offreduccio family, had the prospect of a flourishing and successful life. But after hearing a Lenten sermon preached by Francis of Assisi she gave her heart and her whole life to the imitation and love of Christ. Responding to the Gospel call, like Francis, she chose to live the simplest life possible. With her grew a community of sisters and they were provided a house by St Francis. This community of sisters, living by the rule of St Francis, came to be called the Order of Poor Clares.

All her life, Clare lived in Assisi, poor, simple and contemplative. As a result, she grew in divine wisdom and so people from many walks of life came to visit her with their spiritual as well as material problems to benefit from her wise counselling. Her parents thought that she was foolish in throwing away an enjoyable future in the family and become a pauper. But what is foolish in the eyes of the world is wisdom before God. Clare clearly saw that through a life of humility, simplicity, austerity and prayer, she had found the greatest treasure in Jesus Christ. On her deathbed, Clare was heard to say to herself: "Go forth in peace, for you have followed the good road. Go forth without fear, for he who created you has made you holy, has always protected you and loves you as a mother."

AUGUST 13 * MEMORIAL

PONTIAN AND HIPPOLYTUS
Pope, and Priest, Martyrs (d. 235)

Pontian was a Roman. In his reign as Pope, he held a synod which confirmed the excommunication of the great theologian Origen of Aexandria. Pontian was banished to exile by the Emperor. He was sent to the unhealthy island of Sardinia where he died of harsh treatment. With him was the antipope Hippolytus. Both died reconciled. The bodies of both martyrs were brought back to Rome and buried with solemn rites as martyrs.

The words of Hippolytus found in his Treatise on Christ and Antichrist have a lesson for all of us: "Christ, like a skilful physician, understands the weakness of men. He loves to teach the ignorant and the erring he turns again to his own true way. He is easily found by those who live by faith; and to those of pure eye and holy heart, who desire to knock at the door, he opens immediately."

MAXIMILIAN MARY KOLBE
Priest and Martyr (1894-1941)

Maximilian was born in Poland; His family was very poor under the Russian rule. In their utter poverty, they took refuge in their religion. Maximilian's father, after running a bookshop for a time, joined the Polish patriots and was hanged as a traitor by the Russians. Maximilian joined the Franciscans and was ordained a priest. Returning to Poland, he began energetically to publish Christian magazines, though suffering a severe attack of tuberculosis.

He worked in Japan, and when he returned to Poland he was made superior of a monastery whose numbers grew in his time to 762 friars. During the Nazi invasion, he dispersed his friars to their homes. Together with four others, he was arrested as an "intellectual" and sent to Auschwitz, the labour camp, the horrors of which everyone knows about. It is in that camp he made the following heroic sacrifice. After one of the prisoners tried to escape in July 1941, ten men were selected to be put to death by starvation. Maximilian offered to take the place of the one of the condemned: a married man with a family. His offer was accepted. He prayed with his fellow "death companions" to the Lord of life. He died on 14th August. At his canonisation in 1982, John Paul II said that Kolbe not only saved one man, but he also showed many other doomed men how to die.

ASSUMPTION

On 1 November, 1950, Pius XII defined the Assumption of Mary to be a dogma of faith: "We pronounce, declare and define it to be a divinely revealed dogma that the Immaculate Mother of God, the ever Virgin Mary, having completed the course of her life on earth, was assumed body and soul to heavenly glory." The Pope proclaimed this dogma only after a broad consultation of bishops, theologians and laity. There were few dissenting voices. But what the Pope solemnly declared became an article of faith.

As Mary was assumed into heaven, so shall we be one day – though in a different manner. The great promise held out to the disciples of Jesus is that those who are united with him in the likeness of death will also share with him in his resurrection. The difference between Mary and the rest of us is that she did not have to wait until the end of the world for her resurrection; but we have to wait. This is because we are conceived in sin, whereas Mary was not. Thus Mary is the authentic instance of realised resurrection. Death is not the end of everything. We are destined to live for all eternity. May we continue our Christian journey in this certain hope.

AUGUST 20 * MEMORIAL

BERNARD
Abbot and Doctor (1091-1153)

Bernard was born near Dijon in France. He joined the Cistercians. Three years afterwards he was elected Abbot of the monastery of Clairvaux and ordained a priest. He was outstanding in directing the monks in virtue both by word and example. On account of divisions in the Church he travelled through Europe trying to restore peace and unity.

He was perhaps the most authentic and complete representative of the monastic tradition in the current of mediaeval civilisation. His monastery was a thriving religious community with a constant flow of new recruits, a fervent and well-ordered life, and daughter houses sprang up at a great rate. Bernard was a dynamic personality and a great religious leader. As a young man, he was famous for his charm, wit, learning and eloquence; great gifts for making one's way in the world. But at the age of 22, he led four of his brothers and 27 of his friends into the austere life of the Cistercian Order.

Bernard's following words are great impetus to love God: "When God loves, he wishes only to be loved in return; assuredly he loves for no other purpose than to be loved. He knows that those who love him are happy in their love."

AUGUST 21 * MEMORIAL

PIUS X
Pope (1835 -1914)

Joseph Sarto, the second of 10 children in a poor Italian family, was born at Riese in the province of Venice. After successful studies at the school in Castelfranco he entered the seminary in Padua and was ordained priest in 1858. He was nine years assistant parish priest, eight years parish priest, nine years spiritual director of the major seminary and Chancellor of the diocese, nine years bishop of Mantua, ten years Patriarch and Cardinal of Venice and the last eleven years Pope. On the eleventh anniversary of his election as Pope, Europe was plunged into World War I. Pius had foreseen it but it killed him: "This is the last affliction the Lord will visit on me. I would gladly give my life to save my poor children from this ghastly scourge." He died a few weeks after the war began.

Pope Pius X is perhaps best remembered for his encouragement of the frequent reception of Holy Communion, especially by children. But the aim of his Pontificate was to "Restore all things in Christ". In reality there was no aspect of the Church in which Pius X did not enter, to discern, direct, determine, and relaunch. In each of these spheres Pius X intervened with an able and firm hand, with providential and decisive choices. We too, are called to help "restore all things in Christ", especially the wounded people of God.

AUGUST 22 * MEMORIAL

QUEENSHIP OF MARY

At the Annunciation, Gabriel announced that Mary's Son would receive the throne of David and rule forever. At the Visitation, Elizabeth calls

Mary "mother of my Lord". As in all the mysteries of Mary's life, Mary is closely associated with Jesus. Her queenship is a share in Jesus' kingship. Thus, Mary is queen because she played a unique role in the kingdom of God, in the Saviour's work of redemption. Mary is queen not by birth but by the grace of God and by conquest. She conquered the devil and she conquered death. She collaborated with her divine Son for the establishment of the kingdom. She continues to collaborate with Jesus Christ for the coming of the kingdom in the hearts of men and women. To honour Christ the King and Mary as Queen of Heaven means that we dedicate ourselves to a life of love and service as faithful subjects of the kingdom.

AUGUST 24 * FEAST

BARTHOLOMEW
Apostle

In the New Testament, Batholomew is mentioned only once, in the list of Apostles. Some scholars identify him with Nathanael, a man from Cana in Galilee, who was summoned to Jesus by Philip. Jesus paid him a great compliment: "Behold, an Israelite indeed, in whom is no guile." (Jn 1:47). When Jesus said, "I saw you under the fig tree", Nathanael exclaimed: "Rabbi, you are the Son of God; you are the king of Israel." (Jn 1:49). After Jesus had departed from this world, Bartholomew preached the Gospel in the East and was martyred by the Caspian Sea.

Jesus called Nathanael a true Israelite. By calling him a true Israelite, Jesus meant that Nathanael believed in Jesus; he was faithful to God. Like him we must also be true and faithful to God. In Nathanael there was no guile, no duplicity, no double-dealing, no cheating, no cunning, no bluff, no untruth, no lie, no deception, no trickery, no fraud, no disguise. Like him we too must be sincere, open, frank, truthful, honest and faithful. We must not only be Christians, but true Christians.

AUGUST 27 * MEMORIAL

MONICA
(c. 322-387)

Almost all we know about St Monica is in the writings of St Augustine, especially his Confessions. Monica was raised as a Christian and married Patricius who turned out to be of a dissolute and violent temper. She had constant quarrels with him as well as with her mother-in-law. In order to forget her troubles she began drinking, but later she overcame this addiction and raised three children in an unhappy home. As his father, Augustine too began to live a dissolute life. And so, unable to content her son, she threw him out of the house. But she quickly repented for her action and sought the help of a priest.

From that point onward, she began to live a new life. She stopped arguing and turned to the power of prayer. She began to live a healthier life, and to function in a normal way. As a reward to her patience and long-suffering, God brought about a reconciliation between Monica and her husband and also her mother-in-law. Her prayers for her son, too, were answered, as Augustine himself stilled the violent passions in his own heart and found peace in Christ. Mother and son met in Rome and were reconciled; peace of Christ filled the hearts of them both. She became ill. Realising that her time had come to go, she said to her two sons who were with her: "Lay this body wherever it may be. Let no care of it disturb you; this only I ask of you that you should remember me at the altar of the Lord wherever you may be."

AUGUST 28 * MEMORIAL

AUGUSTINE
Bishop and Doctor (354-430)

Augustine, the son of St Monica, grew up in a stormy and troubled household, and so developed a troubled but dynamic personality. He became a teacher and philosopher and put his gift to use for rhetoric and languages, but in the process, he discarded his early Christian formation received at home, especially by his Christian mother Monica. He spent many years of inner struggle before he finally fell a captive to the love and the light of Christ. His conversion was greatly due to the friendship he had formed with St Ambrose in Milan. As a Christian, Augustine returned to Africa and was made bishop of Hippo. His abundant affection for his flock was the result of his great pastoral heart. He put his natural powers of the intellect to work in his writings, which are even now regarded as treasures of the Church.

Many of Augustine's words have become famous: "Unless you believe, you will not understand." "You have made us, Lord, for yourself; and our hearts find no rest until they rest in you." "Late have I loved you, O beauty both ancient and new, late I have loved you. You called, you cried out and you rid me of my deafness." Augustine is an example of what the grace of God can do in a person. He also teaches us how easy it is to go astray and how difficult it is to discover the path of truth and holiness. But the grace of God, humility and love of truth can keep us on the right track.

AUGUST 29 * MEMORIAL

BEHEADING OF JOHN THE BAPTIST

When Herod Antipas ruled a part of Palestine, he was a law unto himself. He defined the truth and justice as it suited him. John the Baptist, a "voice in the wilderness" was attracting unnecessary and unwelcome attention. He was also saying things that were hurtful to the king. So it suited Herod to imprison him. But in spite of all this, Herod liked to listen to John: because, however corrupt may be a human heart, it tends to be attracted by the truth. But in the end John paid with his life for speaking the truth. How did John die? The drunken oath of a king with a shallow sense of honour, a seductive dance and the hateful heart of a queen combined to bring about the martyrdom of John the Baptist.

John's mission was to point the way to Christ. His life and death were a giving of self to God and for other people. His simple style of life was one of complete detachment from earthly possessions. His heart was centred on God and the call he heard from the Spirit of God speaking to his heart. Confident of God's grace, he had the courage to speak words of condemnation or repentance, or redemption. No one of us will ever repeat the mission of John, and yet all of us are called to that very mission. It is the role of the Christian to witness to Jesus. Whatever our position in the world, we are called to be the disciples of Christ, and by our words and deeds, others should realise that we live in the joy of knowing that Jesus is the Lord.

SEPTEMBER 3 * MEMORIAL

GREGORY THE GREAT
Pope and Doctor (c. 540-604)

Gregory was born in Rome. His first career was in politics as a Prefect of the city. In his mid-thirties, he turned from politics to prayer, founding monasteries and becoming himself a monk. But his talents for leadership and administration were too great for him to be left in his monastic home. He was extremely brilliant, humble and likeable and so made his mark in the great affairs of Church and State. The Pope sent him as envoy to Constantinople for five years. Soon after his return, Gregory himself was elected Pope and ruled for thirteen years.

He was responsible for sending missionaries to England. During his reign as Pope, he guarded and guided the faithful in times of famine, flood and foreign invasion. He wrote at great length on Scripture, morals and pastoral care. He set in motion a renewal and enrichment of the Church's liturgy and music. Gregorian chant takes its name from him. In his homilies, he calls us to surrender our entire self to God, though it may be the most difficult thing to do: "Perhaps it is not after all so difficult for a man to part with his possessions, but it is certainly most difficult for him to part with himself. To renounce what one has is a minor thing, but to renounce what one is, that is asking a lot."

BIRTH OF MARY

Every human birth is a call to new hope in the world. A child is born when the love of two human beings is joined with God in his creative work. Loving parents sow hope in a world filled with anguish and travail. Any new child has a potential to be channel for God's love and peace to the world. This is all true in a sublime way in the birth of Mary, mother of Jesus. Because Jesus is the perfect expression of God's love, Mary is the foreshadowing of that love. Because Jesus has brought the fullness of redemption, Mary is its dawning.

We are called to imitate Mary. Though she was great she did not choose to remain far away from ordinary people like us. Like God whose characteristic is being great while at the same time remaining close to us, Mary too is close to us. That is why we can all imitate her in our ordinary life. Her greatness is from within. Externally she lived an ordinary life. She is not said to have worked miracles, like her son Jesus. And yet, she was great in grace of God. Our greatness likewise consists not in doing extraordinary things, but doing ordinary things in an extraordinary manner, according to God's will, according to our status in life, according to what opportunities we have. Mary teaches us that true virtue consists in doing things in silence, without much glamour.

JOHN CHRYSOSTOM
Bishop and Doctor (d. 407)

Chrysostom had a gift for words and his name means "golden mouth". He was born in Antioch. After a brilliant education in law and rhetoric, he went to the mountains to join a monastery. Due to the austerity of his monastic life, his health greatly suffered and hence after eight years, he returned to city life. Years of prayer and silence on the mountains had produced honey in his speech. His captivating words not only attracted the ears of his listeners, but moved their hearts to the love of God.

The Emperor of Constantinople made him his Archbishop. Since he was not only a man of words but also of action, Chrysostom called for moral reforms both in the court and among the clergy. The result was that he gathered enemies around him and so he was exiled. He died in exile at the age of sixty. We can consider him a martyr of pastoral courage. But what we remember above all is that he succeeded in forming a Christian people, Christian communities worthy of the name.

John had no fear of harassment or defamation. These only made him more firm in his proclamation of the Gospel. Yet, unshakeable as his inner strength was, it never caused him to go against charity either in word or deed. About charity he speaks to us: "You wish to honour the body of Christ? Do not hold it in contempt when it is naked. Do not honour it here, in the church, by wearing silken robes, while you allow it to remain outside suffering from the cold and lack of clothes. Begin by feeding the hungry, with what is left, you may decorate the altar."

SEPTEMBER 14 * FEAST

TRIUMPH OF THE CROSS

Throughout the world the cross stands as the instantly recognisable symbol of Christianity. It stands on cathedral spires and above high altars. It is attached to prayer beads and even ladies' necklaces. The crucifixion of Jesus was the defining moment in the life of Jesus as well as in the life of the world, since he redeemed the world through his cross. "When I am lifted up," said Jesus, "I will draw all people to myself." But, in order to draw all people to himself, Jesus had to go down to the very depths of suffering, even crying to his Father, "My God, my God, why have you deserted me?" But the Father did not abandon him forever; Having accepted his sacrifice for the sake of all humanity, he raised his Son from the dead after three days. We believe that the risen Jesus is with us offering his new life. Yet the sign that leads the way to new life is the cross.

Making the sign of the cross is an act of profession, a prayer, a dedication, a benediction, for it brings life, not death, light, not darkness,

Paradise, not its loss. It is the wood on which the Lord was wounded in his hands and feet and side, and thereby healed our wounds. A tree destroyed us; a tree now brought us life. Therefore let us embrace our daily crosses. Let us have the firm hope that our suffering on earth will lead us to glory.

SEPTEMBER 15 * MEMORIAL

OUR LADY OF SORROWS

For a while there were two feasts in honour of the Sorrowful Mother: one going back to the fifteenth century, the other to the seventeenth century. For a while both were celebrated by the universal Church: one on the Friday before Palm Sunday, the other in September. When Jesus was hanging upon the cross and all his friends had fled, there stood his Mother at the foot of the cross, with two other women and the disciple John. They could not do anything for Jesus except to look at him dying in agony. But they loved him and so faithfully stayed with him through these long and lonely hours. By their presence, they supported Jesus and shared his sufferings in some way.

This feast of the Sorrowful Mother speaks to us not just of Mary's afflictions in life, but also about her readiness to be part of the sufferings of others. In our service to the sick, what is more important than any treatment or therapy is the tenderness and love that we show in our caring. People can feel lost and alone when they fall ill. They might withdraw into themselves and separate themselves from the arena of life, which could be more harmful than physical illness itself. Therefore, let us give them fruit and flowers if we can, but more than that, let us give them our love and affection to help ease their isolation. May Mary's compassionate love for all of us move our hearts to care for and help each other.

SEPTEMBER 16 * MEMORIAL

CORNELIUS AND CYPRIAN
Pope, and Bishop, and Martyrs

Cornelius became Pope in the year 251. He was called to shepherd the universal Church at a time of religious persecution and a time of painful dissension within. His efforts to strengthen the Church's communion were greatly aided by the persuasive talents of the Bishop of Carthage, St Cyprian. Cornelius was sent into exile by the Emperor Gallus and he died in the year 253. Cyprian was born in Carthage about the year 210. Later he was converted to the Catholic faith. Soon afterwards he was ordained a priest and in 249, a bishop, the bishop of Carthage. He guided the Church excellently during troubled times, both by his deeds and his writings. During the persecution of Valerian he was martyred for the faith. When the proconsul pronounced the judgement that Cyprian be put to death, Cyprian simply said, "Thanks be to God".

Cornelius and Cyprian were men of different backgrounds and temperament, but were united by a mutual love for the Church and by their zeal for the unity of the faith. We will do well to remember the words of Cyprian: "One cannot have God for his Father who does not have the Church for his Mother."

SEPTEMBER 20 * MEMORIAL

ANDREW KIM TAEGON AND COMPANIONS
Martyrs (1821-1846)

In the 19th century, a curtain of hostility fell upon Korea, as Korean rulers forbade all foreigners from entering their territory. There was a ban on religion, too. Thus anyone professing Christianity was regarded as an enemy of the state. Some missionary priests from France had come into the country in the 1830s and had worked quietly for a while. Then a violent persecution broke out. Three French priests and 78 Korean people died in the persecution. Among them was the first Korean priest, Andrew Kim Taegon. His great-grandfather and his own father too were martyred before him. Andrew was sent as a youth to train for the priesthood to a seminary in Southern China, 1300 miles from home. He spoke English, French, Spanish and Chinese fluently, was ordained at 24 and came back to work in Korea. He ministered for only six months before he was captured, tried and sentenced to death.

When Pope John Paul II visited Korea in 1984, he canonised Andrew, Paul, 98 Koreans and three French missionaries who had been martyred between 1839 and 1867. Speaking at the canonisation, the Pope said: "The Korean Church is unique because it was founded entirely by lay people. The fledgling Church withstood wave after wave of fierce persecution. The death of these martyrs became the leaven of the Church and led to today's splendid flowering of the Church in Korea."

SEPTEMBER 21 * FEAST

MATTHEW
Apostle and Evangelist

Matthew as a tax collector was to the Jews an outsider, because he had become a collaborator with the Romans against his own people and thus had lost any privilege he might have had among his own people. His only company were other tax collectors. When Jesus saw him and called him, he was very ready to go with Jesus for in Jesus' call he found a way back into the human community. Since money cannot buy human warmth, he was not unwilling to give up his job in order to follow Jesus.

We learn at least two lessons from Matthew's positive response to Jesus' call. Firstly, if we follow Jesus, we have to know that we have a difficult road to travel, but a disciple does not concentrate on the road but on the person they are following, because the Master knows the destination towards which he is leading. Secondly, when we join the company of Jesus, we have to keep in mind that Jesus' community does not have boundaries or no-go areas. It makes no distinction. No matter who we are, no matter what we have done, there is a place for every one of us in his company. The community of Jesus is bound by an all-embracing love. In Jesus' company we love even our enemies. In fact, mercy towards human beings is one of the themes that Matthew emphasises in his Gospel.

SEPTEMBER 27 * MEMORIAL

VINCENT DE PAUL
Priest (c. 1580-1660)

Vincent came from a humble peasant family, but was sent to university and then became a priest at the age of 19. He became close to wealthy people and served as chaplain at the French court in Paris. He enjoyed all the comforts which he could get from his privileged position. But then came a definite conversion in his life. When he met St Francis de Sales and another person who were working for the poor, Vincent questioned his own comfortable life and gave himself totally to Christ and to serve the poor in his name. The love of Christ brought about a dynamic change in Vincent. The focus of his energy was Jesus Christ present in every poor person.

When we leave our parish church after Sunday Mass, we usually notice a small wooden box with the letters SVP written on it. People drop into it charitable donations because they know that the money will go towards the work of helping the poor in the immediate parish community. It is a direct action for local needs. SVP was started by Frederick Ozanam in 1833 and it takes its name from Vincent de Paul, who had inspired great concern for the poor two hundred years before. Vincent founded two congregations, the Sisters of Charity and the Congregation of the Mission, to advance his work. His name lives in these two religious families as well as in the wooden box that awaits us all as we leave the church.

SEPTEMBER 29 * FEAST

MICHAEL, GABRIEL AND RAPHAEL
Archangels

The Archangels whose feasts we celebrate today appear frequently in Scripture. Michael appears in Daniel's vision as "the great prince" who defends Israel against its enemies; in the book of Revelation, he leads God's armies to final victory over the forces of evil. Devotion to Michael is the oldest angelic devotion. Gabriel also makes an appearance in Daniel's visions, announcing Michael's role in God's plan. His best known appearance is an encounter with a young Jewish girl named Mary who consents to conceive the Messiah. Raphael appears in the story of Tobit. There he appears to guide Tobit's son Tobiah through a series of fantastic adventures which lead to a threefold happy ending: Tobiah's marriage to Sarah, the healing of Tobit's blindness and the restoration of the family fortune. Thus each of these archangels performs a different mission in Scripture: Michael protects; Gabriel announces; Raphael guides.

Let us pray to the angels to help us to be faithful to God. May they teach us to choose God. Divine realities seem so far away from us. Let us ask them to grant us fervour in prayer, a taste for meditation, and perseverance in the service of the Lord until the end of our life. God has given us three angels as our protectors, our guardians, our companions, our assistants, our teachers and our advocates. Let us invoke them often in our needs. They will certainly help us.

SEPTEMBER 30 * MEMORIAL

JEROME
Priest and Doctor (345-420)

Jerome was born about the year 345 in Dalmatia. He studied in Rome where he was baptised. Then he began to lead a life of asceticism. He lived for some years as a hermit in the Syrian desert. At Antioch he was ordained a priest. He lived in Constantinople for some time and then returned to Rome, where he became secretary to Pope Damasus and at his request began translating the Bible into Latin. Pope Damasus died in 384 and Jerome went and settled down in Bethlehem. He spent the last years of his life studying, dictating, and writing. His scholarship was unparalleled in the early church. He knew three languages very well: Latin, Greek and Hebrew. He had a thorough acquaintance with biblical history and geography, Church history and the lives of the Fathers of the Church. In the Church today it is our continuing duty to do as Jerome did: to study the Scriptures and interpret them correctly for the people of our own time and to feed on those sacred texts every day at the "table of the Word" so that we can grow in the fullness of Christ.

OCTOBER 1 * MEMORIAL

THERESA OF THE CHILD JESUS
Virgin and Doctor (1873-1897)

Theresa of Child Jesus was a French girl. Her father was a watchmaker and jeweller and her mother ran a small business in embroidery. She was the ninth and the last child in the family. At the age of four, she lost her mother. When she was ten, she contracted a serious sickness which lasted three months with extended deliriums and prolonged spells. She implored the help of the Blessed Virgin Mary and was cured. She entered the Carmelite convent at the age of 15. In spite of her frail physical condition, she worked hard in the laundry and refectory of the convent. Psychologically she endured prolonged periods of darkness when the light of faith seemed all but extinguished. She wasted away slowly during the last year of her life from tuberculosis. She died at the age of 24.

Life in the Carmelite convent was indeed uneventful and consisted mainly of prayer and hard domestic work. But Theresa had that holy insight that redeems time, however dull that time may be. She saw in quiet suffering Christ's redemptive suffering which was indeed her apostolate, for which she was later declared by the Church Patron of Missions. We have become obsessed with appearance, glamour and status.

We have become dangerously self-conscious people, craving for self-fulfilment, knowing all the time that we can't achieve it. But Theresa, like many other saints, sought to serve others, to do something outside herself, to forget herself in quiet acts of love. She is one of the great examples of the Gospel paradox – that we gain our life by losing it for God and others.

OCTOBER 2 * MEMORIAL

GUARDIAN ANGELS

The idea of an angel assigned to guide and nurture every human being is a development of Catholic doctrine and piety based on Scripture but not directly drawn from it. Jesus' words in Matthew 18:10 best support the belief: "See that you do not despise one of these little ones, for I tell you that in heaven their angels always behold the face of my Father." Perhaps no aspect of Catholic piety is as comforting to parents as the belief that an angel protects their little ones from dangers real and imagined. Yet guardian angels are not just for children. Their role is to represent all individuals before God, to watch over them always, to aid their prayer and to present their souls to God at death. In all these, we recognise God's constant care of, and attention to, his creation. It speaks to us of God's desire for our welfare, his concern to guard us and guide us in the right direction. His guardianship, his message of love and goodness is already implanted in us. The mystery of angels only strengthens this belief of ours, that we are God's children, and blessed children, if only our eyes of faith can open and see.

OCTOBER 4 * MEMORIAL

FRANCIS OF ASSISI
(c. 1181-1226)

Francis was the son of a wealthy merchant. From being a light-hearted youth, he changed the course of his life. Important in this respect was his meeting with a leper and Christ's words to him when he was praying before a cross in the tiny church of St Damiano. He embraced poverty, lived the life of the Gospel and preached to all the love of God. Francis' new way of life in poverty and simplicity led to an almighty row with his father, who saw his family lineage, fame and fortune disappearing before his eyes. At the height of this row, Francis discarded his clothes, wanting nothing to do with his old life or his worldly wealth. The incredible reality of God born poor was vividly demonstrated to the world by Francis when he made the first crib. Not only did he reform his own personal life on the model of Christ poor, he also did his best to reform the Church. Together with his Friars, he set himself to this task through preaching and example, of course, in perfect obedience and reverence to the legitimate authority of the Church. This was the mark and guarantee of the authenticity of his work of reform. Since then, Francis has inspired innumerable groups of believers in the course of the centuries. The Franciscan movement has travelled Europe, crossed the ocean, permeated different cultures and produced a continual flowering of charitable initiatives and marvellous fruits of Christian sanctity.

OCTOBER 7 * MEMORIAL

OUR LADY OF THE ROSARY

Once a university student found himself seated by the side of a gentleman who was praying the Rosary. "Sir, do you still believe in such outdated things?" asked the student. "Yes, I do. Do you not?" asked the gentleman. The student burst out into laughter, and said, "I do not waste my time with such stupid practices. If you like I can supply you with some books." Then the student asked the address of the gentleman. He gave to the student his visiting card. On the card he read, "Louis Pasteur, Director of the Institute of Scientific Research, Paris." The student bowed his head in shame.

The Rosary is a perfect form of prayer, it is a profession of faith. It is a tribute to the Holy Trinity, a prayer of hope and confidence. The Rosary touches the heart, enkindles charity. It is a source of grace and enlightenment. It gives comfort in trials, strength in temptation and is a powerful aid in every need. While praying the Rosary, as we contemplate the mysteries of Christ, we are led into the mystery of our own life. It describes the joys and sorrows of life and gives us the promise of eternal glory. Jesus himself is our light as we journey through life. Our life is full of joys and sorrows, and in praying the Rosary we find help and consolation from the experiences Jesus and Mary themselves had in their lives. The quiet repetition of the "Hail Mary", acting like a mantra, can soothe the spirit into silent contemplation and bring us close to the Lord.

OCTOBER 15 * MEMORIAL

TERESA OF JESUS
Virgin and Doctor (1515-1582)

Teresa was born in Avila, Spain. She entered the Carmelite Order. In the beginning she lived a tepid life. But from the age of 40, she began to enjoy a vivid experience of God's presence within her. She made a vow always to follow the more perfect course and resolved to keep the rule as perfectly as she could. However the atmosphere prevailing in the monastery in which she lived did not favour the more perfect type of life for which she longed. Hence she set herself the task of reforming the Carmelite Order itself. When she moved to a more simple and fervent lifestyle, she was ridiculed not only by the sisters of her own Order but also by the Church and the civic authorities. Still Teresa set up the first house of her reform and came to be acclaimed as the great reformer of the Carmelite Order, and was declared as Doctor of the Church in 1970.

The gift of God to Teresa in and through which she became holy and left her mark on the Church and the world is threefold: She was a woman; she was a contemplative; she was an active reformer. As a woman, she stood on her own feet, even in the man's world of her time. She was her own woman entering the Carmelites despite strong opposition from her father. As a woman for God, she was a woman of prayer, discipline and compassion. In the midst of her struggles, she clung to God in life and in prayer. As a woman for others, she founded over half a dozen new monasteries. She travelled, wrote and fought – always to renew and to reform.

IGNATIUS OF ANTIOCH
Bishop and Martyr (d. 107?)

Born in Syria, Ignatius converted to Christianity and eventually became bishop of Antioch. When Emperor Trajan forced the Christians of Antioch to choose between death and apostasy, Ignatius would not deny Christ and thus was condemned to be put to death in Rome. Ignatius wrote seven letters on his long journey from Antioch to Rome. In his letters he warns the Christians to remain faithful to God and to obey their superiors. He warns them against heretical doctrines providing them with the solid truths of the Christian faith. In the final letter he begs the Christians in Rome not to try to stop his martyrdom: "The only thing I ask you is to allow me to offer the libation of my blood to God. I am the wheat of the Lord; may I be ground by the teeth of the beasts to become the immaculate bread of Christ." Ignatius bravely met the lions in the Circus Maximus. His martyrdom calls us to be ready to pay the price, whatever it might be, to persevere in our commitment to Christ.

LUKE
Evangelist

Luke, the Gospel writer, was himself a doctor and Jesus appropriately called him to the vocation of human compassion. A convert to the faith, he became a companion of Paul on his missionary journeys, and he is one of those who wrote the Gospel story. In his Gospel, he brings out the heartfelt compassion of Jesus to everyone. It is a Gospel of Mercy, and contains the great stories of compassion: the parables of the Good Samaritan and the Prodigal Son, and the words of consolation spoken to the women of Jerusalem and to the Good Thief during the hours of Jesus' Passion. His Gospel, besides being the Gospel of Mercy, has other features. It is the Gospel of Universal Salvation: Jesus died for all. He is the Son of Adam, not just of David, and Gentiles are his friends too. It is the Gospel of the Poor, for little people are prominent in his Gospel and he is concerned with "evangelical poverty", as we call it today. It is also the Gospel of Joy: Luke succeeds in portraying the joy of salvation that permeated the primitive Church. He also wrote the history of the early Church, called "The Acts of the Apostles", a work full of historical detail, which situated the Christian story in the secular world of the time. Whatever ills our world may suffer, Luke offers in his writings the remedy for our sorrows and a cause for our joy in Jesus Christ.

OCTOBER 28 * FEAST

SIMON AND JUDE
Apostles

Jude is so named in Luke and Acts. Matthew and Mark call him Thaddeus. He is not mentioned elsewhere in the Gospels, except of course where all the Apostles are referred to. Simon is mentioned in all the four lists of the Apostles. In two of them he is called "the Zealot". The Zealots were a Jewish sect that represented an extreme of Jewish nationalism. For them, the Messianic promise was made only to the Jews. However, Simon had to learn later that Jesus came not just for Jews but for all people on earth.

These men, called by Jesus to be his apostles, began their following of Jesus in uncertainty, as we all do in life, and they were led by the Lord into experiences of confusion, confrontation and downright fear. When Jesus was arrested and killed, their whole world was shattered. But in the days of the Lord's resurrection and appearances, their faith in the Lord was restored, and fired by the Spirit, they went out to preach the Gospel of the Lord, thus becoming the foundation stones of the Church. It is said that Simon and Jude journeyed together into Persia where they were martyred. These two Apostles, helped by the Spirit, slowly matured in Christ. Detaching themselves from a desire for soft living, morbid fear of death, foolish self-importance and self-preoccupation, they surrendered themselves joyfully to live by the teachings of Jesus until their death and spent every ounce of their energy for spreading the Gospel. May the Holy Spirit lead us to the same kind of maturity in Christ Jesus.

NOVEMBER 1 * SOLEMNITY

ALL SAINTS

There is an unusual rejoicing today in heaven. Though some of the saints have been allotted particular days during the liturgical year, today there is universal celebration in the Church for all the saints. The Catholic Church has an amazing galaxy of saints, canonised or beatified. Each age has produced its crop of holy men and women. Today we celebrate the great harvest of them all, including the millions and millions the Church has not canonised. We remember them all today. They come in all sorts, shapes and sizes. They come from all walks of life, from royalty to working class. They range from serious and angelic doctors to humorous types, from the aristocratic to the poetic backgrounds, from great Popes to humble curates. And standing above them all is our Blessed Lady.

Saints are masterpieces of God's work. Admiring the painting, we admire the artist. The praise and the admiration of the painting does not detract anything from the praise and admiration we owe to the artist. On the contrary, when we bestow admiration and praise on the painting, in reality we praise and admire the artist who, in the case of saints, is God, who works always with the co-operation of human beings. If so many have become saints why can't we? The countless number of saints in heaven were men and women of flesh and blood like us. They had the same weaknesses, the same human inclinations, the same human nature. They had also the same means of holiness.

NOVEMBER 2

ALL SOULS

The need for purification stands to reason. The following example illustrates the point. Once two people went out for walk. They had a vehement discussion on the existence of Purgatory. One of them said, "I do not believe in Purgatory". The other could not convince him of its existence. Both came back. Supper was ready. The one who tried to prove the existence of Purgatory said, "Let us go for supper". The other said, "How can I eat supper like this. I am all perspiring. My hands are dirty. Let me at least wash my hands and my face." "You see," the other at once remarked, "You are not ready for supper. Do you think that one will be ready at once to participate in the heavenly banquet soon after death, with all the dust and stain of life's journey?"

Belief in Purgatory is founded on the acknowledgement of human frailty. Since few people achieve perfection in this life and go to the grave still scarred with traces of sinfulness, some period of purification may be necessary before a soul comes face to face with God, and the prayer of the living can speed up this process of purification. That is why we pray not only today but daily for the souls in Purgatory.

All Souls' Day also reminds us that we are immortal, that we shall not really die, that we have an eternity to live. Our eternity depends on how we live here on earth. Our works follow us. There is a real connection between this life and the next. This brings a great responsibility. We are forming the physiognomy of our eternity. Every action of ours has a bearing on eternity. No action of ours is lost.

NOVEMBER 4 * MEMORIAL

CHARLES BORROMEO
Bishop (1538-1584)

Charles was born in a castle in Northern Italy. He came from an aristocratic family, was educated at a nearby abbey, and graduated at 22 in civil and Church law. His uncle became Pope Pius IV. Tonsured since the age of 12, he inherited privileges, positions and appointments in the service of the Church, together with a large and lavish household. However, Charles felt discomfort at his luxurious outward circumstances and longed for a simpler lifestyle. In the course of time, he broke away from the pomp and riches, was ordained a priest and became bishop in Milan. Charles became a great reformer, putting into practice the decrees of the recent Council of Trent. He literally wore himself out in the work of reform, died at the age of 46, and was proclaimed a saint 26 years later.

 In order to give a good example of what he preached, he allotted most of his income to charity, forbade himself all luxury and imposed severe penances on himself. Thus he sacrificed wealth, honours, esteem and influence to become poor. During the plague and famine, when the civil authorities fled at the height of the plague, he stayed in the city, where he ministered to the sick and the dying, helping those in want. Like Charles, may we try to make the words of Christ our own: "I was hungry, you gave me food, I was thirsty, you gave me drink, a stranger and you welcomed me, naked and you clothed me"!

NOVEMBER 9 * FEAST

DEDICATION OF ST JOHN LATERAN

In the city of Rome where there are hundreds of churches, there is a special one called St John Lateran. This is the home church of the Pope as bishop of Rome. As the Pope stands for the unity of all the local churches, so his special church stands for the unity of all Christian people all over the world. It was first built by the Emperor Constantine, a basilica full of history. Most Catholics think of St Peter's as the Pope's main church, but they are wrong. St John's Lateran is the Pope's church, the cathedral of the Diocese of Rome.

 Every church is the sign of Christ who became man in order to reconcile the world with God, and who has achieved this through the cross and resurrection. It is a sign of the world reconciled with God in Jesus Christ. We proclaim here that Christ has overcome the alienation between God and man and between man and man. The true centres of the world are not the big capital cities of the world which are the hubs of politics and business, of money and power. The true centres of the world are the quiet places where we go to pray. This is where the earthly world particularly comes into contact with the supernatural world, the Church of pilgrimage on earth with the eternal and victorious Church in heaven. St John Lateran, being the church of the Bishop of Rome, fulfils in an excellent way all these qualities of a church and is, indeed, the spiritual home of all the people of God.

NOVEMBER 10 * MEMORIAL

LEO THE GREAT
Pope and Doctor (d. 461)

Leo was born in Rome at the beginning of the 5th century, became a deacon in the Church and a very able diplomat, negotiating peace between warring generals in Gaul. It was during this period of negotiations that he was elected Pope. In his twenty-year reign as Pope his powers of negotiation were called for to resolve the theological and political difficulties of the time. The doctrinal dispute was over the nature of Christ; the Council of Chalcedon accepted Leo's teaching about the two natures of Christ in one person, and this became the defining moment in the history of the Church. In the political sphere, he persuaded the Huns to withdraw beyond the Danube (451) and secured concessions when the Vandals took Rome (452).

As the universal Pastor, he was God's instrument of the call to holiness. Well-versed in Scripture and endowed with great ecclesiastical awareness, Leo had the ability to reach the everyday needs and interests of his people. We hear today criticism that bishops and priests – indeed, all of us – are too preoccupied with the administration of temporal matters. Pope Leo is an example of a great administrator who used his talents in areas where spirit and structure are inseparably combined, so that doctrine, peace and structure go together in harmony. Leo is rightly called "The Great".

NOVEMBER 11 * MEMORIAL

MARTIN OF TOURS
Bishop (c. 316-397)

Martin of Tours was born about the year 316 in Upper Pannonia, the present-day Hungary. He was a Roman official converted from paganism. He received baptism at the age of about 20. He later became a deacon, then a priest and finally bishop of Tours, France. It is said that on a bitterly cold day Martin met a poor man, almost naked, trembling in the cold and begging from passers-by at the city gate. Martin had nothing but his weapons and his clothes. He drew his sword, cut his cloak into two pieces, gave one to the beggar and wrapped himself in the other half. Some of the bystanders laughed at his now odd appearance; others were ashamed at not having relieved the man's misery. That night in his sleep Martin saw Christ dressed in the half of the garment he had given away and heard him say, "Martin, still a catechumen, has covered me with this garment."

Martin died in the year 397. In France 3602 parishes are dedicated to him. In his birthplace Hungary, more than 100 churches and villages bear his name. We must be like Martin, courageous in living and bearing witness to our Christian faith. May we be like St Martin, generous to everyone and show love, charity and the spirit of sacrifice, believing that our true joy is found in loving and giving.

NOVEMBER 12 * MEMORIAL

JOSAPHAT
Bishop and Martyr (c. 1580-1623)

Josaphat was born in the Ukraine. Tension between the ecclesiastical traditions of the Roman and Orthodox Churches had long existed in that region. It was Josaphat who played the role of mediator between them; but he paid for his noble efforts with his life. Though born into a wealthy family, Josaphat became a monk, was ordained a priest, and developed into a very gifted and popular preacher. After becoming the abbot of his monastery, he was made bishop of Polotsk. For the following few years, he spent himself in works of reform, holding synods, publishing a catechism, and visiting his people. But in the course of his campaign of reform, he made a lot of enemies among those who saw his activities as a betrayal of Orthodox customs and a selling-out of local power to the alien Bishop of Rome. Determined to put an end to Josaphat's influence, they murdered him in 1623. Although born into Orthodox tradition, Josaphat became a Catholic and did his best to promote unity among the two traditions. May we also, following his inspiring example, bear with one another in charity and do our part to bring unity wherever people are divided by religious or other affiliations.

NOVEMBER 17 * MEMORIAL

ELIZABETH OF HUNGARY
Religious (1207-1231)

Elizabeth lived about eight hundred years ago. Born a royal princess in Hungary and betrothed at the age of four to a prince in Thuringia in Germany, she was sent to live with that family. She later married her prince, Louis, at the tender age of fourteen. She bore him three children in her teenage years, and was a widow at twenty when her husband died while on a Crusade. Shattered by the death of her husband, she never married again, fulfilling the promise she had made to her husband, and with that her earthly career also was over. She turned her heart totally to God to whom she always had great devotion, showing her love for him by serving the poor. She now became a Franciscan tertiary, gave her whole self to the service of the poor and the sick. Having lost her husband and after providing for her children, her life really became otherworldly.

When Jesus washed the feet of his disciples at the Last Supper, he taught the lesson that a Christian is one who serves the humblest needs of others, even if they serve from an exalted position. Elizabeth clearly understood this lesson from Jesus. Of royal blood, Elizabeth could have forded it over her subjects. Yet she served them with such a loving heart that her brief life stands as a shining example to all for Christian charity.

NOVEMBER 21 * MEMORIAL

PRESENTATION OF MARY

As with Mary's birth, we read of Mary's presentation in the temple only in apocryphal literature which is recognised as unhistorical. It tells that Anna and Joachim offered Mary to God in the Temple when she was three years old. This was to carry out a promise made to God when Anna was still childless. Mary's presentation was celebrated in Jerusalem in the sixth century. A church was built there in honour of this mystery. The Eastern Church was more interested in the feast but it does appear in the West in the eleventh century. Although the feast at times disappeared from the calendar, in the sixteenth century it became a feast of the Universal Church.

Though unhistorical, Mary's presentation has an important spiritual message. It continues the impact of the feasts of the Immaculate Conception and of the birth of Mary. It emphasises that the holiness conferred on Mary from the beginning of her life on earth continued through her early childhood and beyond. It also points out that from the beginning of her life, Mary was dedicated to God. She herself became a greater temple than any made by hands. God came to dwell in her in a marvellous manner and sanctified her for her unique role in God's saving work. At the same time, the magnificence of Mary rebounds upon her children. They, too, are temples of God and sanctified in order that they might enjoy and share in God's saving work.

CECILIA
Virgin and Martyr

Cecilia is said to have lived in third-century Rome. She dedicated herself to God, but was betrothed against her will to Valerian. She converted her husband to Christ, and soon afterwards, he and her brother were arrested and martyred. Cecilia gave their bodies a Christian burial, and was immediately arrested herself. Required to offer sacrifice to the gods, she refused and was put to death. Even then there was great suffering: because the executioner was incompetent, Cecilia lingered on for three days before she died.

Cecilia is the patron saint of the musicians. St Augustine says that he who sings prays twice. He also says that it is the mark of a lover to sing. We all love God and our neighbour. Therefore we must sing. Our life should be a song. We must sing not so much with our voice, but rather in our heart. In music there is harmony. Many notes harmonise. There should not be discordant notes. Sin is a discordant note. When there is sin we will not be able to sing with our heart. Our life will not be a song. Therefore, let our life be a life without a discordant note.

ANDREW DUNG-LAC AND COMPANIONS
Priest and Martyrs

During the first two hundred years of Christianity in Vietnam, it is believed that about 100,000 people were put to death for their faith. Among them were bishops, priests and laypeople who lost their lives for the sake of Christ. Two great waves of persecution in the nineteenth century under two different kings brought hardship and pain to the budding Christian Church. Foreign missionaries were banned from the country, and native Christians were ordered to renounce their faith by trampling on the crucifix. Churches were destroyed and the teaching of the Gospel was forbidden. Many people died. The records we possess tell of 117 martyrs, whose feast we celebrate today. Andrew was one of them who met death in Vietnam between 1820 and 1862. Members of this group were beatified on four different occasions between 1900 and 1952. All of them were canonised by Pope Paul II in 1988. If it is true that the blood of martyrs is the seed of Christians, then the Church in Vietnam should be assured of a great future because no particular Church in the world has had to endure over 260 years of persecution, all for the love of Christ. Do we love Jesus Christ?

NOVEMBER 30 * FEAST

ANDREW
Apostle

Andrew was St Peter's brother, and was called with him by Jesus: "As Jesus walked by the sea of Galilee, he saw two brothers, Simon who is called Peter, and Andrew his brother, casting a net into the sea, for they were fishermen. He said to them, 'Follow me, and I will make you fishers of men.' Immediately they left their nets and followed him." (Mt 4:18-20) John the Evangelist presents Andrew as the disciple of John the Baptist who introduced Jesus to Andrew and another disciple. Following Jesus, they "stayed with him that day" (Jn 1:38-39).

Andrew's vocation seems to have been to introduce people to Christ. He first of all introduced Peter to Christ. He later introduced the boy with five barley loaves and two fishes to Jesus, which Jesus multiplied to feed more than five thousand people. Later, together with Philip who was also from Bethsaida, he introduced some Greeks to Jesus. The Greeks who had come to worship at the festival said to Philip, " Sir, we wish to see Jesus." Philip went and told Andrew; then Andrew and Philip went and told Jesus. Are we introducing anyone to Jesus, to the Good News or to our Christian faith?

DECEMBER 3 * MEMORIAL

FRANCIS XAVIER
Priest (1506-1552)

Francis was born at the castle of Xavier, in Navarre. While studying at the University of Paris, he first met Ignatius Loyola who repeated to him the words of Jesus: "What profit would there be for one to gain the whole world and forfeit his life?" Being captivated by these words, Francis, a teacher of philosophy who had a highly promising academic career, with success and a life of prestige and honour before him, left all of them behind and became a Jesuit. In the next ten years, he achieved outstanding results in his work of preaching the Gospel to the pagans.

He first arrived in Goa, spent some months there and renewed the spiritual and moral life of the Portuguese Christians on that island. From there he went to South India and spent seven years living as a poor man among the people of India, of Sri Lanka, of Malacca, of the Molucca Islands and of the Malay Penisula. After making many converts among the poor people, he left behind him strong, well-organised communities. In 1549 Francis went to Japan where he planted the seeds of the faith which in latter years would prove brave and resilient under persecution. Francis set out again from Goa in 1551, this time for China, but he was taken ill on the island of Chang-Chuen-Shan, and died there worn out by his apostolic labours. His body was brought back to Goa where it is enshrined to this day.

All of us are called to "go and preach to all nations" (Mt 28:19). Our preaching is not necessarily on distant shores but to our families, our children, our husband or wife, our co-workers. And we are called to preach not with words, but by our everyday lives.

DECEMBER 7 * MEMORIAL

AMBROSE
Bishop and Doctor (340?-397)

Ambrose was born at Trier. He studied in Rome, entered the civil service and became governor with his residence in Milan. He was noted for his uprightness and blameless character. On the death of the bishop of Milan, he was unanimously chosen as bishop of that city although he was still a catechumen. He received baptism on 30 November 374 and already on 7 December he was consecrated bishop! He immediately distributed his share of the family wealth to the poor and set an example of strict asceticism in the episcopal household. He applied himself to the systematic study of theology and became a zealous pastor.

His writings on ethics and asceticism, his letters and sermons – all reveal a Christian bishop of great faith and energy. He championed also the rights of the Church. He enunciated the principle that the Church is supreme in its own domain and is the guardian of morality, and that even the Emperors are subject to the moral laws as taught by the Church. It was he who received Augustine into the Catholic Church. Let us have the courage to stand by the teachings of the Church on all questions of morals.

DECEMBER 8 * SOLEMNITY

IMMACULATE CONCEPTION

In 1854 Pius IX declared it to be irreformably true that "the Most Blessed Virgin Mary, in the first instant of her conception, by a singular grace and privilege granted by almighty God, in view of the merits of Jesus Christ, the saviour of the human race, was preserved free from all strain of original sin." This is one of the Church's teachings that arose more from the piety of the faithful than from the insights of brilliant theologians. Mary's Immaculate Conception enhances Jesus' redemptive work. Other members of the human race are cleansed from the original sin after birth.

In Mary, Jesus' work was so powerful as to prevent original sin from the start.

Living in the world we feel as if we are stranded on a desert island. For we experience the constant struggle between good and evil, between light and darkness. And so, like long-lost castaways we scan the far horizon, and thank God, on this day, in the Church, for the sound of music, a hymn of praise to Mary Immaculate. This music is for deserted people, a true song for our race, because Mary is the true image of every human being, as God created us, and as we shall be. God is good and we are all his children. Hence, though the world may look like a deserted island, we are not alone. Like Mary, we also have been chosen for holiness and purity so that we can live one day through love in God's presence.

DECEMBER 12 *FEAST

OUR LADY OF GUADALOUPE

On 9 December, 1531, the Blessed Virgin Mary appeared to an Indian convert named Juan Diego, by a hill called Tepeyat, in a small village called Guadalupe, near Mexico city. The Lady asked Diego to build a church on the spot of the apparition with the promise: "No one who seeks me here in true need or affliction shall go away unconsoled". The message was conveyed to the Bishop of Mexico; but the Bishop asked for a sign to verify the claim. The visionary was told by our Lady to go and collect flowers from the place of the first apparition – though it was not the season for flowers – and Diego brought them back to the bishop in his cloak. When he opened the cloak a miraculous image of the Madonna was to be seen. With the giving of this sign, our Lady's message was accepted, and soon a small chapel was built. Today it is a magnificent shrine and basilica, and there Our Lady of Guadaloupe is celebrated as patroness of all the Americas.

Mary's call to build a church, as she had given in her other apparitions, is symbolic of a deeper call, that is, it is a call to gather people together in faith, hope and love, with the promise of help and consolation to the poor and the weak of this world. As recipients of these messages of Mary, it is our vocation in this world to convey these messages to others, and to be a sign of God's love and life here on earth.

DECEMBER 13 * MEMORIAL

LUCY
Virgin and Martyr (d. 304)

Lucy was born in the city of Syracuse, Sicily, where she was later martyred during the persecution of Christians by Diocletian. Her name lives on to this day in the popular song, "Santa Lucia". The ancient Canons of the Roman and Ambrosian Rites, Greek liturgical books and ancient churches testify to the name and to her cult. She decided to be a virgin all her life and not to get married. To be pure before marriage was an ancient Roman ideal, rarely found, but not to be condemned. To exclude marriage altogether, however, was too much. So, people thought that she must have something sinister to hide. But Lucy knew of the heroism of earlier virgin martyrs. She remained faithful to their example and to the example of the Son of God. Pope John XXIII, in a Letter to Women Religious, wrote: "May your conduct prove to all that chastity is not only a possible virtue, but a social virtue, which must be strongly defended by prayer, vigilance and mortification of the senses."

DECEMBER 14 * MEMORIAL

JOHN OF THE CROSS
Priest and Doctor (1541-1591)

Born in Northern Spain, John joined the Order of Carmelite Friars and studied theology at Salamanca. Ordained at 25, he wanted to pursue the spiritual life in a more austere Order, but on meeting Teresa of Avila, he was persuaded to stay and to reform the Carmelites. In his work of reform, he made a lot of enemies among his Friars. They had him arrested and imprisoned in Toledo and kept in appalling conditions. It was while there that John wrote his finest poetry, including "The Dark Night of the Soul". He later escaped from prison, and his reformed group escaped from those who opposed to them. After some years, as leader of the reformed houses and as a teacher, he again suffered harsh treatment at the hands of his superiors and was banished to the south, to Andalusia where he died aged 49.

John is a saint because his life was a heroic effort to live up to his dedication: "of the cross". The folly of the cross came to full realisation in time. The paschal mystery – the journey through death to life – strongly marks John as reformer, mystic-poet and theologian-priest. But as agony leads to ecstasy, John had his own "Ascent to Mt Carmel" – the title of one of his masterly works. As a Carmelite he experienced in himself this purifying ascent; as spiritual director he sensed it in others, and as psychologist-theologian he described and analysed it in his prose writings. We learn from him that the path of union with God leads us through rigorous discipline, abandonment, and purification.

DECEMBER 26 * FEAST

STEPHEN
First Martyr (d. 36?)

Stephen was a man filled with grace and power, who worked great wonders among the people. Certain Jews, members of the synagogue of Roman Freedmen, debated with Stephen but proved no match for the wisdom and spirit with which he spoke. They persuaded others to charge him with blasphemy. He was seized and carried before the Sanhedrin. In his speech Stephen recalled God's guidance through Israel history, as well as Israel's idolatry and disobedience. This speech brought anger from the crowd, who threw him out of the city and stoned him to death. As he was dying he asked God to forgive his executioners.

In Stephen's martyrdom we have the same confrontation between good and evil, hatred and forgiveness, meekness and violence which is found in the cross of Christ. The commemoration of the first martyr, therefore, quite opportunely reveals to us the demanding depth of Christmas, linking Bethlehem to Calvary, and reminding us that divine salvation necessarily implies the struggle against sin and inevitably passes through the mystery of the cross.

DECEMBER 27 * FEAST

JOHN
Apostle and Evangelist

John had a special place in the apostolic college. He describes himself as "the disciple whom Jesus loved". He is one of the three who witnessed the raising to life of the daughter of Jairus, the Transfiguration and the Agony in the Garden of Gethsemane. It was John together with Peter, James and Andrew who asked Jesus about the destruction of Jerusalem. It was again John together with Peter who was sent to prepare the Passover supper. It is said that in his old age John never changed the topic of his sermons and that he limited them to a single phrase: "My dear little children: love one another".

The Lord gave to the Virgin Apostle three things: he gave John his heart by allowing him to rest his head on his chest; he gave him his passion by calling him alone of all the other Apostles to witness to the drama of calvary; and finally, he gave him a mother, his own mother. The heart of Jesus, the Cross and the Virgin Mary are indeed the triple gift which Jesus gives to the chosen ones. John enjoyed a special intimacy with Jesus and Mary. Let us also cultivate a special intimacy with Jesus and Mary.

DECEMBER 28 * FEAST

HOLY INNOCENTS
Martyrs

Life was considered very cheap at the time Jesus was born. One day in Rome 400 slaves were put to death because their master had been found dead in his home. The life of a newborn child was worth nothing. The father of the child had power over the life of his child. He could dispose of it at his pleasure. No wonder, then, that Herod who was by nature a cruel man, ordered the killing of all male children in order to dispose of the child Jesus. These children are venerated by the Church as the holy innocent martyrs.

The feast of the Holy Innocents calls before our minds all the children of the world who die before their time, including the unborn, still in the womb, by abortion. We remember today children who are victims of accidents, the victims of war, the victims of abuse, children murdered, children molested, children who do not die but have their childhood stolen from them. To every child thus suffering there are the tears of the parents and guardians in sorrow. We are never far away from the sound of lamentation, "of Rachel weeping for her children", because they are no more. May we give generous financial support to all the agencies that work for children, both local and international. May we give generously of our time to help in voluntary work for children. Perhaps we can also do something else. We can see in every other person the loveable and vulnerable child that surely lives hidden therein, and allow tenderness to grow in us, that will help to wipe away the tears of those who cry.

Alain Ducasse is one of the most celebrated chefs of his generation and the author of several cookbooks. Born in 1956 on a farm in Les Landes, France, he went on to train with great chefs including Michel Guérard, Gaston Lenôtre, Alain Chapel and Roger Vergé. He received his first three Michelin stars in 1990 at the Louis XV restaurant in Monaco. Since then, he has set up schools, created artisan factories and opened restaurants across the world, most notably in Japan, the United States and London.

Jay McInerney is an American novelist, screenwriter and wine critic. His novels include *Bright Lights, Big City, Ransom, Story of My Life, Brightness Falls* and *The Last of the Savages*.

Clare Smyth MBE is the first and only British female chef to hold three Michelin stars. Born on a farm in County Antrim, she moved to England at the age of sixteen, building a career that included working at Alain Ducasse's the Louis XV in Monaco and with Gordon Ramsay for thirteen years. Her first restaurant, Core, opened in London in August 2017.

Polly Mackintosh is an editor and a translator from the French.

GOOD TASTE
A Life of Food and Passion

ALAIN DUCASSE

With introductions by
Jay McInerney and Clare Smyth

Translated by Polly Mackintosh

Gallic Books
London

A Gallic Book

First published in France as *Une vie de goûts et de passions*
by Éditions Jean-Claude Lattès, 2022
Copyright © Éditions Jean-Claude Lattès, 2022

English translation copyright © Gallic Books, 2023
Foreword copyright © Jay McInerney, 2023
Introduction copyright © Clare Smyth, 2023

First published in Great Britain in 2023 by
Gallic Books, 12 Eccleston Street, London, SW1W 9LT

A CIP record for this book is available from the British Library

ISBN 978-1-913547-67-7

Typeset in Garamond by Gallic Books

Printed in the UK by CPI (CR0 4YY)

2 4 6 8 10 9 7 5 3 1

To Gwénaëlle and to our children

CONTENTS

FOREWORD
by Jay McInerney

I was lucky enough to spend a few days with Chef Ducasse more than a decade ago, exploring Provence with him and visiting his two properties there, and I was struck over and over again by his exquisite sense of taste, not just at the table, but at the antique stores and art galleries and bookstores we visited – his finely tuned and joyful aesthetic sensibility, the pleasure that he took in a carved antique wooden door or a piece of rustic pottery.

He collects antique doors, luggage, cars, books, art and much more. Sharing five successive meals with him over the course of those days, I could see that he truly enjoyed eating and he had a wonderful facility in explaining and sharing his enthusiasm at the table.

Dining at Noma in Copenhagen with some friends recently, I heard a story which confirmed the extraordinary acuity of his sense of taste, in the most literal way – his ability to detect and parse flavours and nuances. The story comes from Dan Barber, the celebrated American chef of Blue Hill at Stone Barns, situated on a bucolic property in Westchester where much of the restaurant's produce is grown. A few years back, he heard from Ducasse's office that the chef was coming to the property for a sunrise photo shoot: the chef only had twenty minutes in his schedule to devote to eating.

Barber, boldly, decided to serve bread and butter. 'I was particularly excited about the butter because it's from the farm my brother David and I took over from our grandmother and reconfigured into an all-pasture dairy. Since we had done so much work to improve the pasture, I thought the quality of the butter was better than ever.' Arriving promptly at 7 a.m., Ducasse took several minutes to eat the bread and butter. 'It was clear,' Barber said, 'that he did not find the butter to be the best butter of his life. He said "I have a question. Has it been raining recently?"' In fact, Hurricane Irene had just doused the area. 'He was suggesting that the butter was washed out. Dude could taste the weather. Then he said, "I have another question for you. Was the butter made by hand or in an electric mixer?" I said, "By hand." "And was the butter from cows pasturing near the barn or far away from the barn?" he asked. I said, "Near the barn." Because I always see them near the barn.'

'A week later I saw my pastry intern making butter in an electric mixer.' Barber asked him what he was doing. 'The intern turned to me and said, "Chef, I've discovered I can make the butter a lot faster in an electric mixer."' Score two for Ducasse's palate. A week and a half later Barber was up at the dairy farm and he didn't see any cows. 'And I turned to Sean the farmer and asked, "Where are the cows?" He said, "I've been trying an experiment for the past month. I'm pasturing them in Field seven, the field farthest away from the barn. It's in bad shape, it's all weeds, it needs manure and I want to bring it back to the shape

that the pasture right here next to the barn is in."
It's human nature if you're a dairy farmer that at
five in the morning you are least inclined to walk
your cows out a mile and a half to Field Seven. You
keep them close to the barn. So the fields closest to
the barn are the most fertilised, the most diverse,
the healthiest, resulting in the fattiest milk and
cream and the most delicious butter. Ducasse
could taste Field Seven.'

His feel for ingredients was cultivated as a child
growing up near Castel-Sarrazin in the south-
west of France; he was mesmerised by the smells
coming from his grandmother's kitchen directly
below his bedroom; of ceps sautéing with garlic,
of braised veal cooking with peas and spring
onions. 'My grandmother didn't care to teach
me to cook,' he told me over lunch at his inn in
Moustiers. His constant questions and criticisms
annoyed her, not least when he pronounced her
food to be overcooked. But he was allowed to
gather produce from the garden, which is where
he developed his famous ability to pick the tastiest
and the freshest ingredients. After working at a
truck stop restaurant in nearby Mont-de-Marsan
he had a brief stint at the Lycée Hôtelier de
Bordeaux-Talence before talking his way into some

of the best kitchens in France, including Michel Guérard's in Eugénie-les-Bains and Roger Vergé's Le Moulin de Mougins, where he fell in love with the Mediterranean landscape and cuisine.

The apprenticeship he describes as the most influential took place at Alain Chapel's restaurant outside Lyon. Ducasse credits Chapel with teaching him the supreme importance of fresh ingredients. While it may be a cliché now, forty years ago the idea that a meal was only as good as its raw materials was radical, even in France, or especially in France, where heavy sauces could cover a multitude of sins. The concept dovetailed with Ducasse's passion for sunny Provence and the Côte d'Azur's bounty of fresh vegetables and seafood. After two years with Chapel he returned to the south, working first as head chef at La Terrasse in Juan-les-Pins. Putting Chapel's lesson into practice, he told me, 'I got to know the fisherman and the farmers, and I went to the market every day at five in the morning for seven years – apparently an unusual practice for a head chef in those days.' A few years later, at the behest of Prince Rainier, he moved down the coast to the Louis XV in Monaco, the restaurant that sealed his reputation as the greatest French chef of his generation. He promised the prince that he would garner three Michelin stars and less than three years later he achieved that goal.

In these pages Ducasse describes receiving a phone call at the restaurant of the Hotel Okura in Japan informing him that Michelin had awarded him that third star. 'I can remember the feeling of delight and success,' he writes, 'of having achieved an aim I had set myself and had promised Prince Rainier thirty-three months previously – an aim that I had promised myself several years before that, even. But as soon as I hung up, the delight, celebrations and fulfilled promises were offset by questions. Now what? And what about after that?'

Serendipitously enough, Joël Robuchon had received a similar phone call at the exact same location six years previously, informing him that his restaurant in Paris had been awarded three stars. And it would be Robuchon who would provide Ducasse with the answer to 'Now what?'

In 1996 Robuchon called to say he was thinking of retiring, and Ducasse, on an impulse, offered to take over. A crazy suggestion, since he was intending to remain at the helm of the Louis XV. But take over he did, in August 1996. It was here, a year later, that I first tasted Ducasse's cooking and became a fan. I can still conjure the taste and texture of the Bresse chicken breast with white truffles in Albufera sauce – a cream-based concoction turbocharged with foie gras and port. For all its luxury, the dish is actually fairly straightforward, based on the perfect provenance of the humblest of fowl, highlighted by, rather than smothered in, a perfect sauce. This for me is the signature of Ducasse's cooking: the freshness of ingredients and the relative simplicity of presentation (if not preparation). As Walt Whitman remarked, it's incredibly difficult to achieve the appearance of effortless simplicity. Ducasse's clean cuisine rests on a solid foundation of classical technique. (The chicken was poached in a pig's bladder, a traditional method that helps keep it moist.)

Ducasse was greeted with some scepticism in Paris; in those days the idea that a chef could operate two different major restaurants in two different cities was considered absurd. When Michelin gave him three stars in Paris, it initially stripped a star from the Louis XV, as if out of spite. But that star was eventually restored, making Ducasse, at the age of forty, the first chef to simultaneously helm two separate three-star establishments. When I was travelling with him in Provence in 2005, the chef told me a story I'd never heard or read before, which he talks about in these pages; in 1984 he was the sole survivor of a plane crash which left him severely injured. For more than a year he was unable to stand or walk. 'Intellectually I was still working,' he told me. 'But it was impossible for me to go back to the kitchen. It was necessary for me to do the job in a different way. From that time I had to start cooking in my head.' Which may explain how, with the help of extraordinary collaborators, he was able to essentially be in two places at once. Or thirty-six at once, which is the number of restaurants he is currently overseeing, in France and around the globe.

But as he has continued to expand, he has also been engaged in a kind of paring back, a search for simplicity. This was noticeable in the menu at the Plaza Athénée, where he moved to from the 59 Poincaré in 2000, and where he sought, as he writes, 'to dare to create a natural kind of cuisine, to make something great out of something simple, to pare down the preparation process and to put technique back where it belonged so that the real flavours of nature could shine through.' In

2014, Ducasse took the concept even further, developing, in concert with the chef Romain Meder, 'a nature-forward style of cuisine [...] serving essentially vegetables, grains and a small amount of fish that was sustainable or whose source, seasonality and breeding season we knew exactly.' He called it Naturality.

As with most of the big changes Ducasse has instigated in his career, this was met with resistance, although, almost ten years on, this concept has entered the mainstream. I encountered an early example seventeen years ago when I had a simple sauté de légumes at his Provençal inn, La Bastide de Moustiers. Every vegetable seemed to sing the lead even though it harmonised with its neighbours. When I raved about the dish to Ducasse, he said, 'The Mediterranean sun gives the taste to the vegetables.' Naturality, indeed.

INTRODUCTION
by Clare Smyth

It's hard to put into so many words the greatness of Alain Ducasse – his achievements, his legacy, and the way he transmits his passion and knowledge through the food he serves. His influence on gastronomy cannot be overstated, and his empire extends to all corners of the globe, across every facet of hospitality, as a flagbearer for our profession at its highest level. And his influence on me – first as an idol, then as a mentor – has been immeasurable, something that has driven me all the way through my career and still pushes me on today.

I don't think I'll ever forget my first impression of Chef Ducasse. I was twenty-three years old when I first saw the grand dining room of the Louis XV in Monaco, in the pages of a book compiling the best restaurants in the world. I'd never seen anywhere look so glamorous, so beautiful – it appeared, to me, as the pinnacle of our profession, and I knew straight away that if I wanted to work in the very best kitchens, with the very best chefs, I had to go there and be a part of it.

So, I did what any enterprising young chef would do: I went there to eat, and begged for a job. Before dinner, the team invited me into the kitchen for a look around, and the glamour in there was just as breathtaking as the dining room. Spotless counters, gleaming copper pans, crisp white toques adorning the heads of the brigade. The way they moved, the way they worked, was all so elegant. And yet, for how haute and opulent everything seemed, the food was more than pure luxury: it was honest and humble yet extraordinarily refined; proudly vegetable-forward and centred on the purity of each ingredient. This, I would come to learn, was

Chef Ducasse's unshakeable culinary identity, one that endures to this day, and one that continues to set his food apart.

Mind you, this purist approach is by no means simple. It is, in fact, incredibly challenging to execute night after night, service after service, in the Louis XV and in all of his kitchens. Behind the effortless, near-silent movement of the kitchen brigade is a tightly organised choreography, in which even the slightest misstep can throw the whole dance out of order. To cook à la minute is to cook on the edge, bringing anything you're responsible for – a risotto, three spears of asparagus – to the absolute point of perfection, and then sending it straight out to the dining room. It's real cooking for real cooks, where you live and die on the strength of your technique and ability.

Cooking this way would not be possible were it not for Chef Ducasse's skills as a teacher, someone who has trained so many young talents across his empire to embrace his philosophy and embody his values in the kitchen. He is, in many ways, the grand conductor of his orchestra. Calm and considered in everything he does, yet a man in constant motion, going from restaurant to restaurant all over the world ensuring that the highest standards – his standards – are being maintained. Whenever he arrived at the Louis XV, he would cast his eye over everything, and such is the quality of his training that he could leave again more than satisfied, safe in the knowledge that his team were fully committed to upholding his levels of excellence.

He also retains, and imparts, an incredible breadth of knowledge about the produce he works with. When he would taste things in his kitchen, he would know exactly what it was, what it should be, where it came from and what it needed in order to be perfect. Better still, he would always explain why, and it was those moments that I never took for granted: to learn from him is to learn from the best. And I know how important these moments are for Chef Ducasse, too. He has always endeavoured to encourage his young chefs, to share in their journey, and to show how rewarding this profession can be.

When I first arrived to work at the Louis XV, I was given a handbook outlining the twelve values that Chef Ducasse expects of his staff. The one value which resonated with me most deeply, and, in my view, best embodies Chef's philosophy, is respect. Respect for the produce, and the producer.

Respect for nature: its beauty, its bounty, and the urgent need for its preservation. Respect for the guest, who has spent months in expectation of the meal they're about to receive. Respect for the colleagues all around you who depend on your total commitment, and in turn give you theirs. And respect for the chef's whites, the profession and its traditions, for those who came before you and those who will succeed you. 'My move moves the other,' he says – act with grace, and leave things better than you found them.

And yet, the value that always impressed me the most – the one I see him demonstrate like no other – is 'audacity'. Chef Ducasse is still leading the pack and a giant of our profession, because he is completely unafraid of facing the future. Less meat, less sugar, less fat, less salt and more vegetables and more grains; sustainability over luxury, and nature above all – these positions might seem scary for our profession to embrace, but time and again, he has proved right.

I've held on to that old handbook all these years, and still read through it today; its principles have served me well, and are the foundation of what I pass on to my team. Looking back over my twenty-plus years in the kitchen, I am still learning from

Chef Ducasse. He is just as inspirational to me now as he was at the beginning of my career, and I'm certain that this book, with all the knowledge it contains, will guide and inspire generations of chefs to come.

GOOD TASTE
A LIFE OF FOOD AND PASSION

EARTH AND WOOD

I was born on a farm in the south-west of France, in the Chalosse, in the middle of the undulating countryside between the Adour and Gave de Pau rivers that is often likened to Tuscany. My memories are of the vegetable garden, the surrounding forest, our modest lifestyle and the simple food the land offered us.

So many memories. The vegetables we grew. The way my grandmother cooked them. The forest of oaks where I would walk with my grandfather, who was a joiner and carpenter. The family meals every Sunday. The first strawberries. The lettuce, still soaked in dew, that we would go and pick before lunch, and its milky-white sap that would appear when we pulled it from the ground...

It was there on the farm that my first tastes were formed, there that the seeds of my life were sown. It is my native land. Other places and other flavours came along to influence me, and to add to my obsessions, but it was that part of Les Landes where it all began, and which still inspires me to this day.

From my childhood there, came two major passions which can be found in all my restaurants and in my cuisine.

First of all: make do with what you've got. With whatever nature offers us; with whatever is available. Each of my restaurants is linked to a vegetable garden, and each of my chefs has a connection to the land, to local markets and growers. Our culinary school in Meudon, near Paris, also has a herb garden, 'The Garden of Flavours'.

Secondly, oak is very important to me. All my restaurants feature oak in tribute to the forests of my childhood, and to my grandfather and his woodworking. In fact, our name, Ducasse, means 'he who lives at the foot of the oak'. And when I opened an auberge in the Basque country I called it Ostapé, meaning 'beneath the oakleaves'.

These two passions guide my work.

At 11.30 a.m. my grandmother would say, 'What shall we have for lunch?' She would go off to the vegetable garden, returning with peas, a lettuce, green beans and potatoes. Sometimes she would add bacon and a spring onion, but that was it. We went to the butcher once a week and some weeks not at all. On Sundays she would cook one of the poultry from the farm.

The farm was passed down through the generations and it is now my sister who manages it. You can imagine just what hard work it was for my parents and grandparents. It was from being around them, watching them tend the land, feed themselves from the fruits of their labours, collect mushrooms in the forest, make preserves and shape the wood, that the notion of work came to occupy a central place in my life.

My bedroom was right above the kitchen. We had no extraction or ventilation system so the smells would spread through the house, and especially into my bedroom. Even more so than the tastes of childhood, it is the delicious aromas that have stayed with me. In particular, I remember the smell of roast chicken, of sautéed veal, of vegetables cooking and dishes simmering. Those are the smells that made me want to cook.

That, and watching my grandmother cook. She did it because she had to. It was a necessity: she had to feed the family. No one talked about healthy eating, or even how well done your meat should be. But the produce was good, and, in our garden, everything grew. It is impossible to forget the flavour of that freshly picked lettuce, of carrots straight from the ground, scrubbed for immediate consumption, of sun-drenched tomatoes, of peas gathered and eaten raw. These are essential flavours. I know because I grew up in that garden. It's where I discovered the best combinations and where my quest for the perfect flavour began – a quest that still preoccupies me today. Every product is affected by the place where it comes from, the environment of that place; the person who cultivates or grows it; and the person who prepares it. These factors must be combined correctly for the perfect taste.

In our kitchens, we are first and foremost interpreters of nature.

We aim to preserve the original taste of each ingredient. We do not try to transform a turnip to make it taste like a carrot. And we don't try to suppress the very strong taste of chicory root. On the contrary, we peel the root, dry it out and make a feature of its strong flavour in the recipe. In the past, people would blanch chicory to remove its bitterness. Just as with carrot tops: instead of discarding them, we chop them up and make use of them. We try to extract everything we can from a vegetable without ever distorting the original taste which nature has given us.

The first vegetable from my grandmother's garden to make an impression on me were the peas. A pea plant is perfect for less than a week, so you have to plant peas every eight days for several weeks. I loved, and still love, tasting peas from the garden – eating them raw – just as I still love visiting vegetable gardens, learning, taking a leaf in my hand and crushing it, smelling it, tasting it.

I am certain that 'Naturality' – a style of cuisine I created with the chef Romain Meder at the Plaza Athénée restaurant in Paris in 2014, combining grains, vegetables and sustainably sourced fish – owes much to the first vegetable garden of my childhood, to the farm, to the producers I met and the forests I explored for hours on end and in every season, admiring the trees and searching for hidden treasures at their feet. Vegetables were not in fashion, and they were often dismissed or used badly. At the time, the idea of placing them at the centre of a dish, restoring their authentic flavour and their dignity, and serving only a small amount of meat, was truly groundbreaking. But it had already become a passion of mine, something so obviously worthwhile and something that I would always offer.

In 1987 at the Louis XV restaurant in Monaco, I devised an entirely vegetarian menu which I called 'Les Jardins de Provence', or 'The Gardens of Provence'. If I think even further back, I can recall that the first menu I ever designed, when I was twenty-three, not long after becoming a chef at L'Amandier de Mougins – where I was met with an audience of chefs including Jacques Maximin and Roger Vergé – consisted mainly of exceptional vegetables. I bought all the vegetables that I could at the Marché Forville in Cannes and made spaghetti with vegetables, followed by a wonderful herb-stuffed fowl and stuffed vegetables. I wanted to preserve the flavour of every vegetable, its warmth, its crispness, its unctuousness. It had to be an explosion of nature. Even back in 1976, I helped chef Michel Guérard develop his slimming cookbook at his restaurant in Eugénie-les-Bains, and the first recipe I worked on was a cake made with tender carrots and chervil.

My vegetable-forward approach is obvious from my signature dishes, one of which is the cookpot, designed by Pierre Tachon. It is both a dish and an object, providing a modern take on the traditional farmer's cooking pot. Seven vegetables are simmered together in a white porcelain casserole dish made in Le Berry by Pillivuyt, the oldest porcelain cookware company. The vegetables vary according to location and season, but they always take centre stage.

Ever since my very first dishes, I have endeavoured to highlight the importance of vegetables, grains, gardens and the land. But I had to persevere. These dishes were not hugely popular at the time, as vegetables were not à la mode and were often used only to garnish meat or fish dishes. Even today, Naturality is still avant-garde, because we are constantly innovating and trying to push it even further.

For years, the dishes at the Plaza Athénée, which often used only vegetables, reflected the importance of the region where I spent my childhood. You only have to look at their names: quinoa d'Anjou, roots, mushrooms with wild quince, harking back to forest walks in autumn; grand roux corn from the Basque country, a grain that started to be grown again in the late 1990s; casserole of spring vegetables and wild mushrooms; buckwheat groats with peas and broad beans, evoking the freshness of a garden in the first days of spring; and vegetables from the gardens of the Palace of Versailles with black truffle, a dish that varies according to what the garden delivers each day.

I came up with the idea for the 'Nature' series of cookbooks in 2009, which was divided into vegetables, fish and desserts. I wanted to put forward a simple kind of cooking that was full of feeling, using seasonal produce smartly and rediscovering the true flavours of nature. From the very first pages, I thanked the suppliers with whom we have worked, sometimes for over twenty years, including market gardeners, breeders, fishermen and mushroom pickers. Men and women whose work I admire, such as Jean-Louis Nicolaï, a market gardener from the Apt region. And I came up with our first commandment: 'Thou shalt get closer to nature and respect its seasons.'

The terroir of my childhood is important, and yet I am not at all nostalgic for those years, nor am I nostalgic for the flavours of the past. Our roots are essential, but accumulating layers, experiences, journeys and cultures is just as valuable. To that you must add hard work, curiosity, a desire for a challenge and an interest in discovering other regions and other flavours. Regions different to Les Landes and the south-west, such as the Mediterranean – which is so dear to my heart as an adoptive Mediterranean ever since I lived in Moustiers, Mougins and Monaco – and Japan, Thailand and America helped me discover new flavours, new producers and new vegetables. I am very grateful to those producers.

Other connections to the earth and to nature have since been formed. I remember a vegetable dish I had in Japan, in Kyoto to be precise, in which every flavour came through. I wasn't familiar with half of the vegetables in it. Everything was in perfect harmony, with perfect contrasts, structures, temperatures and warmth, impeccable seasoning, different flavours and a balance of colours, as if the chef had tried to create a portrait of nature.

Nonetheless, that first layer, that first terroir is important to me – not because of nostalgia or any wish to preserve it in memory, but because I am constantly striving to evolve it further. I know how much I owe to it. It lives within me: I refer back to it and I seek to transform it.

I am conscious of what I learned over those years and how they shaped my vocation, as well as the values they inspired in me that I still hold today.

I started cooking in my head when browsing the markets of Les Landes. But in France, and throughout the world, markets were also my education. I had the same obsession wherever I went: that which the land offers us, that which nature affords. I wanted to understand the land and its produce, and so for several years I went to the market every day. I spent a long time listening to the people who worked there.

Talking to them will tell you a lot about a region, a country, its condition, its people, its natural resources, and about what those who live there eat. The colour of a fruit or vegetable can tell you everything, revealing whether the land is bountiful or dry. It is another connection to the land.

I am not nostalgic, also because cooking gets better every year, and we get better at it too, rich with the knowledge of where we come from and the new things we are discovering, and with a connection to nature that we make stronger every day. We now pay more attention to produce, techniques and cooking than we did before. We are refining things. As a child, would I have dared tell my grandmother that she had overcooked the green beans or that her blanquette would have been better, the veal more tender, if she had cooked it for longer? I think sometimes I did tell her, but I also learned a lot more from each of her movements just by watching her, remaining silent.

That is another value that I pass on to students and young chefs: spend a long time watching, taste things, keep your eyes open, leave, get away from where you grew up and return richer, more curious and with higher standards than anyone else.

That kitchen of my childhood was my first education, with its techniques that were not quite perfect, methods that were somewhat basic and produce that was somewhat humble. It was much later than I learned precision, elegance and accuracy in everything. But before that, being attentive, curious and full of love was a crucial stage.

At the age of twelve, I had never even been to a restaurant, but I had had that unspoken education, those smells, those tastes, the vegetable garden, the forest and my mother's magazines, like *Cuisine et vins de France* (*French Food and Wine*). Together these things sparked my passion.

The lessons I learned on the farm and from my grandmother's hard work have stayed with me. With every restaurant and every new adventure that I pursue, I reflect on what I have, what I know, where I have got to and what I have at my disposal. And I do it with rigour, stringency and discipline. It is a toolbox and a code of conduct that I try to pass on to everybody.

As for my grandfather, he was the one who forged my connection to wood, to what we build and to what endures. You will find this wood in all my restaurants, in my home and at the culinary school – the wood of the ceiling, the floor, the shelves that bear collections of objects, and the wood of all the doors of which I am an avid collector. These doors are heavy, solid, and shaped with all the finesse of the craftsman. They are magnificent. I remember that my grandfather would choose the oak trees he wanted before cutting them down and leaving them to season for three years. One day I wanted to build a house, and together we squared off the timber for the framework. He promised me that this timber would withstand anything, that it was made to last, as if he were offering me both time and memory.

It was through seeing my grandparents and my parents at work that I got a taste for labour, and the importance of taking pleasure in this labour. If you have never spent all day picking vegetables, you have no idea just how low down the ground is, nor how hard it is. When I am speaking to producers, I never forget how difficult it is to grow fruit and vegetables. This also guides my work and is a founding principle of my restaurants.

For that reason, I have a very specific memory of René, a wild strawberry producer in the hills of Nice. One day he had no one to pick them, but I needed them that evening. He suggested that I pick them myself and left his greenhouse open for me. It was unheated, but the fruit was safe inside and in the evening the greenhouse would retain the heat of the day. I picked two kilograms of wild strawberries that day, and I still remember it. Since then, I have never argued over the price of wild strawberries. Likewise, when our butter producer at Le Ponclet in Brittany, David Akpamagbo, increases his prices by 20 euros per kilo this year, I know I must accept it because his butter is the best and his work is worth the price. And even so, he has not managed to make a living from his excellent craftmanship.

I learned an essential lesson from my grandmother: that of labour that goes beyond simple work. She found meaning in her life and her work through such labour. She showed me that vegetable gardens only bear fruit if you take care of them and tend to them day and night. That was my education, and it defined who I am. I tell everyone I work with that they must take pleasure in their labour, even though I know it has unnerved many of them, who believed they were already working hard. But I want to push them even further.

I know that the gardeners and producers I work with have the same high standards. For example, the market gardener from the Val de Loire who provides the vegetables for Sapid, amongst others. Sapid is a sort of restaurant-refectory, or canteen, that I opened recently in Paris. It foregrounds plant-based cuisine for all, with vegetable and grain dishes and very little protein. You do not need to add anything to his vegetables. You just have to brush off a bit of soil, cook them and eat them.

My grandmother's vegetable garden, the taste that I later developed for vegetables, and Naturality, what it represented and what it represents today, have always inspired me to tell the story of vegetables so I can offer everybody –

chefs, students, customers – the tools to appreciate them.

In the same vein, I have always sought to create a connection between the land and the dish. This connection was clear to me when I was at the farm, without my ever needing to speak of it or draw attention to it. But that connection has disappeared. I like the idea that our restaurants and chefs, all from their own terroir and all with different sensitivities, are bringing it back into focus.

Today, Sapid is perhaps the place that best brings together these obsessions, that terroir and the importance of nature and wood. The walls are the colour of rust, and the floor is made of oak. On the wall is cob, made of natural, crude earth from Beauvais, and around the tables, which are taken from the refectory of the Lycée Lakanal in Sceaux, are walnut-wood benches that are almost seventy years old. On the wall I have placed watercolours that I've always had in my office. They perfectly express our love for plants. I have always liked them. I think they explain our work better than we can. They capture the image of nature in the same way that we hope to capture its taste.

I invited about fifteen of the producers I work with to come to Sapid when it was still under construction, just before it opened. It was an opportunity for them to meet one another and combine their strengths, understand our approach, reinforce our relationships and for them to grow alongside us.

I remember telling them that the land matters, and that one of my most important values is knowing where you come from; that they were not 'small producers' but have a central role to play: to grow, without growing too large. One of the physically smaller men quipped: 'I know why I haven't grown. It was so I could be closer to my carrots.' I laughed. It spoke volumes about his modesty and his attachment to his land and produce.

At Sapid, even more than at any of my other restaurants, I want to bring together the producers, growers, market gardeners, farmers, fishermen, chefs – the chef at Sapid is the Peruvian Marvic Medina Matos, who trained in Naturality for three years at the Plaza Athénée – and the people who come to eat there.

I have a special relationship with each producer and each woman or man of the earth. I know them and I understand their passion, their high standards. Our lives have been intertwined for a very long time.

That is why I went around France meeting the very best producers in 1999, for my book *Rencontres savoureuses, petit traité de l'excellence française* (*Delicious Encounters: A Short Essay on French Excellence*). I was touched by those encounters, the conversations we had and the stories they told me, and I wanted to pay tribute to them, knowing that some of them were being bled dry just to survive, making a thousand sacrifices for their passion – but also that they embodied a way of life, as well as their land and their produce.

My first meeting was with Henri Dessolas, a truffle specialist, in the Périgord. He was born on a farm near Saint-Front-d'Alemps in the early 1930s. He told me about the work on the farm, the routines, the fields and the forests, the sowing and the harvest. I listened to him with great emotion, realising that my childhood had not been all that different to his. From then on, all my meetings were influenced by that emotion.

Inspired by these *rencontres savoureuses* and by our lunch offering at Sapid, I recently got in touch with Hectar, an experimental farm an hour and a half from Paris that teaches young farmers to make a living and improve their production by co-ordinating with each other. I took the chef Romain

Meder there, thinking it could be a new place for us to take root, an obvious choice of additional terroir, and that we could prepare lunches at Sapid using only produce from this farm.

I also make sure the students of the École Ducasse in Meudon understand the importance of rootedness, of the land, of seasonal produce and local food systems, and that they meet the producers when they visit farms. And in a nod to the important places of my childhood, the restaurant at the school in Meudon is called Adour, and the refectory is called Chalosse.

This is what I tell every chef and every student across the world: you must put forward your land, including its hardest, most arid and most difficult parts. Because from this land, from these terroirs, springs feeling and individuality. You must embody where you come from without looking backwards or being nostalgic, but instead with a modern perspective, using the techniques and outlook of today.

Several years ago, a journalist asked me what my favourite vegetable was. 'If you were a vegetable, what would you be?' A mushroom, I replied. A cep. They cannot grow without trees, they lurk under ferns and dead leaves, and they need a mild, humid climate, with July's sunshine and August's stormy showers. They remind me of my childhood and the hours I spent picking them with my grandfather. Mushrooms bind me to the earth and the wood, to the simple joy of finding them and then cooking them. I like the fact that they are wild and cannot be controlled, that they grow however they want, that you must seek them out and hope to find them, and that they are dependent on the seasons.

I would say the same thing today.

When I was a child, I dreamed of being a cook, an architect or an adventurer. I would also sometimes say I wanted to become a coach driver so I could travel and see the world.

I am not far from my childhood dreams. I travel often, I come up with ideas, I dream up dishes and places. I am like an artistic director – I mentor, I taste, I impart knowledge, I encourage young chefs by sharing what I have learned and am still learning. I try to bring with me stories, a vision and my beliefs. Everything in our restaurants and shops, in the books and encyclopaedias I publish, and in the culinary schools, is connected by the same desire: to nourish, teach, impart, search, and share the food of the earth.

Some common threads have been woven into my work since childhood, linking it closely to the earth and the wood. These threads are referred to in these first pages and in the ones that follow.

This is not a book of memories, nor is it a book of recipes. It is a different way of sharing the emotion conjured by a meal, a dish, a taste; of defining something ineffable; of telling a story; of evoking fleeting pleasures and engraving them within us.

Everything evolves, everything moves. Everything is in motion in a world that is increasingly loud. When it is all too much, I take refuge in the silence and solitude of my home in the south-west, near where I grew up, in a house that looks out on nature, by the woods, by a fireside, all while listening to the sound of the water. I do this for several days, before it all quickly starts up again. Before I discover a new taste or place, before I learn more, tell other stories, think about the challenges of the forthcoming years, break my bad habits and bring everything into question so I can continue my quest once more.

LEARNING, TEACHING

In November 2020, the culinary school we had opened in Argenteuil in 1999 moved to a large campus in Meudon. The school was founded in the middle of the Covid crisis with a risky aim: to host over 400 students of any nationality on one large campus, offering three-year bachelor's degrees to high-school graduates, and culinary programmes to passionate, curious career-changers looking for knowledge, values and skills.

I wanted all the kitchens, laboratories and classrooms in the bright, open buildings of the campus, which is situated next to the forest, to be named after significant people – after chefs I admire and have learned from, or young chefs who have trained with us and whose work inspires me, whose personalities and attitudes set an example. They are also named after important places – my terroirs, my reference points, our roots.

At the school in Meudon, the job of passing on knowledge, something we have been doing for over twenty years, is fully realised. To do this we needed a centre of excellence on an exceptional site, a cooking school that would be the most advanced in terms of culinary technology and tools – it has nine laboratories for cooking, baking pastries and bread, chocolate-making and ice-cream-making. We also needed great teachers to embody who we are, what we know and what our story is, and to showcase our mission of learning, educating and passing on skills, techniques and tastes at the highest standard.

I often wonder about the students of seventy different nationalities studying in the Alain Chapel, Michel Guérard, Anne-Sophie Pic, Guy Savoy and Dominique Crenn kitchens; in the Patrick Castagna, Cédric Grolet, Claire Heitzler and Jessica Préalpato laboratories; in the Naturalité, Juan-les-Pins, Moustiers-Sainte-Marie, New York, Tokyo, Monaco and Mionnay classrooms; in the Yves Thuriès library; and in the Dom Pérignon and Jacques Maximin tasting rooms. I wonder what they think of the masters and the towns and villages these rooms are named after. I wonder about their sense of curiosity and what connection they may have to these things in the future, and also about what they know about my story and what I would like to pass on to them.

Cooks and chefs are go-betweens: we are heirs, masters and students, all at the same time. We never stop learning. And for me, just as for young people, school is a crucial step. You must be willing to learn at school, and you must be willing to learn after you've left, wherever you are and whenever you can.

I remember what my master, Alain Chapel, told me: 'Cooking is before all else a state of mind. It is not just recipes.'

There is a culinary state of mind. There are values, pieces of knowledge, techniques and precise skills that students must learn, and there are no shortcuts. Either you know how to do it or you don't, whether it's choosing the right produce or preparing something perfectly, seasoning something perfectly, cooking something perfectly or reducing something perfectly. It is a toolbox, similar to learning music theory, that enables you to create recipes and to cook, reduce, season and put together a dish; to make an aroma or jus; or to prepare a fish.

Students must achieve a level of mastery which equates to freedom.

There is a moment when everything clicks into place, just as I experienced at Alain Chapel's restaurant.

When I was a child, the farm was my school. The silent lessons of my grandmother, the aromas that came from her kitchen and my mother's magazines provided an invaluable education. At the age of twelve I had never been to a restaurant and I had never had any formal training, and though I sometimes helped out in the family kitchen, it was only occasionally, at parties for example. I have a specific memory of a chocolate log with good egg whites and good chocolate and a well-cooked sponge that did not break on rolling. It was perhaps my first success. Could that moment have decided my vocation? Could that have convinced my adolescent self to say, with the courage of my convictions: 'This is what I want to do, and this is what I will do. I will be a chef'?

I don't know why I announced this to my mother

at that age, nor why I was so sure about it. But I do remember my determination and the disapproval of my parents, who had been hoping that I would take over the farm, or study for longer.

That was the first decision I made. It would be followed by many others, born of one or two nights of reflection – decisions that I made alone and stuck to. Those who know me are very familiar with what I call my 'morning decisions'. They always help me to make choices, be decisive, overcome challenges, turn corners and make progress.

During the Christmas holidays my mother got me a job at a roadside café. I think she was secretly hoping to put me off so that I would give up on the idea of cooking. It was very hard, but just to be contrary, and also to prove to everybody that I could do it and that I had what it took to be a chef, I pretended that I liked it, and I even went back at Easter.

That roadside café no longer exists. It was near Mont-de-Marsan. It had all the usual hallmarks of that sort of establishment: a buffet, a big car park, the coldness, harshness and rigour of the profession. You had to do it all. I remember spending entire days plucking poultry in the yard and making crêpes for hours without a break. It was thankless and repetitive; the motions, tasks and instructions all blurred into one. Yet I learned to endure without complaint and get through the work assigned to me. And above all, I was hopeful that it wouldn't always be that way, that I would soon have other mentors and learn other skills, and that my mother, convinced by my perseverance, would let me do what I wanted.

After the roadside café I did an apprenticeship at Le Pavillon Landais Hotel, on the banks of the Soustons Lake. It is also now closed. When I was there, it had one Michelin star. It was a historic building that had opened in 1934 and attracted politicians and artists – a completely different world to that of the roadside café. The internship only lasted a few weeks, but it was enough to make me want to do more and truly start to learn.

I went to hotel school in Talence with one aim: I wanted to learn quickly, to lap up all the experiences and skills I could. Today, I am able to say that these were not the happiest years of my life – I learned things, but not quickly enough and not well enough. It was not specific to my profession, a lesson I remembered when I opened our first school: you do not learn enough in schools for the amount of time you spend there, and it is often outside of school that you meet your real teachers. That is the relationship we try to establish between students and teachers – one of connection, the broadening of experience, the acquisition of a feeling and a way of understanding the profession. I would go on to have four such masters, and from their teachings I drew an appetite, a curiosity, a rigour and a passion that is constantly evolving: Michel Guérard, Alain Chapel, Roger Vergé, Gaston Lenôtre.

I left the school before I graduated, much to the irritation of my teachers, and started working at Michel Guérard's restaurant in Eugénie-les-Bains in 1975. It had already been established there one year. It was the beginning of so-called 'nouvelle cuisine', championed by Paul Bocuse, Jean and Pierre Troisgros, Alain Chapel, Paul Haeberlin and Jacques Pic.

Michel Guérard embodied this creativity, a new type of freedom and a very different interpretation of the style of cooking defined by Auguste Escoffier. Guérard's book, *Mémoire de la cuisine française* (*The Story of French Cooking*), is fascinating. In 1965, he had bought Le Pot-au-Feu, a restaurant in Asnières-sur-Seine. He earned his first Michelin star in 1967, and then another in 1971, by creating iconic dishes such as the *salade folle* ('crazy salad', typically made with foie gras, crayfish and vegetables) and laying the foundations for nouvelle cuisine. When he moved to the spa town of Eugénie-les-Bains with his wife, Christine, he set himself a new challenge: *cuisine minceur*, offering a lower-calorie version of traditional French food.

I started there as commis chef. I worked in the restaurant, but I also helped develop a book that was to set a benchmark, *La Grande Cuisine minceur* (*Great Slimming Cuisine*), in 1976. Two years later, Guérard would publish *La Cuisine gourmande* (*Gourmet Cuisine*). He also involved me in his partnership with Nestlé's frozen-food brand, Findus. In particular, I worked on the recipe for 'Pithiviers feuilleté mousse de cresson et beurre blanc', or pithiviers with watercress mousse and beurre blanc. You can no longer get it today, but it was on sale for twenty years.

I learned about everything – about *cuisine minceur* and *cuisine gourmande*, about making books and about industry partnerships, which was revolutionary for a major chef.

Michel Guérard taught me how to taste and

how to create. His journey from winning 'Meilleur Ouvrier de France' in patisserie while working as head pastry chef at the Hôtel de Crillon, to earning three Michelin stars as a chef at Le Lido speaks volumes about his open-mindedness, hunger and curiosity: he tried everything, and he dared to do anything.

I spent my summers with him, and in the winter I went to Paris to work with the pastry chef Gaston Lenôtre.

Meeting Lenôtre was a defining moment. He had come to Eugénie-les-Bains to visit for a few days. I wanted to know everything: I wanted him to teach me how to make croissants while he was there. One morning, he came into the kitchen at 7am and taught me. I never forgot the lesson.

During my time in Paris I did everything, including viennoiserie, charcuterie, ice-cream and chocolate. I discovered a whole range of jobs, all of them at a very high standard. I was a student, and I very quickly became an assistant to one of the teachers too. Some of them I remember more than others, especially Monsieur Rey and Monsieur Ponée, who had just opened La Coba, a school in Switzerland that specialised in patisserie. I prepared for my classes and I watched. I was always busy – at the weekend I was working, and I was at school the rest of the time. I took lots of notes and I eagerly observed everything. What I had not yet mastered, I dreamed of conquering. I met the pastry chef Pierre Hermé there for the first time in 1976 – I was a junior ice-cream maker and he arrived as an apprentice. There was also Yves Thuriès, who was ten years older than me and doing a course at the patisserie school. I also met the chocolatier Michel Chaudun there and considered moving into chocolate, but I realised that I found it too intoxicating and I became too immersed in it. Chocolate-making was the style of cooking I liked the most, but I wanted my base of knowledge, techniques and crafts to be as broad as possible.

This is the type of education that is today at the heart of our school and the professions for which we train people – open, generous and multifaceted. But crucially, it was at that point that I adopted a mindset that has stayed with me ever since: I want to learn things I don't know how to do from the very best teachers. I want to master every skill and every craft so I can then bring my own vision to them, rewrite the rules, create connections between crafts, refine the line.

Later on, my restaurants, for example the Louis XV, would have one atelier for bread and another for chocolate, and later still I would come up with 'Les Manufactures', artisan factories that specialise in chocolate, gelato, coffee or biscuits. I opened a salon bringing together these factories in November 2021 on Rue des Petits-Champs in Paris. I am sure that this idea was conceived during those years I spent learning in Eugénie-les-Bains and Paris with Michel Guérard and Gaston Lenôtre, years of hard work that were like a test laboratory for all that I would do next.

The third crucial step in my education was when I discovered the Mediterranean while working at Roger Vergé's three-starred restaurant, Le Moulin de Mougins. He had a talent for passing on knowledge, and he had trained several chefs. It was at his restaurant that I really came to understand how a kitchen is organised. And most importantly, it was where my passionate love affair with the Mediterranean, its regions and its produce all started. This was where a key element of my cooking and inspiration was added to my original terroir of Les Landes. I walked up and down markets; I traced the white paths of Provence; I discovered the most extraordinary growers and magnificent produce – olive oil, elephant garlic, globe artichoke, white aubergine, 'Grisette de Provence' courgette and yellow potatoes from Manosque. I would later be reunited with Roger Vergé and return to my adopted home when he offered me a job as chef at L'Amandier de Mougins in 1980.

But before all that, there was the decisive meeting with Alain Chapel.

When I was at Eugénie-les-Bains, I travelled across France one day with two other chef friends to eat at Chapel's restaurant in Mionnay. The journey was almost 500 miles long, with many hours in the car and a truly memorable meal upon arrival. I particularly remember a thrush casserole that was perfect and yet surprising, far from what you would expect from game. It was a type of rural cuisine that I had never tried before. But most of all, I could feel a question, a doubt, an exciting kind of uncertainty and the beginnings of a quest rising within me. I did not know how to make what I had just eaten. I remember the promise I made myself on the way back: one day I will work with him and learn from him.

While I was working in Mougins with Roger Vergé, I read an article about Alain Chapel that reminded me of the promise I'd made to myself. Now forty years old, he was a role model in the industry and already had three Michelin stars. It was rare to see an article on him since he was a private man who kept away from the media, which made him all the more admirable in my eyes. I took the day off and set out in my little car, a Citroën Ami 8, and several hundreds of kilometres later I pulled up outside his restaurant. I spotted him. He was coming back from the market carrying an armful of flowers and I still remember the first question he asked me, which was just as frank and direct as my answer:

'What do you want?'

'To work with you.'

As we went our separate ways, we agreed upon a date: I would start a few weeks later, on 2 November. I can remember it perfectly.

He was an incredible man. It was at his restaurant that I discovered precision of movement. His personality and outlook came through in even the smallest details: the flavours were perfect, the tone was perfect and there was a perfect harmony between style and content. He had exceptional precision in everything he did, and he passed this lesson on. Through him I learned how to cook perfectly, how to reduce perfectly, how to season perfectly and how to achieve elegance in everything else.

As well as working at the restaurant, I would cook for Alain Chapel and his mother every day. At around 10am, he would find me and tell me what he wanted me to make – sometimes a veal chop, sometimes a fricassee, sometimes veal kidney. He would eat it and give me feedback afterwards. Through him I learned that there are no half measures: either it is excellent or it is a failure; either the dish comes out right or it doesn't. I discovered just how difficult it is to achieve that kind of perfection which involves a precise balance of sharpness, seasoning, temperature and cooking. It is about being able to master the moment; it is very delicate. That is what cooking is: finding the precise point at which the dish is perfect. My dishes were not always perfect and, even when they were, Alain Chapel was economical with his praise. 'It's nice, Alain' was as good as it got.

Those months were so important because I learned so many lessons – lessons from the kitchen, from a man who watched over everything with incredible poise, from a difficult life outside work, where I had a tiny apartment in Fontaines-sur-

Saône that was badly heated and had no hot water, where the pipes froze every winter and I counted every expenditure, and from the sometimes brutal relations in the kitchen with chefs, the competition, the rivalries. One day I made one of my famous 'morning decisions' that was to mark a new chapter in my life. I was so badly paid that my salary didn't even cover the cost of petrol to get from my apartment to the restaurant, thirty or forty kilometres away. I told myself, 'If he doesn't give me a pay rise, I'll give up on being a chef.' He gave me a pay rise and I stayed on.

Chef Alain Chapel's praise for a successful dish, bringing me joy on days when I was close to giving it all up, also provided a lesson. Every student is familiar with these extremes of joy and disappointment, and the passion that remains when the job is over, defeating all else.

Through Alain Chapel, I gained a sense of control that was both precious and liberating. I knew the rules and at the same time I felt free of them. I could pursue my own cuisine, not other people's. And I could leave.

On reflection, it was perhaps during those years that I learned a vital lesson, which is today part of the code of values we give everyone who works with us: Do not be afraid. Just give it a try.

Michel Guérard, Gaston Lenôtre, Roger Vergé and Alain Chapel represent almost seven years of my life. The learning process is a long road. It is made up of so many encounters and lessons; it requires so much work, curiosity, appetite and persistence, and it never lets up. You don't stop learning, even once you have reached that level of mastery. Everything is still to be thought up, built, defined, constantly improved and rewritten. But that stage of mastery is important, and we seek to pass that on in our schools.

When I went to Paris in 1996 to take over from Joël Robuchon at his restaurant on Avenue Raymond-Poincaré, I brought several of my colleagues with me, including Patrick Ogheard, who was the pantry chef at the Louis XV. His wife Véronique, my assistant, told me that her husband was tired and wanted to do something else – teaching, in particular. I had been thinking about it for a long time. I was looking for an opportunity, the right moment and the right person. And so the school in Argenteuil was established in 1999. We wrote up the curriculum and the principles of our dream school, starting with one class, then two, and then five. Since then, teaching and sharing our expertise on all the disciplines has become of

liver the way I ate it as prepared by a chef in Kyoto. Everything about it was new, both the flavour and the consistency. In Japan I first discovered the rough-patterned ceramic mortar that we have since introduced to all our kitchens, changing everything about the way we prepare food. And it was also there that I discovered umami, the fifth basic taste, after sweet, salty, bitter and sour, which can be interpreted as 'savoury'.

Every day we learn from an infinite range of tastes and knowledge. We can maintain traditions and then also transform them, expand them and deviate from them. That is what I tell the students at our schools and the chefs I showcase today. You must focus on what you know how to do, on your region and your history, but also remain curious, observing things and going out into the world to find new influences, remembering them and becoming richer with this new knowledge.

This year I made a resolution, marking a shift that is crucial for me and the rest of the group. I want to encourage a generation of talented people in their thirties and place them in the highest positions. The wonderful team at Restaurant Le Meurice in Paris is emblematic of this revolution, this passing of the baton, and of what I want to start doing with more young people. Olivier Bikao came from the Plaza Athénée and is now director of Le Meurice; Amaury Bouhours, who trained at the Louis XV and the Plaza Athénée, is the chef; Gabriel Viessaire, who also worked at the Louis XV, is the sommelier; and Cédric Grolet, who cut his teeth in our patisserie school in Yssingeaux, is the pastry chef. But it is not just at Le Meurice that the younger generation are demonstrating their talent. Marie-Victorine Manoa is chef at Aux Lyonnais in Paris and Gabrielle Aguilo is the manager, though she will soon be leaving for a new adventure within our business; Charlotte Bringant is chef at Restaurant Allard in Paris; and at the Louis XV in Monaco the chef is Emmanuel Pilon, who previously worked at the Plaza Athénée, and the sommelier Maxime Pastor, also previously at the Plaza Athénée. In addition, Sandro Micheli has been pastry chef at the Louis XV for seventeen years and was previously pastry chef at our restaurant in New York, and Claire Sonnet has been manager for two or three years and also worked at the Plaza Athénée beforehand.

I still dictate the vision, direction and changes, but they are the ones I want to encourage, each of them with a story that has often long been linked to ours, yet with their own unique tastes, curiosity and tenacity. Now we must recognise their talents. Nouvelle cuisine was a quiet development in cooking, an essential progression that seemed almost self-evident. A very codified style of cooking needed updating. But there appears to be almost more personality and creativity in this new generation. The divide is more clear-cut, and there is a risk that these talents and this revolution will pass us by, that critics will not understand and television programmes will not notice. We must be able to recognise it, write about it and push it to the forefront.

I encourage and train these young people; I am there for them, but I am also taking a step back. I don't want to carry on having people believe I'm in the same position as I was before. In this new role, I am much more useful.

There are the schools, and then there are the people we train, who are in turn setting the standard in their restaurants with their personalities and their boldness. There is also the unique connection between myself and these young people, to keep learning and to push our expectations and passions even further. Several years ago, I thought of another way of educating people. I suggested to Valéry Giscard d'Estaing, who was at the time in charge of restoring the Hôtel de la Marine on Place de la Concorde in Paris, that he acquire all the writings on nutrition, gastronomy and everything relating to food – 'the reasoned knowledge of all that relates to man nourishing himself', in the words of Anthelme Brillat-Savarin. It would make all that invaluable knowledge available to everybody, everywhere, either on site or online. France would own all the written expertise on international gastronomy. Having those records brought together in one place, passing down our history, was a dream for me. I probably won't see it come to fruition, but it doesn't stop me from trying to find other ways to pass things on and understand those who came before us, in order to better demonstrate what we are doing and give meaning to it, all while continuing to create.

I have a new project at the Maison du Peuple in Clichy, a historic building built in the late 1930s by Charles Auffray, who was mayor of Clichy at the time. This major industrial centre, a magnificent construction of steel and metal designed by Jean Prouvé, Eugène Beaudouin, Marcel Lods and the engineer Vladimir Bodiansky, was classified as an official historical monument in 1983, renovated between 2000 and 2005, and then fell into abandon. We are going to make ourselves part of this history, and set up everything there, including our equipment, our factories and our head office. The building will become a global culinary centre with a focus on vegetables and sustainability. I often say that food should be fit for thinking about before it is fit for eating. There will be a restaurant, an atelier and a foreign chef in residence who will come and train in the French way of doing things and cook with us. This will force us to learn too, to be curious and alive.

It will be a centre of thought and a laboratory, an extension of the school in Meudon. It will be in dialogue with our schools and chefs, a living museum with all the kitchen utensils we need to train people and teach them new techniques.

This project is a new way of providing an education, by learning from the past and from others, refusing to be satisfied with just doing and instead thinking about the way we cook. And most importantly, producing the cooking of the future.

MEDITERRANEAN VENTURES

In my first book, *La Riviera d'Alain Ducasse*, I used a quote from Predrag Matvejević's *Mediterranean: A Cultural Landscape* for the epigraph: 'Anyone, regardless of place of birth or residence, can become a Mediterranean.' This sentence had great resonance for me.

I am a Mediterranean by adoption. I discovered its regions, its land and its landscapes over several years, first in Mougins, then in Juan-les-Pins, and most notably in Monaco when I became chef at the Louis XV at the Hôtel de Paris on 27 May 1987. This iconic place which is fundamental for me – on a rock that fascinates so many, linking the Côte d'Azur and the Riviera dei Fiori, the hinterlands of Nice and those of Liguria – is where I laid the foundations and built the great opus of my cooking. I travelled the coast and hinterlands of Nice and Liguria by car, by motorbike and on foot. I soaked up the smells and flavours of the region. The landscapes I traversed, the people I met, the markets I never tired of browsing and the Mediterranean recipes I discovered, adapted and worked on repeatedly created a base in me, a constant point of reference and another identity to complement the regions of my childhood.

I have long been under the spell of the Mediterranean. When I left Mougins for Alain Chapel's restaurant near Lyon, in the Dombes, I knew that I would one day return to its landscapes, flavours and people; that it was an important detour but that my story was rooted in the south.

When I decided to leave Alain Chapel's, there was no going back – as is the case with all my morning decisions, whether they are made after a long night of reflection or on impulse. I wanted to leave, to get away, to be free of his wonderful tutelage. I chose the Buckinghamshire village of Aston Clinton, in the most typical of English countryside. The restaurant was called The Bell.

I was sous chef and had only been there for a few weeks when Roger Vergé, who had invented *cuisine du soleil* at the Moulin de Mougins and L'Amandier de Mougins, called me one Friday evening to offer me the role of chef at L'Amandier. He gave me ten minutes to think about it and call him back. I said yes immediately and wasted no time in packing my things and hitting the road at 3 a.m. in my Citroën Ami 8. I got the ferry to Calais and only took one detour, to visit my grandmother in Les Landes, before arriving at L'Amandier at 8 a.m. on Monday morning.

It was my first role as chef and the first time I was entrusted with the keys to a restaurant. I knew that thanks to my teachers, I had enough expertise to be able to express a particular identity and way of seeing things, and I knew that this Mediterranean land, combined with that of the south-west, would enable me to express the values closest to my heart. These would become recurrent themes, shared characteristics – a thread that links every dish, every recipe and every restaurant.

A few days after I arrived, Roger Vergé brought the great chefs of the Mediterranean together for a symbolic photo on a point off the Cannes coast. He was in the middle, flanked by Jo Rostang from

La Bonne Auberge in Antibes, Louis Outier from L'Oasis in Mandelieu, Jacques Maximin from Le Chantecler at the hotel Le Negresco in Nice, Gérard Ferri from Èze and Jean-François Issautier. It was a mixture of major Michelin-starred chefs and promising young talents. I was only twenty-three years old, but I was asked to cook for these great chefs after Jacques-Louis Delpal had taken the photograph and done his story. It was then that I made the spaghetti with vegetables, herb-stuffed Landes fowl and stuffed vegetables. As I had hoped, it was an explosion of nature, preserving the flavour of all the vegetables, and my first proper meal as a chef. Jacques Maximin, whom I met for the first time on this occasion, came to find me afterwards and gave me his encouragement. He put in a word for me with Roger Vergé, saying 'He will go far.' In some ways, this was my initiation into the Mediterranean.

I only stayed at L'Amandier de Mougins for a year. The restaurant was doing very well, but I felt limited – I wanted to do fewer covers and take things to an even higher standard. I went to Juan-les-Pins and took over at La Terrasse, the restaurant in the Hôtel Juana, where I stayed for seven years. I redesigned the kitchens. I wanted them to be bright, white-tiled and equipped for all kinds of cooking. It was there that I earned two Michelin stars. It was also where I met the writer Frédérick E. Grasser-Hermé for the first time, in May 1981. She writes about it in her book *La Cuisinière de cuisinier* (*The Chef's Stove*). She ate at La Terrasse several times and decided to spy on me so she could meet me. She followed me to the Marché de Forville, where I went every morning, and came up to me. She wanted to be allowed into the kitchen to watch and listen. I said no several times before eventually agreeing. In the end she never worked at the restaurant, nor at the Louis XV, because she realised that she wasn't comfortable in a team, but it would mark the beginning of a precious friendship and a long collaboration. She is a great seeker-out of places, produce and recipes, and still today she is always introducing me to new treasures. She took me to the 20th arrondissement to meet a unique baker, Maxime Bussy, who was trained by rural bakers and now opens his boulangerie, Le Bricheton, for just a few hours a day, a few days a week. He kneads by hand using a natural leaven from ancient wheat. I owe that meeting and many more to Frédérick, and I will never forget where it all started in Juan-les-Pins, and later in Monaco.

In Juan-les-Pins I also visited markets and coastal and country roads, discovering these profoundly Mediterranean flavours that would become my essentials. For example, there is the 800g–1kg John Dory that is found near Cap Martin, or the red mullet fished from the rocky depths of the ocean in the morning, perfectly cooked and served with a splash of olive oil, Menton lemon, tomatoes and Taggiasca olives. It has the most delicate flesh in the world. Its size, colour, pearly skin and tender flesh together make it a work of art, and you cannot get it like that anywhere else.

I wasn't yet thirty years old when I met Prince Rainier of Monaco for the first time, through Michel Pastor and Jacques Seydoux de Clausonne. Prince Rainier was looking for a chef at the Louis XV and they had put my name forward. After a long interview at the palace, I still didn't know what it was I could offer him. What could I do that they didn't already have in Monaco? I wrote seventeen pages detailing what I was thinking about – my vision. I had ambitions of earning three stars, but above all, I wanted the Louis XV to be a laboratory, a base, an anchor; I wanted to concentrate all my foundations, desires and obsessions in that one place, and I wanted it to become a reference point as well as part of my perpetual quest. It was where I wanted to focus my Mediterranean passions.

In those seventeen pages, I was already developing the concept of an entirely plant-based menu, and I dared to propose a combination of vegetables and bacon that I would later recreate. I suggested country bacon with tender morsels of vegetables, gently simmered in a cast iron casserole dish, adding that the guests of the Louis XV would never have tried it before. I believed that Prince Rainier would appreciate its obvious simplicity and what was the beginning of Naturality. I wanted to offer Mediterranean cooking in all its rusticity, a country kitchen in a bright setting. I didn't keep that document, but it laid the groundwork for what we are still doing today. I combine my focus on the produce and producers of the Mediterranean with a nod, a heartfelt reference, to the produce of my home – pullets from Les Landes, côtes de bœuf from Chalosse and foie gras from Castelsarrasin. It is a way of bringing together the things that matter the most to me.

When I became chef at the Louis XV, I also took charge of all the kitchens at the Hôtel de

Paris, from Le Grill on the top floor, to the Salle Empire which was only for receptions. Almost seventy people worked in the basement every day, in kitchens we redesigned. I also made myself a sort of office/dining room down there so I could watch, write and taste, and for a long time I kept in sight a quote from the dancer Jean Babilée that had made a big impression on me, like a mantra: 'Go on stage thinking you're a genius and you're guaranteed to look like an idiot.'

These beautiful kitchens had everything you could wish for, including boulangerie, patisserie, chocolate-making, ice-cream-making, a butcher and a fishmonger complete with a fish tank. I wanted an overview of all the jobs and the highest level of control possible. This also foregrounded my passion for manufacturing, which I would later return to when I created the chocolate, coffee, gelato and biscuit factories.

I started working in Monaco on 1 October 1986 and we opened on 27 May 1987. As first in command at the Louis XV, I could try out my role as leader and bearer of a vision and a trajectory, and I was eager to teach and encourage the young chefs I wanted to bring to the forefront. It was there that I built an incredibly strong, indispensable relationship with the chef Franck Cerutti. He had started out alongside Jacques Maximin at Le Negresco and then went to work at Enoteca Pinchiorri in Florence, but in 1980 he joined me at the Hôtel Juana in Juan-les-Pins. He was the first person I hired upon arrival at the restaurant. He came with me to Monaco and then opened Don Camillo, a family-style restaurant in Nice, before taking over the Louis XV in 1996. He was executive chef at all the restaurants in the Hôtel de Paris from 2007 until he retired. Jean-François Piège was eighteen when he arrived in Monaco, and he took a job in the kitchens straight away. Hélène Darroze also cut her teeth in the kitchens of the Louis XV. A great many chefs have passed through these kitchens, and for some they became a school, a home even. Dominique Lory, who was head chef at the Louis XV from 2011 after several years at the Plaza Athénée, has just taken over from Franck Cerutti as executive chef at the Hôtel de Paris. We have been working together for over twenty years. With many of our chefs and employees, we go back a long way – with Jeannot, for example, a lifelong dishwasher I met in Mougins who then came with me to the Louis XV and stayed with me until he retired in 2015.

He was perfect, irreplaceable in his work and his respect for the job.

There is a particular photograph that I am very attached to and which I put in my book *La Riviera*. It depicts my first team and my oldest colleagues, with whom I earned three Michelin stars in 1990, thirty-three months after we took over the Louis XV. Jeannot was there, of course, as well as Benoit Peeters, the head waiter, Sylvain Portay, my second-in-command, Frédéric Robert, the pastry chef, Georges-Marie Gérini, the manager, Mario Muratore, the pantry chef, Frédéric Roemer, the assistant sommelier, and Jean-Pierre Rous, the head sommelier, Bruno Caironi, the chef at Le Grill, and Patrick Roy, the baker.

Every year we had to create a strategy, a sense of solidarity within the team, and we had to set an example, no matter how long each person was with us, so that the experience made an impression and resonated deep within them. I thought about even the smallest of details, from the way the waiters moved around the room, like a dance, with a learned elegance – I brought in a choreographer who taught the art of going into a room as if it were going on stage, to ensure that the service was light and delicate and not too intrusive – to the distribution of tasks in the kitchen. Every Thursday I would rotate the team around stations – fish, meat, dessert, pantry – to keep everyone on their toes and stop people falling into habits, which are for me the same as bad habits, and to encourage us to challenge things and call them into question. Several years later, I would put this rotation of teams and people into practice on a global scale in all our restaurants.

A few years after I arrived in Monaco, I also inaugurated a committee of chefs, with regular meetings to help them work better together and continue to create new things. I asked them to each look out for two young talents and then monitor them. And it was also there that I learned a lesson from the rugby player Daniel Herrero, which for me rings very true: 'Sometimes you have to part with a great man who doesn't carry the team.'

Monaco, the Louis XV, its passionate workforce – to my mind, it's like a school that aims to support everyone and ensure it is always imparting knowledge and creating, while still remaining flexible. As the years went by and we earned more stars and encountered new challenges, this place became my base, my constant reference point and my anchor. Prince Albert of Monaco is today a staunch supporter of our work. He tells me he often meets chefs across the world who trained at the Louis XV and are now taking Mediterranean cooking with them wherever they go. And he adds that in their restaurants, he often has a greater sense of being looked after with the utmost of care.

We have been laying the foundations of our take on Mediterranean cuisine since 1987, constantly reworking it and refreshing it.

I remember my first menus at the Louis XV, on the back of which I wrote: 'Thanks to authentic market gardeners, breeders, farmers, butchers, fishermen and mushroom pickers, we have the great privilege of getting the best produce, which we treat with all the respect it deserves. Every dish has a story, and every producer, breeder and market gardener has their own reason for their search for beauty.'

Against the luxurious backdrop of the Louis XV, I wanted to highlight the producers, breeders and all the people who work the land, who know what labour is and know what their efforts and their passion are worth. In the Mediterranean coastal region, I have met people with whom I have built unique relationships, including René Schmid from the hills of Nice, Jean-Louis

Ruggieri at the Marché du Cours Saleya, who has a banner that says THE REAL PRODUCER, Pierre and Édith Poussou, the producers of the famous Sainte-Catherine olive oil, and André and Gérard Rinaldi, the last fishermen of Monaco.

I wanted to showcase those meetings, those men and women and the landscapes that created them in my first book, *La Riviera d'Alain Ducasse*, which was published in 1992, just after we earned three stars. It occupies a unique space as a book – it is like a manifesto, a summary of everything that mattered and everything that would matter in the future.

The food critic and writer Claude Lebey had come to see me several years beforehand. He wanted me to write a book for his chef series, but I didn't like the idea. I knew that I wanted to make an illustrated book, and I knew that I wanted to work with the talented photographer Jean-Louis Bloch-Lainé, the graphic designer Yan Pennor's, and my friend Marianne Comolli, a journalist and author whose great sensitivity, outlook and writing I knew about. This trio would mark a new era in the history of cookery books.

I spent time with each of them. I remember Jean-Louis's work, which was so delicate and so precise. How do you photograph polenta without it looking like a shapeless mess? He had that talent, that skill. He could capture the look of smoke, just as he could capture the translucent quality of cod. He knew how to photograph the produce that was most important to me, like Taggiasca olives in the Province of Imperia, just before the harvest; clusters of wild asparagus growing at the edge of the woods; the incredibly tender Bellone fig; the fennel flowers that grow in Courmes, diffusing their scent of aniseed; vegetable soup with pesto; peapod, broad bean and radish-top soup; and Mama Lena's torta pasqualina made by Elena Muratore, mother of pantry chef, Mario Muratore.

Jean-Louis and I traversed the Côte d'Azur, the Riviera dei Fiori and the countryside further inland. He captured places that are very special to me, including the old town of Sanremo, Thorenc and the national forests that surround it, the Paillon de Contes, the Col de Braus, the Col d'Èze, the Gorges du Loup canyon in Villeneuve-Loubet and its Escoffier Museum of Culinary Art, housed in the birthplace of Auguste Escoffier, the red rocks of the La Mortola promontory and the Vallée des Merveilles.

We travelled through Pigna in Liguria, a stone village above the Nervia valley which I love, and he took an important photograph of me. I am sitting down, and you can see the words LA RESISTANZA CONTINUA written on the wall behind me. To me it was like a battle cry, a reminder. 'The resistance continues.' You must fight and carry on searching. Don't ever stop.

Marianne came with us on those trips and captured what was so important in her introduction, captions and presentation of the recipes and history of each dish. Together, this made the book an important work, a precious one in my opinion, a written record of my tastes and my landscapes and the men and women who are dear to me, and a memento of what we had been working on over the previous few years.

Many other books would expand on that vision, which I have championed since 1992. A few years later, I published *Méditerranées, cuisine de l'essentiel* (*Mediterranean: The Essential Cuisine*), in which I reflect on what connects me to those places. The book was conceived and produced with Frédérick E. Grasser-Hermé. I wanted to make it for people who cook every day, a step-by-step guide to creating significant dishes, like a sort of ten commandments for making risotto, for example. In it, I wrote, 'Nice, Naples, Tangiers, Barcelona... A curious traveller around a sea that is almost completely enclosed, I have brought back from my culinary journeys a mixture of flavours from all the coasts.' It was a new opportunity to reflect on all my Mediterranean influences, from people to places and produce. There were Jacques Maximin's cromesquis with garlic, which I tried at Le Chantecler at Le Negresco; the purple artichoke from Venice, introduced to me by Reine Sammut at her restaurant L'Auberge La Fenière in Lourmarin; the white aubergine I bought at the Marché de Forville; a courgette scarpaccia I tried in a small restaurant in northern Tuscany whose name I have forgotten; my favourite beans from Pigna and other beans from Figaret; as well as the 'telephone' peas that are harvested by farmers near Ventimiglia.

That book and its recipes were an opportunity to record those regions, giving pride of place to the producers and chefs, and to constantly extend and enrich my memory of the Mediterranean.

Several years later, in 2004, I published another book that I am very attached to, which describes this passion for the Mediterranean, its importance as a point of reference and our quest to enrich it and develop it further. *Le Grand Livre de cuisine – Méditerranée* (*The Great Cookery Book: The Mediterranean*), the fourth volume in the series 'Les Grands Livres', includes over 500 recipes that were discovered and are explained as a result of the impressive work of a dozen historians coordinated by Oscar Caballero; iconic dishes that were photographed by Thomas Duval on thermoformed metal plates. Thomas had done a lot of research on the colours and light of the south.

The book built on *La Riviera* and *Méditerranées, cuisine de l'essentiel* by charting the culinary history of six countries in the western Mediterranean, recording its foundational recipes. It was no longer just about France and Italy, but also about other countries that share their soil and their flavours.

The publication of those books is among the important moments uniting me with the Mediterranean. But there were other events that cemented our connection and enriched this relationship. Among them was our twenty-five-year anniversary at the Louis XV in 2012, which played a big role. It was an opportunity to bring together the great talents of French and international cuisine in Monaco for three days. There were 240 chefs and 300 Michelin stars, from every continent. We organised a pop-up market of Mediterranean produce, giving centre stage to our twenty-five top producers and breeders, and fourteen chefs cooked with these magnificent products for the occasion. Franck Cerutti, Dominique Lory and I also organised a reception dinner. Our aim was to celebrate what had been achieved, the passion of the producers and chefs, and to introduce all these chefs to the recipes and products, continuing to create and pass ideas on.

The Mediterranean is an endless quest, composed of landscapes traversed and the places where I feel at home; the people I meet on each journey; the books; the parties that, rather than just being celebrations, helped us think about the future; the recipes collected, shared, refined and explained; and the daily lessons of this challenging region. Its cuisine is vital to me because it takes nothing for granted. It acts as a role model: we must continue doing what we know how to do and preserve our own DNA, but we must also be open to other influences and explore other regions. One of my favourite words, and a word that my colleagues are very familiar with, is *l'aggiornamento*: constant renewal.

I have other moorings in the Mediterranean besides the Louis XV. The first, I visited monthly for ten years before we left to pursue other adventures. The second one was, and still is, a place for which I feel a deep affection, though it was turned into an inn in 1995.

For the ten years between 2004 and 2014 I partnered with Vittorio Moretti, a great Italian winemaker who produces what is undoubtedly the best Champagne-style wine, and we opened the Trattoria Toscana, a restaurant in the Grand Dukes of Tuscany's old hunting estate in Castiglione della Pescaia. This beautiful town is between Pisa and Rome on the Tuscany coast, in the Maremma, a region which is so dear to my heart, a historically communist area where people have a strong attachment to their land. There is an incredible kilometre-long avenue, lined with cypress trees, pine trees, grapevines and olive trees, which leads to the house and gives it its name, L'Andana (The Windrow). Our chef Christophe Martin served a spectacular menu of land and sea produce, earthy and rooted in tradition. I was fascinated by the rather insular food culture of this region, which, like all those very anchored in tradition, had succeeded in conserving the original DNA of its produce. I visited the trattoria for ten years, and I also drove across Tuscany, Liguria, Umbria and Campania – not the whole of Italy as I would have liked, but a good part of it.

And then there is La Bastide de Moustiers, my refuge and beloved home. It is a place that embodies who I am, and is so much like me that there is a saying among my colleagues: if you really want to know me, you must go to La Bastide. I chose every object in it, and designed all the bedrooms and the garden. But I could not keep it to myself. I realised that I didn't go there enough, so in 1995, after several months of construction, we opened it up to the public.

I discovered the area for the first time in 1977, when I was working at L'Amandier in Mougins. I motorbiked across Alpes-de-Haute-Provence, arriving via the road that runs through the Gorges du Verdon. It took my breath away. I went into the village, roamed the white paths amongst which I would lose myself so often afterwards, and the plateau where lavender, wheat, poppies, sage and curry plants grow. What struck me was not just the obvious beauty of these places, but also their fragrances. The smells were truly unforgettable.

I went back to the area ten years later. I was

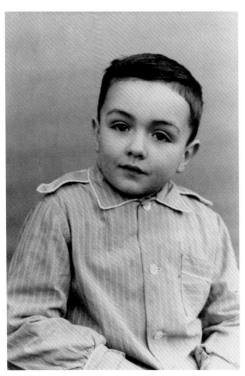

Alain Ducasse aged 5 at the family farm in the south-west of France

The cookpot, containing rock fish, fennel and black olives in a bouillabaisse broth
© Pierre Monetta

The École Ducasse Paris Campus in Meudon
© École Ducasse

Alain Ducasse and Alain Chapel in Mionnay, 1979

The women of the 'Femmes en avenir' philanthropic project, Paris, 2015

The original Louis XV team in Monaco, 1987, including Frédéric Roemer, Jean-Pierre Rous, Alain Ducasse and Sylvain Portay

The dining room of the Louis XV, Monaco, 2018
© Pierre Monetta

The team at
the Louis XV,
Monaco, 2022
© Matteo Carassale

La Bastide de
Moustiers,
Moustiers-
Sainte-Marie
© Matteo Carassale

La Bastide de
Moustiers,
Moustiers-
Sainte-Marie
© Matteo Carassale

Alain Ducasse and Romain Meder in the kitchens of the Plaza Athénée, Paris, 2014
© Pierre Monetta

The dining room at Benoit, New York
© Pierre Monetta

Vegetables from Kamakura, with top condiment and green *jus* at Esterre, Tokyo
© Tokyo Palace Hotel

The artisan chocolate factory on Rue de la Roquette, Paris
© Pierre Monetta

The dream team from the artisan factories, including Veda Viraswami, Quentin Francis-Gaigneux, Alain Ducasse, Flora Davies and Matteo Casone

© Ilya Kagan

Fresh biscuits from the
artisan biscuit factory
© Atelier Mai 98,
Thomas Dhellemmes

Plans for the Maison du
Peuple, Clichy
© Perrot & Richard Architects

The ADMO team, including Jessica Préalpato, Albert Adrìa, Vincent Chaperon, Alain
Ducasse and Romain Meder, at the Musée du Quai Branly – Jacques Chirac, Paris, 2021
© Atelier Mai 98, Thomas Dhellemmes

working at the Louis XV and travelled the area as soon as I could, this time not by motorbike but in a 4×4. The house belonged to a farmer and then to a master potter from Moustiers. I bought it in 1994 and we spent two years on construction, though sympathetically with the main country house, La Grisolière. We went to the plateau to find stones to refurbish it, and for its colours, which have evolved over the years, we were inspired by blue – the favoured colour in Moustiers pottery and the colour of lavender – and pink, in keeping with the light on the rocks of Moustiers and the distinctive shade of the whitewashed walls. The great landscape architect Jean Mus designed the garden that is at the foot of the cliff and the village. There is a vegetable garden, a herb garden, a meadow and two donkeys.

All the objects in the bedrooms, lounges and restaurant were bought second hand, carefully chosen as if it were a family home. There are the famous oak-and-walnut doors, rare and magnificent, that I collect like beautiful travelling trunks. In the dining room is a collection of Japanese lacquer works; silver-rimmed Lalique plates dating from 1920; watercolours; Jean Luce porcelain plates; plates with a sinking boat on them; illustrations by Tonia Peyrot, an interior decorator friend; and on the tables are modern, Japanese-style lanterns. I know the history of all the objects and where I found them, and I like to arrange them and move them around the place. Sarah Chailan is now the manager, having started out as an apprentice, and is today the perfect hostess.

The chefs who have worked at La Bastide are aware of its demands and its idiosyncrasies. I remember the first chef, Sonja Lee. She burst into my office at the Hôtel de Paris and said, 'I won't leave until you hire me!' It worked! Then there was Benoit Witz, Christophe Martin, the chef from the Trattoria in Tuscany who managed La Bastide's kitchens from 2012 to 2017, Vincent Maillard and Éric Santalucia, and then Frédéric Garnier, Thomas Chambraud and today, Adrien de Grigny. The house is also a school, and often chefs who have spent time at the Louis XV end up at La Bastide, and vice versa. They swap one climate, region and mood for another; they can learn, and reinvent themselves.

Here, at La Bastide, time passes differently. In this magnificent countryside, there is a different relationship between people and produce. I savour every minute of it. It is a refuge that enables me to reflect on everything I want to do, on my numerous projects, and to start again, but do things better.

It is perhaps here that I have most often told the employees something I truly believe in. Doing something well and doing something badly takes the same amount of time. So, better to do it well, do it as best you can, and always choose the most difficult path.

That is the main lesson I have learned from this place, this land and all my Mediterranean adventures.

PARIS, NEW YORK AND TOKYO

One day in February 1990, I was at La Belle Époque, the restaurant at the Hotel Okura in Tokyo. I was there for the Week of Gastronomy and was using the opportunity to discover Japan, a country that would go on to be such a big part of my life. At that point, it was too early for me to understand what I was seeing, perceiving and tasting. I let myself be carried along by my instincts, though I felt that to fully appreciate my surroundings, I needed to be initiated, to be guided through, and to return there often. But even in 1990, I was struck by the precision of Japanese gastronomy, the precision of its flavour and form, and the harmony between style and content. I promised myself that I would go back and turn this initial charm into passion.

My assistant in Monaco called me that day. The Michelin Guide was trying to reach me to tell me that the Louis XV had been awarded three Michelin stars. Six years earlier, via that very same telephone in Tokyo, they had called Joël Robuchon to tell him about the same three stars. It was as if there was something magical about that place and that phone.

I can remember the feeling of delight and success, of having achieved an aim I had set myself and had promised Prince Rainier thirty-three months previously – an aim that I had promised myself several years before that, even. But as soon as I hung up, the delight, celebrations and fulfilled promises were offset by questions. Now what? And what about after that?

I was not sure I would find the answers immediately, but I knew that I would eagerly search for them. It was the next stage that now interested me. In Japan, a country far from Monaco, which I was fascinated by and yet did not fully understand, these questions became crucial, and the beginnings of an answer began to form. I wanted to do what I had never done before, to go where I had never been before and to taste things I had never tasted before. I wanted to do more, even if it meant failing or making mistakes. There is no doubt in my mind that it was then that a conviction emerged that has stayed with me for years and would go on to become my guideline, a sort of code or personal commitment: never stop creating, understanding and trying new things, or you go backwards.

Where did this quest, this hunger, this desire to unsettle things, even within myself, come from? There are many possible answers – my personality, my education, the landscapes of my childhood, the strength and endurance of my role models, my passion for making and my years of learning. And then there are the tests we have faced, which I usually try to make light of, giving them distance and countering them with a philosophy: it would have been better if this didn't happen, but since it has happened, we might as well do a good job, a better job even, despite the setbacks and mishaps. We must counter every brush with death and every moment we survive, all the things that remind us that time moves quickly and everything is uncertain and fragile, with effort, determination, action, movement, words, tastes, places, feelings and decisions that endure.

There was the knife incident in Alain Chapel's kitchens, one of those all-too-familiar cases of jealousy and competition. Fortunately it all ended well, but it was incredibly telling of how high emotions can run in kitchens, and of how passion and rivalry can predominate within them.

There was the motorbike accident on the Antibes seafront as I was approaching the Hotel Juana in Juan-les-Pins, where I was chef at the restaurant. I was speeding along when a wire got stuck in my wheel and I came to among the pebbles on the beach. The following week I sold my motorbike and resolved never to ride them again.

And then there was the plane accident on 9 August 1984, a crash I refused to talk about for a long time. We were flying to Courchevel from the coast. The weather suddenly took a turn for the worse and a string of bad decisions were made, simple human errors – leaving, turning back, carrying on despite the summer storm, mistakes in navigation... I knew we were going to crash a few seconds before it happened thanks to my flying lessons, and I curled myself up on my seat. That was perhaps what saved my life. Luck, chance, destiny. I was the only survivor. Everything came crashing down. I had to cope with mourning as well as the pain and the memory of it. During the long months of hospitalisation, surgery and physiotherapy that followed, I discovered that the only real problem in life is physical and mental incapacity, when you can no longer be independent. All other problems have solutions.

After the accident I could not be independent, and I didn't know whether I'd ever be able to walk or see again. I have never been that alone. But you have to make do with what you've got, and I learned a lot from that test. It made me more sensitive, more curious, more eager to discover, to feel, to meet new people and keep learning. And after months and then years in which it seemed impossible, I decided one morning to get on a plane again. So as not to be held back by my fears. I got on a plane again, and it wasn't just once a year – it was sometimes two or three times a week.

During those months in hospital, I had to learn how to live differently. I was still in charge of the restaurant in Juan-les-Pins, which had just received two Michelin stars. I could no longer go to the market every day like I used to, so I had to give other people strict instructions so they could do it instead. Since I could no longer cook,

I carefully wrote down all my recipes, first in my head and then on paper, for others to bring to life. I could only taste things and rely on my memory, my recollections and my ideas, things that I could also teach and pass on. I am sure it was then that I really learned how to delegate and to have faith in teaching, the knowledge I could pass on, and what others could reproduce and create in turn. This radically changed my way of living, of course, but it also changed my way of thinking about the job and about cooking. I realised that I didn't want to be a chef at one restaurant and stay there for years, and that I had the resources, experience and desire to invent my own way of being a chef.

Six years after the accident, I earned three stars. Did I think about that accident when I received the call in Japan? Did that accident and what it changed, what it taught me, influence what I wanted to do afterwards? I am certain that it did.

It took a while to find answers to the questions, 'And what about afterwards? And now?' Each thing I accomplished called for another challenge, another project. That's still true today. And of course, when I no longer have the energy or the drive to look for the answers, I will have to stop and turn my attentions to something else.

One of the first answers came out of a phone call with Joël Robuchon in 1996. We were talking and, just before we hung up, he told me he was thinking about retiring soon and was looking for someone to replace him. I remember saying 'Yes.'

'Yes what?' he replied.

'Yes to taking over from you.'

I have often made big decisions before even hanging up the phone, in the heat of the moment, and sometimes, as was the case with Joël, before the other person has even put their question into words. To replace Robuchon you needed a little of that kind of madness and recklessness.

I took over his restaurant on 59 Avenue Raymond-Poincaré in early August 1996. It was a challenge, a demanding establishment on five different levels; it was in Paris, a city I did not know well; and it was the legacy of a much-admired master. At the restaurant Joël had developed a French haute cuisine that was sophisticated, intricate and finely tuned, and to succeed in the role I had to continue his legacy but also set myself apart from it, bringing my own touch to the restaurant and its dishes. And create a narrative, just like Robuchon had done. I recall dishes that were symbolic and unusual at the time – lardons and potatoes for example, a dish that was to all appearances very simple and was like a statement of intent, or an affront – and I also recall wanting to tell people about what we were offering and to put it all together in a landmark illustrated book.

Le Grand Livre de cuisine was prefaced by Jean-François Revel and coordinated by Jean-François Piège, whom I had known since he was eighteen years old, and was written in collaboration with Didier Elena, Franck Cerutti, Patrick Ogheard and Benoit Witz. It came out in 2001, and included over 700 recipes along with our impressions of and ideas about French haute cuisine. Meeting the Académie française member Jean-François Revel had made a big impression on me. We often had lunch together and it was not uncommon for us to order two bottles of wine. When the maître d' came to offer him a 'little digestif', Jean-François Revel lost his temper with an outburst that I enjoyed. 'Why little? Little in quality? Little in quantity? Bring me the best and I will serve myself!' His appetite, education and knowledge were superb. He told me he could only write well after eating and drinking well. I haven't met many men like him and I haven't forgotten the lesson. 'Why little?! Never little! I hate the word "little"!'

When I arrived in Paris, I was expected to fail. A long time had passed since my days in the attic room, near the Michel-Ange–Molitor metro station, that I left at 3am every morning to get to Lenôtre, living off meagre savings since I wasn't being paid, and surviving on bananas. Seen from the Avenue Poincaré, Paris was like a dream to me, a blank slate. Claude Lebey, the journalist from *L'Express* I had met when I was at Michel Guérard's, had come to see me two months after I took over the restaurant. He told me he thought that I would soon go back to where I came from, that I wouldn't even have time to settle in, that he didn't know what I doing in Paris, that I didn't have the skills. I asked him if I could count on him to help me and he replied, 'We'll see.' I said thank you and told him I would make do without him. We met again several months later and, seeing that I was still there, he almost apologised: 'I was wrong. But I'm not often wrong.'

Such doubts would plague nearly all my ventures. When I opened my restaurants in the United States, London and Japan, when I embarked upon the journey of the factories, there would always be a barrage of criticism and reservations at the beginning, sometimes frank and sometimes brutal. I came up with a sort of maxim to counter such conflict: 'You could also do nothing' – or rather, 'It is always easier to do nothing.' Though I do not enjoy this kind of conflict, I also know that I thrive off it, that it also makes me learn faster, that it sometimes redirects me from the wrong path, or the opposite – it reinforces my determination and certainty and encourages me to go even further towards the criticism in response. If it is too provocative, provoke people even further; if it is too bitter, make it even more bitter still; if it is too expensive, take the prices even higher. Because there is no such thing as luck, and everything will explain itself and be retold, and it all fits into the story.

Le Grand Livre de cuisine was also made during those years when everything was a challenge. I created my own publishing house to publish this collection, this encyclopaedia. The editors I had been to see about the project all said it was an impossible risk – it was too expensive, too monumental, too crazy. Who would want it? It was a huge amount of work for the people writing the recipes, and it was twice the price of other similar books at the time. But I was convinced that we had to do it, that we had to be able to offer people objects that were out of the norm, encyclopaedias – nothing 'little', in the words of Jean-François Revel.

We set up a publishing house, found a distributor, learned about buying paper, binding books in canvas, finding a thirty-ton lorry to transport the first print run of 5000 copies and offering bookshops a sales strategy – if they took ten, I would give them an eleventh for free so they could leave it open for their readers to peruse. I also launched a subscription for professionals, including producers and colleagues. And in the end, it was a success. The book sold out. The incredulous boss of a big publishing group called me to ask how I had managed it. And I believe that it is precisely because of the problems that were raised beforehand that the book appealed. It was an encyclopaedia, a tome, a book about gastronomy, which was rare at the time. It was about giving someone, or buying for yourself, a piece of excellence.

We would later publish other books in same vein in the 'Grands Livres' series, including *Desserts et pâtisserie* (*Desserts and Pastries*) in 2002 with Frédéric Robert, *Le Grand Livre des bistrots, brasseries et restaurants de tradition* (*The Great Book*

of Bistros, Brasseries and Traditional Restaurants)
in 2003, prefaced by Jacques Chancel, adopting
the same ambitions and the same standards, and
Méditerranée in 2004.

The saga of these encyclopaedias reminds me
of a memorable lunch which was perhaps the best
lunch of all, and one of the most delicious in all
senses of the word. Nathan Myhrvold had designed
and written the illustrated 'Modernist Cuisine'
book series that was published in France in 2011
by Taschen, an encyclopaedia in six volumes that
was presented as an absolute benchmark text, an
analysis of international cuisine. He had built a
laboratory in Seattle which had all the ovens in
the world, from which he drew techniques and
reports that were almost mathematical in order to
create the very best food. Nathan wanted to meet
me, and we ended up at the Plaza Athénée for
lunch, both of us with our encyclopaedias. It was
like a duel, a boxing match without the punches,
or a cockfight at least, a fight of enthusiasts. It was
spring, and I remember there being remarkable
peas at the lunch. The produce and the wine were
perfect. Asparagus, veal, morels – everything was
as it should be. Christophe Moret was the chef
at the time. Everything he served that day was so

delicate that Nathan was blown away. It wasn't the highly technical nature that was important, nor the culinary display, but touches that were simple, controlled and delicate: perfect cooking, perfect produce, perfect balance, *jus* that was perfectly reduced and wines that were perfectly paired. The finest gastronomy pushed to its highest level. I believe that only the French can achieve this level of excellence, and that is why I fight for and defend French gastronomy so much: to preserve and champion this art.

I asked Nathan if what I would taste in Seattle with him would be better than what we had just eaten. He replied, 'No, we cannot do this. We don't have the produce or the expertise.' This perfect yet radical balance of all the elements, that brings us back to the terroir, to the original taste, to the product. His laboratory was exceptional, but it would never be enough. Technology should support, but never take centre stage or dominate, the cooking.

In 1996, we had a considerable challenge on our hands. We had to keep two restaurants alive, the Louis XV in Monaco and the 59 Poincaré in Paris, and for a year I spent my days commuting between the two cities – I would buy plane tickets in their hundreds. It was the first step towards what I was hoping to offer and to be – not claiming I was doing everything alone, instead offering menus that had different nuances but were united by the same standards and carried forward by talented young chefs who embodied this passion, this modernity, this work ethic. Laurent Gras, my chef in Monaco, came with me.

Several years later, in tribute to Joël Robuchon, I bought the rights to a book that brought together his most iconic recipes and life story but had only been published in Japan. *Le Grand Livre de cuisine de Joël Robuchon* (*The Great Book of Joël Robuchon's Cuisine*) came out in 2013 and became a sort of reference work with its beautiful black jacket. For the preface, I asked him what he thought makes a great chef. He told me, 'Someone who can express their vision through others and have them bring it to life... Aiming for three stars on your own is not feasible. You must have a team with you. You must be very demanding and uncompromising with yourself... Being a chef means being strict with yourself at all times.' And he left me with a few words that I also like very much: 'A great chef is someone who manages to express with their hands what they have imagined in their head', words I could have written myself. Yet the two encyclopaedias clearly demonstrate our differences. And show that despite having a different sensibility, different ambitions and different ideas, it is possible to create a conversation, to honour a legacy, to create something together and to leave your mark.

In my 'J'aime...' book series, from 2011, which is a homage to much-loved cities, to restaurateurs and producers, there is of course a *J'aime Paris*, a city that never ceases to surprise me. It was the first book in the series. In the preface, I wrote that although a far cry from my cities of the south, it gives me a stronger sense of disorientation and it takes me on imaginary journeys; that the city has always sparked in me competition, creativity and renewal. I believe that was precisely what I was looking for when I took over from Joël Robuchon. And at every stage of my relationship with this city, what was important was the renewal, the disorientation and the creativity it offered. Never ceasing to create and move forward. And being able to offer different cuisines in different places, like a fashion house with different lines, both haute couture and ready-to-wear, but connected by the same obsession, the same passion and the same high standards.

In 2000, we left the 59 Poincaré for the Plaza Athénée. We opened at a legendary venue on 25 Avenue Montaigne, which is one of the most beautiful venues in Paris, on Jean-François Piège's thirtieth birthday, after extensive renovation of the Régence room which Patrick Jouin and Sanjit Maku redesigned. It was looking tired, and we wanted to bring the same level of modernity to the décor as there was in the kitchen. The chair frames were given a metallic finish and the impressive chandeliers were hung with metallic veils. Ten years later we removed the metal and it was as if they had been set free, the light bursting out. We also added a cabinet of curiosities using ancient materials and objects, including silverware, crystalware and books, with the intention of emphasising modernity at the front of the restaurant, and the ancient towards the back. The tables were covered with leather and stainless steel. How many people notice these details that are barely there, the choices that have been made? We removed the tablecloths, and that too was a big development.

I wanted this place to evolve and for each chef, within clear editorial lines, to be able to develop a personality. From Jean-Francois Piège, great scholar and great technician, to Romain Meder, via Christophe Moret and Christophe Saintagne, everybody has made their mark on the Plaza Athénée restaurant and helped it evolve.

We are composers of transient pleasures; we seek to fix something intangible in the memories of those who come to spend time here for a lunch or dinner. And at the Plaza Athénée, the relationship between chef and customer has always been strong. It is not without resistance, periods of adjustment and changes, but it is never neutral and never ordinary. That is without a doubt what is most important to me.

In *J'aime Paris*, I wrote that at the Plaza Athénée I wanted to go back to basics, start from the beginning, and rediscover real flavours and original fragrances. It was not yet time for the Naturality revolution of 2014, but the concept was already radical: to dare to create a natural kind of cuisine, to make something great out of something simple, to pare down the preparation process and to put technique back where it belonged so that the real flavours of nature could shine through. For example, I challenged Christophe Saintagne, who had joined me at the 59 Poincaré in 1999 and was chef at Aux Lyonnais before taking over the kitchens at the Plaza Athénée in 2010, to create one product using no more than three ingredients. He had to refine things, remove what was unnecessary, surprise people with its very simplicity. We wanted – and this was pioneering at the time – to offer 'sustainable high gastronomy'. It was a movement that prefigured Naturality.

I had been thinking about a new development in gastronomy for several years. It would be an extension of what we had already started but would open new horizons and new ways of doing things, of eating and of being. It was about pushing a nature-forward style of cuisine even further by serving essentially vegetables, grains and a small amount of fish that was sustainable or whose source, seasonality and breeding season we knew exactly. I was following the career of my young chef Romain Meder. At the time he was chef at the Museum of Islamic Art in Doha, having previously worked at the Plaza Athénée, where he was at La Cour Jardin in particular.

The restaurant at the Plaza Athénée closed for several months in 2014 for renovation. It was time to give it a new lease of life. I called Romain and asked him to come and see me in Paris. In Doha, Romain had proven his talents and ability to adapt, taking into account limited resources and several restrictions – there was no pork, no alcohol, and many products had to be imported. But at the restaurant he had developed a cuisine with influences from Lebanon, North Africa and India, from an eastern Mediterranean food heritage that was both spiced and colourful. It was very good. I told him about my vision for the Plaza Athénée. He had never been a chef at a three-star restaurant, but I reassured him, explaining that everything would be new and that he had the skills to carefully shape this new style of Naturality cuisine. I hired Jessica Préalpato as patisserie chef a year after Romain, following an interview that lasted three minutes as she remembers. I had the same plans for her as I'd had for Romain: to start a revolution in desserts, using much less sugar and fat and playing with fruits and grains, with their bitterness, sourness, texture and unique qualities. We wanted to create Desserality as well as Naturality. And with this new pursuit came much resistance and criticism; customers who thought the desserts were 'ugly' or were perturbed by the new flavours. But Romain, Jessica and all the other teams stood their ground.

A few years ago, Jessica wanted to drop everything. But I suggested that instead of handing in her notice and leaving for a new life, she could change her hours, stop working evenings, write a book (that she published in 2018) and go even further with her research and the radicalism of what she had to offer.

You must be able to forge new paths and support those who set out on them, knowing the price you must pay and not allowing talented people to get disheartened or lose their way. Romain earned the three stars at the Plaza Athénée, and in 2019, several years after her period of discouragement, Jessica was named the best patisserie chef in the world.

Between 2014 and 2021 at the Plaza Athénée, we were able to think about, create and develop these new ideas. There were many protests at the beginning. Customers would come looking for old classics and meat, game and sugar – all the things that were traditionally associated with high gastronomy. It was a battle to get people interested in Naturality and Desserality. In *Le Grand Livre de la Naturalité* (*The Great Book of Naturality*), published in 2020, we were able to gather together the new recipes and record this story. Such developments are, of course, fragile. We left the Plaza Athénée in 2021, and the restaurant will now serve a different kind of cuisine.

With the help of Romain and Jessica, we took Naturality elsewhere, to other places and in other guises. We took it to the Sapid refectory, for example, and to Les Ombres, the restaurant at the Musée du Quai Branly – Jacques Chirac, first as part of the ADMO pop-up restaurant and then within the new menu at the restaurant. Again, we must never stop being curious and open, never stop creating and never allow ourselves to stand still or become closed off.

Paris was a dream and New York was another dream. Of course, the projects, ideas and challenges did not come about with the same clarity as those morning decisions. Chance and luck had parts to play, obviously. And when I earned the three stars in Monaco, and then three stars in Paris, I certainly didn't think, 'And now, New York.' Stories are born of meetings, memories, experiences you want to prolong, being playful and being reckless.

I went to New York for the first time as a fresh young chef in 1976. I was working for Michel Guérard, who was a consultant for the Regine restaurant group. A Regine's had just opened on Park Avenue. He offered me work there during the two-month winter closure of the restaurant in Eugénie-les-Bains, and at twenty years old, I jumped at the chance. I found the cheapest flight to New York with Pakistan Airlines. We were put up in shared accommodation and paid in cash at the end of every week on Fridays. I remember it being extremely cold, and dangerous too – we were constantly in fear of being robbed – and it being an incredible experience. I suppose I couldn't have understood the city, its rhythms and its personality in those two months, but I had an enduring urge to go back.

Years later, in Monaco in 1991, I organised a birthday celebration at the Louis XV for the American critic Craig Claiborne, who practically invented restaurant criticism while he was at the *New York Times*. He had helped to raise my profile in the United States, as did the front page of the *Wine Spectator* accompanying an article by the journalist Thomas Matthews. I invited several young American chefs into the kitchens at the Louis XV, and then to eat as guests in the dining room along with other tourists who had come to discover our gastronomy. That's what happened with Dan Barber, today one of the most influential American chefs, who was the first to set up on a farm outside of New York and devise a locally sourced menu, breeding pigs and chickens and cultivating his own vegetables. In the early 1990s, at the age of twenty-four, he came to Monaco after several months of apprenticing in Paris. He said he had put aside 1000 francs for the train, the youth hostel and a dinner at the Louis XV. We had just crossed paths that once outside the restaurant. Several years later, I would cook for him and several other foreign chefs. I also remember a wonderful meeting with the writer Jay McInerney, who had written about our journey from Monaco to La Bastide de Moustiers for *Departures* magazine.

As well as those important encounters and those charming, talented Americans, there was my first proper encounter with New York and the United States. There was the opening of a first restaurant, the failure of a restaurant, a lesson, and the determination to persevere.

I published *J'aime New York* in 2007, and in the introduction, I wrote that New York is a city that simultaneously blends, repairs and tests. I feel that way with every new adventure in the city, with every restaurant and every stay. The city changes me, forces me to question myself and always learn more – and often to do things differently. I also wrote that I had never felt as alive as I did in that city, propelled by a hunger for discovery and never certain of knowing what things should taste like. It is a source of learning about food, people, and about myself.

I met the journalist Jean-Christian Agid, who was working for Canal, for an interview. It was a wonderful meeting, and after the interview I asked him if he wanted to go to New York. I was convinced that we needed to make a book before we opened a restaurant over there, and that we needed to seek out the very best produce in the United States. *Harvesting Excellence* was released in 2002, published by Assouline. Jean-Christian travelled over 50,000 miles to find all the produce – bison, pig, chicken, turkey – creating something akin to a map of the best American producers and a tribute to American food from the people who produced, bred and sustained it day after day.

Before we came along, Jean-Louis Palladin had been the trailblazer for French chefs in the United States. He was from Gers in the south-west of France; I knew him well. He had opened a restaurant in Washington in the late 1970s. He was passionate about American produce and land, and he travelled the country trying to show Americans how rich their territory was. In 1989, he published a book called *Cooking with the Seasons*. He was the chef who developed the best recipe for Caesar salad. To me, who dreamed of America, he was a role model.

I wanted to create a very high-quality French gastronomy using American produce. Only perhaps the truffle and olive oil were imported. It was up to our restaurant to showcase the very best of French culinary expertise – through the tableware, hospitality, silverware, all the gestures and details, and how we worked with all the produce. After the publication of *Harvesting Excellence*, I was ready.

On 19 June 2000, we opened the Alain Ducasse at the Essex House restaurant, in the Essex House hotel in Central Park. Chef Didier Elena came with me. The managing director of the Essex House, Ibrahim Fahmy, had asked me on the phone if I would be interested in opening a restaurant there. I immediately replied, 'I'm coming next week!'

He rented us the restaurant and we renovated it. For its opening I was spending almost a third of my time in New York. To say it was difficult would be an understatement. We had to learn everything from scratch – and then learn it again, from New Yorkers' tastes, to waste management. It was another world, but that was also exactly what I was looking for. News of the restaurant's opening had triggered a long waiting list – we had more than 2000 bookings, envisaging that the restaurant would be full for months. And then the critics arrived, and all of them, or nearly all of them, didn't like the restaurant. It was too expensive, too sophisticated and too pompous, they said. I read them all. Some of them joked that you'd be better off going to the pizzeria opposite for example, or made fun of the collector's pens used to sign the bills, or the shape and size of the knives for carving beef or cutting pigeon. Over several months we had almost 1400 negative reviews. It was the size of the bills that attracted the most criticism – these days prices have gone up significantly in New York, but in 2000 our menu was the most expensive in the United States – making me so notorious over there that one day at the airport a customs officer who recognised me asked: 'Is that you, Monsieur L'Addition?'

One critic, Marian Burros, a food columnist at the *New York Times*, was particularly virulent towards me. I bumped into her a few years later in Washington, just before I opened my restaurant near the White House. Contrary to my press officer's advice, I couldn't resist letting her know that I was still around, and that the vehemence of her article had not destroyed me. It was like Claude Lebey telling me I would be back in Monaco in six months when I took over Robochon's restaurant.

It was at this first New York restaurant, before Dominique de Villepin gave his speech against the Iraq War at the United Nations, that I hosted President Chirac, Dominique de Villepin and Kofi Annan, who came in through three different entrances. For the first time, it occurred to me that the kitchen was a fabulous vantage point from which to watch the world, as I would later do with numerous heads of state in the dining rooms of my other restaurants. I had one principle: greet them and then disappear. The day after the speech, France became the enemy, and for months and months we received only cancellations. People brandished signs saying: FRENCH, GO HOME.

We learned. We changed the menu; we adapted to American demands without compromising on our relationship to gastronomy, nor our standards; we kept going despite the harsh critics; and little by little, over the years, the bookings started coming in again, and so did the praise and the stars. William Grimes, a critic at the *New York Times*, gave us four stars, the highest mark of distinction that the newspaper could give a restaurant: 'The kind of food that brings diners to their knees. Mr. Ducasse, a chef in the classic French tradition, promised New York a great restaurant. Now he has delivered it.'

I think opening a restaurant and then persevering with it takes a mixture of pride and recklessness, but it is mostly about passion for creation and taking on new ventures.

In 2003, two years after the Essex House, I opened Mix, a second restaurant in New York, on West Fifty-Eighth Street in Manhattan. The idea was to create 'a mix', offering a bridge between France and the United States, the past and the present, and a mélange of seasons and cultures. Patrick Jouin and I discussed our hopes for the place and settled for a design that was resolutely modern – we imported wagon boards and kept the old bricks, and the concrete façade featured a chain mail curtain. We wanted to demonstrate the influence of the past, the industrial surroundings. But our enthusiasm did not stop us making mistakes. Before it had even opened, my partner Jeffrey Chodorow and I were in disagreement about everything: the price of the menu, of the cocktails, what the waiters should wear. It was the first sign of trouble. The restaurant opened and the tension only increased. One day I went to see my friend Tom Matthews, who had become editor-in-chief of the *Wine Spectator*, and he said, 'You can tell you didn't have enough money to finish the restaurant. It's sloppy.' It was the exact opposite. I remember coming out of a crazy meeting and immediately realising in the taxi on Park Avenue that we had made a mistake, that we would not be understood. That we had – and it happens – got it wrong. The venture lasted two years, but in some ways, it was already doomed to fail. And I have always remembered the lesson it taught me: you must understand where you are and not be too early, too ahead of the times or the fashion. In that respect, the United States taught me a lot. And we didn't stop trying new things after those 'mistakes'. After the Essex House, we opened Adour restaurant in the St Regis Hotel, a stone's throw from Fifth Avenue, with yet another proposition. And then in 2008 we opened Benoit in New York, which is celebrating its fifteenth anniversary in 2023.

In 2016, I hired a young chef there whom I greatly admire, Laëtitia Rouabah, who went from the kitchens of the Plaza Athénée to our London restaurant, before becoming sous chef at the Jules Verne and then executive chef at Air France's La Première lounge at Roissy-Charles de Gaulle airport. I recall that my flight was an hour late and I ordered a chicken fricassee with chanterelle mushrooms, which was perfect. Having seen her execution of a dish that required such great skill, I had the idea of appointing her at Allard and then at the restaurant in New York. She saw everything – its ten-year anniversary, Covid, two years of working with the teams singlehandedly since I couldn't go and see them, plus a bike accident. She kept the restaurant going, and she did it perfectly.

That is also one of the things I like the best about these openings and this passion for taking on new ventures: launching things and handing them over to young, equally passionate people who can put a stamp on the place. The chef Alberto Marcolongo from Cucina in Paris has now taken over from Laëtitia. It's a passing of the baton, a chance to offer people and the restaurants a breath of fresh air, but it is always about transmitting knowledge and continuing the search.

When I go to New York now I am still searching, tasting and learning, just like how I used to roam the city's five boroughs in search of culinary adventures. I always wander the aisles of the legendary Fairway Market, the fine grocer's shop Russ & Daughters or the Kitchen Arts & Letters bookshop; I treat myself to Memphis-style marinated pork ribs or pastrami at Katz's Deli or fries at J. G. Melon. When I was able to go back there in December 2021 after the lockdowns and border closures, I wanted to visit Daniel Humm's restaurant, Eleven Madison Park, to try his radical all-vegan menu. He had brought in a Japanese chef whom I like very much and whom I had brought to Paris myself. Together they unveiled a noteworthy offering that, just like with Naturality in 2014, attracted a fair amount of criticism, from the *New York Times* in particular, who paid no attention to their high level of vegan expertise. Yet I am sure their gamble will pay off. It also encompasses everything that I admire: putting forward something that hasn't been done yet or hasn't been pushed far enough, inventing, being radical, standing your ground, allowing yourself to be inspired by a powerful city that encourages you to be daring, to reinvent yourself and to try everything.

All of this explains what feeds my relationship with New York and with the United States in general. Every encounter, every venture, every failure or mistake makes me want to improve, to do better, to dare and to start again, in an enormous territory where everything differs from one city to the next, from one year to the next. It is a constant reminder, even more noticeable there than in Paris or London, to be vigilant, curious and open, to keep reinventing yourself in order to maintain who you are and what you believe in.

The relationship I have cultivated with Japan is entirely different. I can no longer count how many times I have been there, since the culture shock of my first encounter with the country, its history and its food. Many years later, in December 2004, I opened my first restaurant there, Beige, in the Ginza district in Tokyo, then Benoit Tokyo in 2005 and Esterre in the Palace Hotel Tokyo in 2019. Each place has its own story, its own unique identity and method of showcasing French gastronomy while incorporating Japanese produce, art and gastronomy. But to me, what is important is the sense of the unknown and the fascination of it. When I discovered Japanese cuisine on that first trip, I knew that I could not do it and did not have the ambition or the audacity to become a true Japanese cook, but that I could try to understand, and take inspiration from as many influences as possible to build on my existing knowledge. Every trip is an opportunity for an additional layer, for learning more. And it is probably in Japan that I have had my most memorable and most inspiring encounters.

One of these was with the chef Toshio Tanahashi, famous for his plant-based Buddhist temple cooking, whom I met in Kyoto upon the advice of my assistant in London who had a real passion, a real intellectual interest in cooking. I decided to go and see him with Fabrice, my office manager in Tokyo, and when we got there, we arrived in front of a garage door. We thought it was a joke; the restaurant must not exist. But the chef was waiting for us in traditional clothing and his sense of hospitality dictated that he also offered us a bottle of Dom Pérignon before we had lunch and saké.

That lunch is one of my most vivid memories. I search and I work so passionately and so relentlessly, precisely so that I can experience such moments. It is the entire object of my quest: to arrive in a surprising place, knowing nothing about it, to taste what I have never tasted before and to leave transformed by those flavours and that encounter.

It was an extraordinary place, composed entirely of wood and so perfectly modest. I remember having an incredible vegan lunch, a lunch of temperatures, textures and flavours that were neutral, somewhat tasteless even. It immediately sparked my curiosity because I did not know how to make what I had just eaten, and I wanted to learn straightaway. My mind was made up: this incredibly talented chef had to come and work with me in Paris. I could not leave the restaurant without his word. We spoke and he told me that we were his last customers; his restaurant was closing and he was going to San Francisco to join a Japanese friend there. I insisted; I wanted to hire him. He didn't say yes, but he said he would stop off in Paris after his trip to the United States.

He came to work with us in Paris for two months. Romain had just got back from Doha, and together we prepared for the reopening. With the Japanese chef there, I had an even stronger sense that the menu at the Plaza Athénée needed to change. He taught us about that neutrality of taste that so fascinated me, as well as the art of working with textures and temperatures, his incredibly precise gestures, and most notably, how to use a Japanese mortar. We incorporated the technique into our recipes. For those two months we all worked at Le Meurice and he stayed there too. He didn't speak a word of English or French and the owner of a Japanese deli in Paris, Issé, had to interpret for us. He quickly made it clear that he was not happy at Le Meurice; the kitchen was too noisy to work in and he wanted to be alone, at one with his vegetables. We found him a furnished apartment near a market, and a kitchen in my cooking school on Rue Ranelagh in which he could work. Every two or three days, Romain and I went to see him. We did not understand his recipes, but we discovered amazing things about taste, and we absorbed the feelings and the emotions that emanated from every dish.

He lived in a bubble, in his own world, and he gave us the tremendous gift of allowing us inside it. He was wonderfully radical in his absolute love of nature and intense focus on plants, a radicalness that he shared with us and we then added to our skills, techniques and inspirations. I am sure that the Naturality movement we later chose to explore benefitted from his expertise and his personality.

That's what influence is for me. It means being able to encounter that which you do not know, paying attention to it, not copying what you see but incorporating it to effect change and become even richer. Of all the lessons I learned from Japan and the other countries I explored, the cuisines I tasted for the first time, for me that was the most important.

I didn't hear anything more from Toshio Tanahashi, but I knew he was still working in the United States and I thought to myself that I'd love to publish a book about him. And then when I returned to New York in November 2021, I found out that he was working with Daniel Humm at Eleven Madison Park and had helped him come up with that unique vegan menu. It is exciting to see that what Daniel Humm took from his lessons is again different to our approach, to the things we admired and worked on with him.

I had other exciting encounters in Japan, even though the one with the Kyoto chef was the most memorable. In particular, I remember a tiny restaurant under a bridge in Osaka, a soba restaurant. One man worked there on his own with just a handful of ingredients; he had one method of cooking, some sheets of nori and nothing more.

The motion was so simple and repeated again and again, and right in front of us he made something that was perfect, at its very best.

Another great Japanese chef, Hirohisa Koyama, also came to visit us. I had persuaded Marianne Comolli and Jean-Louis Bloch-Lainé, with whom I did *Riviera*, to produce a book on Japanese cuisine with him. *Saveurs du Japon* (*Flavours of Japan*) was published in 1998 and has become, like *Riviera*, a reference text. I remember cooking with Hirohisa several times, including a wonderful, perfect method of cooking an egg that has set the standard ever since, as well as his small, black lacquer boxes containing unforgettable amuse-bouches. Those were also perfect dishes.

After Beige and Benoit, we opened Esterre in Tokyo in 2019 on the sixth floor of the Palace Hotel, facing the gardens of the Imperial Palace. It was a tribute to 'Mother Earth', the 'meaning of the land' and Naturality, which the young chef Martin Pitarque and I wanted to showcase. Martin, who grew up near Cahors in Quercy, had been working with us since 2014 at the Plaza Athénée and then as sous chef at the Dorchester in London. We decided to make the restaurant thoroughly modern, showing off the magnificent seats that the incredible Jean Nouvel had designed for my friend Jean-Marie Amat's restaurant, Le Saint-James, in Bouliac. They looked like clouds of leather and I thought they were perfect against the backdrop of the Imperial Palace. We'd had them redone. I liked everything about them, the armrests, the backs, the cushions – everything. And yet it was a gamble. The owner of the Palace Hotel did not like them and looked at me in shock when he discovered them. I promised him that if people didn't like the chairs on opening night, if I had made a mistake, I would take them back myself.

I didn't take the chairs back. They are still there and have made a lasting impression. I thought they were the perfect fusion between French and Japanese culture; you could be in Tokyo just as easily as you could be on the banks of the Garonne. The chairs helped us introduce a little bit of edge to a place that was so beautiful and harmonious and to tell a memorable story. It is the opposite of decoration. It is about being a part of history, for objects to acquire the patina of time and create places that are lived in. It is the same for the kitchens, dishes and moments we have created that are preserved in memory and speak of an encounter, a moment, an emotion, an inspiration and a tenaciousness.

Those are the lessons I have taken from all my journeys, from all the countries and all the cuisines I have discovered. We have restaurants in the United States, in London, Japan, Qatar, Singapore, Bangkok and other cities, and each of those destinations presented me with a challenge, a new question, a desire to take French gastronomy everywhere and place it into dialogue with others.

They do not cook fish in Hong Kong the way they do in Paris or Los Angeles. In Hong Kong it is cooked in its moisture, in its stock. If I served it like that in Paris or New York, nobody would eat it. Each place has a different way of appreciating fish, just as they do for all the other dishes. It is an eternal lesson in humility.

The force that drove me towards those countries, chefs and different cuisines has changed me. I would never have known about all the different ways fish can taste, nor about what true bitterness is, nor neutrality. I would never have had the desire to share those tastes with other people and make them known everywhere, in Paris and in other places, and for them to make up part of our expertise, a sort of personal library that is always richer, more open and in motion. I am also in motion, and I hope to be so for as long as I can.

THE FACTORIES

When I met Gaston Lenôtre in Eugénie-les-Bains, and asked him to teach me how to make croissants, I was a very young chef but was already convinced that it was important to be curious, to discover everything there was to discover, and to be able to do it all. That is why I went back to Paris and to his school, where the diversity of teaching, skills and expertise available filled in all the gaps for me. I went from station to station. I started with cold buffet, then moved to sugar work and cream desserts, and I learned about all the skills, techniques and tools associated with each job, including charcuterie, pastry, ice-cream and chocolate, a group of areas at a high level of excellence. I liked everything, to the extent that I wasn't sure what I wanted to specialise in. In the end it was cooking that I chose, but I still thought about the whole range of disciplines, and I cherished the idea of having a place and an opportunity to use what I know but also bringing my own vision to it, refining its characteristics, searching for other flavours and honing a flavour until it is perfectly refined. I like the word 'manufacture', which is the French term for 'artisan factory', and the etymologically linked Italian phrase 'fatto a mano' (handmade).

These factories would represent a new departure for me, as I continue to learn, search and discover both the flavours I carry with me and ones I do not yet know.

When I left the École Lenôtre, I had done enough work and had enough passion to know that I would one day return to each skill, each area of expertise, each field, and explore them further. I had been the teachers' assistant and it was then that I learned the most and then committed to it. In that school, the instinct, idea and desire for the ateliers was born. And this idea would be nurtured and strengthened with every passing year. I reiterate that the real danger is when you stop being curious, and the fact that the factories require knowledge, expertise, research and attention, guarantees that we remain curious, on the alert, and constantly in motion.

And so, I threw myself into the adventure of manufacturing to see if I knew how to do it, to learn and to do things differently, from chocolate to coffee, gelato and biscuits. To make them different. Soon, we will have a go at manufacturing seafood. This quest excites me just as much as the search for the perfect equipment. And for the right execution. And for a shop whose look embodies what we sell, with a story, an atmosphere and a tone that is unique. And the fact that none of this is the product of a big factory or large-scale manufacturing, but of ateliers where every touch matters.

The first factory we created was for chocolate. When I set out on this challenge, it was part recklessness and part courage. Nobody expected us to do it. It was new, we had to learn everything from scratch and we certainly did not try to please everyone. It was not about coming up with one all-encompassing flavour or one that would win over the majority of people, but instead a flavour that had personality, differences, irregularities. I would have that same ambition for every factory. For example, I often say that an industrially produced ice-cream will always be popular: it is soft, and high in fat and sugar. It ticks all the boxes for addiction. And it costs less to buy than what I spend to produce a handmade gelato. The same goes for chocolate and coffee. What we are offering is something else. And it starts with something different, with control over every element, from the choice of cocoa bean, coffee bean and the other ingredients, all of which are carefully selected with knowledge of their provenance, to the sale of the product.

Creating a factory is like creating a restaurant. They come with the same issues, the same obsessions and the same difficulties, and with the question that governs everything I do: Are we really going to be different? Are we going to be better?

The venture into manufacturing chocolate began in 2013. Later there would be coffee in 2019, gelato in 2021 and biscuits in 2022. It is a big undertaking and an extraordinary quest. I wanted to start from the raw product and rediscover its original flavour, while carefully controlling every stage of manufacture, just like in the kitchens of great restaurants.

In 2022 we prepared to open our twentieth chocolate shop, on Rue de l'Annonciation in Paris, less than ten years after we started making chocolate on Rue de la Roquette. I remember every step perfectly, and everything that enabled us to bring this to life.

I had worked with chocolate at Lenôtre and was fascinated by it. By the time I got back to my attic room in Paris, I would be so immersed in it that I felt drunk on chocolate. I was also fascinated by the chocolatiers I had met who taught us their art, like Michel Chaudun and Robert Linxe, who founded La Maison du Chocolat. He taught me a lot. He had pioneered the concept of hospitality in his shops. He had very precise ideas about chocolate, about what he wanted to offer and about service, and about how each customer was greeted and taken care of. Maurice Bernachon was another one of the master chocolatiers I encountered. I was working at Alain Chapel's and on my days off I would go and train with him in Lyon. His grandson still works in the same place, using the same recipe for *palet d'or*, a disc-shaped chocolate ganache topped with gold, that left such an impression on me. It still tastes the same. The *palet d'or* ages like good bread, like a fine wine. I learned a lot from those men. I made a note of every touch, every technique and every flavour, and I knew that one day I wanted to come up with something different still, a new flavour. The flavour I am looking for is not one from my childhood – from my grandmother's chocolate mousse, for example – nor is it one I learned from those masters. It does not yet exist. I am searching for it and when I have found it, I will know straight away.

When we created the chocolate factory, we didn't yet know how to make chocolate. We had the basics, some recommendations and the desire, but we had to learn it all alongside Nicolas Berger. I met him in New York, and he was pastry chef at the Essex House before becoming executive pastry chef of the entire group. He came to see me in 2012 and told me he wanted to do something else. Within five minutes we had decided to make chocolate. I felt that it was the right time. And so we began: I sent him off to train with the very best master chocolatiers, and he visited Philippe Bernachon in Lyon and Domori in Turin in particular. We also set out to find the perfect equipment, including the famous 'tarare', a sort of winnowing machine that is vital to the craft. We have since replicated it to make an exact copy. We had to pre-empt this old machine disappearing.

We built a team of people including Quentin Francis-Gaigneux, who was Nicolas's assistant before taking over the production of chocolate when he left. There is also Adonis Bioud, who is today the best cocoa roaster in Paris and who started out with us as commis chef. He knows and speaks about his equipment and his art as if they were people. I like to say that they are both rare assets in their respective fields.

We also travel to better understand and achieve mastery of everything we do. We go to Brazil in particular, to learn about cocoa, fermentation and sun drying with the Tavares family of Fazenda Leolinda, who have been harvesting cocoa for many years and know every region and every vintage and its particular flavour according to its exposure and its steepness, just like the grands crus of Burgundy. In addition to their magnificent land and their beans which are naturally sweetened by the sun, they have complete mastery and the right techniques.

At the start of each venture, I want to understand and see everything. It is better to know something for yourself than to depend on somebody else who knows. That is my golden rule.

I wanted to open a factory where we could make chocolate using traditional methods and control every stage of creation, like goldsmiths at work. To do this, we carefully choose beans from around fifteen different sources to get as much flavour and personality as possible. And we roast each bean differently according to its character. Thus we are able to control every crucial stage, from roasting to grinding, then from grinding to refining, conching and tempering.

It all takes place at our workshop on Rue de la Roquette, which was the first one and the flagship. And since we did not yet have any other shops, we also started selling there.

That location where we first created and started to sell things would go on to set the standard for us.

I picture myself in every location. Whether it is a restaurant, a factory or a shop, you have to think about the space and the décor and commit to it, so that it radiates certain characteristics, a shared DNA, but also has its own particularities and original features that make it unique. It is the opposite of standardisation: every shop is different, with meaningful objects and a different story to tell. That way, we're not tempted to repeat ourselves or follow the path of least resistance.

My trusted architect from the south-west of France, Patrick Laforgue, and I thought about the atmosphere we wanted to create at the factory on Rue de la Roquette. We decided we should evoke the look of a factory by using materials like steel, brick, wood, concrete and industrial lamps. We wanted the laminated, patinated steel in particular to be very noticeable, so that the patina finish added to the place, giving it character and history. So that it was no longer just decorative. So that as soon as you arrive you feel like you are looking into the soul of the workshop and the people working there. As the designer Philippe Starck likes to say, 'There is no substitute for the patina of time.'

We have the same standards for every shop. I went to the twentieth one, for example, on Rue de l'Annonciation in Paris, several weeks before it opened and studied every detail. There was a new lamp on the cash desk that clashed too much. And the shop didn't have any unique, characterful old elements. Every shop needs to have at least five old, original elements. Very few customers will notice, but for me it makes all the difference.

We choose a location and do not try to change its identity, but we also bring to it a little of who we are.

The essence of the workshops – small manufacturing sites instead of big factories, with every touch and product carefully controlled – is palpable in both the production areas, which feature unique, rare, traditional equipment, and in the shop areas. This extends to the packaging of the chocolates, which also tells the story of the factory, with the roughness that so unsettled my colleagues and investors – 'When do the real chocolate boxes arrive?' they asked me upon receiving the unusual packages, which are now so important to our identity.

And so we started selling our first chocolates at the end of the courtyard on Rue de la Roquette. It helped me gauge what customers wanted and how curious they were. It worked, and that shop still makes the most money even now.

New shops and other manufacturing workshops are gradually being created. An old garage in Paris's 20th arrondissement houses the workshop for making high-quality *couverture* chocolate, and another garage the range of bonbons, but the idea has remained the same over the years: small operations that are independent and individual, with workshops and large-scale craftmanship, as well as masters who come in, teach, share their knowledge, refine traditional equipment without sacrificing ancient techniques, and continue to search and experiment.

The coffee factory was created several years after the chocolate factory, with the same idea and the same aim.

I was introduced to coffee over the course of several years by the managing director of Malongo coffee, Jean-Pierre Blanc, who told me about the people he'd worked with from coffee-producing regions, about filters, roasting, cultures and producers. As with chocolate, I was fascinated by the product. In the end we partnered with Giuseppe Lavazza and made a premium coffee with them, Alain Ducasse & 1895 by Lavazza, in a designated workshop with beautiful equipment on a human scale. If you made coffee by the ton, you would not get the same result. It requires precise human control over a small output. We have the same principle when we make gelato and biscuits.

In this way, with respect for the beans and every stage of production, you can create a haute-cuisine coffee using exceptional crus and blends of unique flavours. And then the moment of serving coffee becomes perfection.

As with the chocolate, we had to demonstrate the artisanal nature of the coffee even from the look of the factory on Rue Saint-Sabin. Patrick Laforgue designed it, with bay windows that allow visitors to look in on the production area. We do the blending, the 'haute couture' production, in the Paris workshop, and then everything is recreated in Turin by Lavazza on a special site for roasting.

We also needed somebody well-versed in the art of coffee-making to go alongside the traditional equipment. Veda Viraswami, French roasting champion in both 2017 and 2018 and third in the world championships of 2019, became our roaster. He is familiar with the terroirs and knows everything there is to know about roasting. He is a rare man: he knows exactly how long to roast the coffee before the taste is ruined. We do not cook it to excess: we take what the plant has given us.

It always comes back to learning and education. Today we overcook coffee because it is often served with milk and overcooking gives it more flavour, but this is sacrilege. Most customers are used to drinking coffee with lots of milk and lots of sugar, just as they are used to ice-cream and chocolate that is too high in fat and sugar. For big companies this is the kind of coffee that performs the best. You lose its original flavour, and yet that is the flavour I am interested in. We must conserve the original flavour of the plant.

Just as with the cocoa beans, we choose the very best coffees from the finest regions, such as Guibert Boulanger's farm on La Réunion, or the Mil Cumbres farm at the foot of a volcano in Panama.

In 1975, I was nineteen years old and a junior ice-cream maker at Lenôtre. The ice-cream chef was called Nadler. I can still remember the taste of the vanilla ice-cream Nadler made, and everything I learned there. But in creating the gelato factory, I am looking for another taste within vanilla gelato. I want it to be unique and even better than what I learnt to do.

Quentin Francis-Gaigneux is at the helm of the chocolate factory, Veda Viraswami of the coffee factory and Matteo Casone of the gelato factory, which was founded in 2021. I met him in Bologna. He was a young man and a salesperson for Cattabriga, the greatest brand of gelato makers and machines. We had a chat and I took him on straight away. He arrived in Paris several months before the shop opened with a bag of recipes he had already written and tested. My pastry chef, Jean-Marie, gave him a word of warning: 'I know Alain Ducasse. If you turn up with all your recipes it won't work – he'll put them straight in the bin. He cares about your expertise, your technical skills, your professionalism and how you use the equipment. Together you will come up with new recipes and create what doesn't yet exist.' He was right. Things that are known and have already been done are of no interest to me. I knew what I wanted to find, the flavour that interested me. I knew the kind of coffee gelato I was looking for – how harsh, how bitter it should be.

I think Matteo was a bit lost at the beginning, but he stayed. He put away his bag of recipes and we made extraordinary gelatos, by searching and tasting. My entire life is tasting, including things that aren't very good. And searching for different, bitter, strange tastes; for there to be accidents and for the curious enthusiast to think: 'Hold on, I don't know what this is, and I'm intrigued by it.' That is how you shake up people's memories and leave an impression.

There aren't any ancient machines for making gelato like there are for chocolate or coffee. On the other hand, there are traditional machines for making gelato as it was made 100 years ago. The gelato is always extracted by hand using a scoop. And with all this work, research, carefully chosen ingredients, Matteo's art, his movements and handiwork, we can make unique gelatos and sorbets. That is what I am looking for in every factory.

In 2022, we made several key decisions about the factories. They can be summarised in just a few words and one overarching idea: persevering; growing; opening new shops; inventing a new factory and a place where all of this can come together; refusing to be satisfied with what we've already done.

I am often asked whether I want to carry on opening new shops. And I say yes, of course. It is slightly provocative: I know how much work every opening and every shop requires, and the care that is needed to deliver what we want to the standard we expect. But this is the reason for these factories: they question one another, they nourish and complete one another.

Le Salon des Manufactures was born on Rue des Petits-Champs in Paris in 2022, above a chocolate shop and restaurant that serves both food and gelato. This site brings together everything we do already, with coffee and chocolate tasting, and soon shortbread and artisan biscuits. That was our other great achievement of 2022: after the chocolate, coffee and gelato factories, we opened a biscuit factory. It is led by Flora Davies, who was my pastry chef in London and Hong Kong before joining Matteo on gelato the previous summer. She will become our Madame Biscuit under the watchful eye of Pascal Ferraud and Arnaud Coutret. Again, we had to start from practically nothing and invent it all – finding a site and inhabiting it so that it represented everything a biscuit factory should be, and finding a person to channel this story and our plans. It was new, and when you do something new you are never sure what you will feel when you open that door for the first time, and you are never sure that you will even get there.

The idea was to make shortbread, unique biscuits, biscuits that nobody would ever have tried before and that would set the standard – the best pistachio biscuit, the best coffee biscuit, the best vanilla, chocolate, almond and lemon biscuits and so on.

I was already grinding almonds at Lenôtre back in 1975. In storage I had an old mill that I'd had restored, an almond-grinder with an adjustable gauge for coarser or finer grains according to preference. When I spoke to Flora, I had in mind a very simple, perfectly delicious shortbread with a pinch of salt, a shortbread that needed to develop and mature for several days like Bernachon's *palets d'or*. We hadn't yet created it and I had never tasted it, but I wanted us to reach for that and try to find it. And we did.

The magic lies in the fact that we never know beforehand whether we will succeed, and this encompasses everything I enjoy: uncertainty, pressure, hard work, hours of tasting and questioning yourself, and the moment when you know that you've hit the nail on the head. And then every day we will try to do better, to refine the flavour even further.

We are not guided being sure of pleasing people or being understood, but this does inspire us to carry on creating. It inspires us to invent chocolates that are specially designed for the East; to conceive of a chocolate shop in Switzerland, the home of Lindt; to dream of setting up a pasta factory based on an old machine found in Sicily and restored piece by piece over several months, without knowing whether it will ever work again.

THE MAISON DU PEUPLE

When I don't have the appetite anymore, when I don't have any more answers or desires, when I stop being curious, always elsewhere and already elsewhere, I will have to stop. I often say this to myself, and I say it to other people just as often. Life is made up of cycles, conquests, achievements, grand plans, failures, departures and new directions. I am preparing myself for this. I try to anticipate all the changes and every day I ask myself, 'What do you want now?'

I knew that I wanted to become a chef, that I wanted to be the best, that I wanted to earn three stars and then even more stars, that I wanted to set myself other challenges and not remain tied to my home in Les Landes, to Monaco, Paris or France, but instead to travel, see the world and taste the world.

I knew that I wanted to come up with a flavour, an element specific to everything that nourishes.

I knew that I wanted to build a group that was daring, that brought together places which were seemingly contradictory but which were in fact in dialogue and completed one another. You would think that there is a huge difference between the splendour of Versailles and the refectory at Sapid, with histories that are difficult to reconcile, and yet everything is linked. The earth brings them together and so do our aims – to feed, to be remembered and to come up with a different take. It is a group that we've built with generosity and honesty, and everyone who works with us is important to me. I am aware of my responsibility: it is up to me to think about the future, about the group I will leave behind, about a business that we want to be sustainable and enduring, constantly evolving in order to keep up with the times, its demands and its issues. I have never had a plan or a strategy, nor have I ever really done any market research; I wanted to start something, to be open, to dare, to respond to my instincts. We've had more success than we've had failure, but this requires work and concentration on a daily basis. I will also know when the time comes to hand over this business to others and take on a different role. What is most important is that we preserve the expertise we have developed in a fair, honest way, and that every person who works with us is aware of our story and our commitments. Everyone I work with is a rare resource. But we must not allow ourselves to become paralysed by respect for what has been done before: we must continue to take risks, to acquire new expertise, to succeed, lose, evolve and think about the future.

I knew that I wanted to bind myself to places that were powerful and symbolic, like the Louis XV in Monaco, La Bastide in Moustiers and the foot of the Eiffel Tour with the boat, *Ducasse sur Seine*. On the other hand, I knew when it was time to unbind myself from places where I had been very happy but had become less so, like with the Plaza Athénée.

I knew when it was time to take a step back from what I had been doing initially, to no longer claim to be 'doing the cooking' and posing in chef's whites, and instead highlight the younger generation, the great chefs of the future.

And I knew when I discovered the Maison du
Peuple (The House of the People) in Clichy, that
this incredible place would become an obsession,
my next dream and my next battle.

Every day I make decisions for myself and for
the people I work with. Every day I question my
profession, our professions and our gastronomy
– the place it occupies, the direction it seems to
be taking, what makes me happy and what makes
me scared. I am not somebody who is bound to
the past; I am not particularly melancholic, and
I am even less nostalgic, and I do not often look
backwards: telling my story in the preceding pages
of this book is another way of interrogating myself
and questioning our present as well as our future.

How do we want to feed ourselves?

How do I feed my contemporaries?

What do we want to serve in our restaurants?

What does a lunch or a dinner represent today?

What place does French gastronomy occupy?

What is my place, my role?

The answers to these questions are open
and in flux depending on feelings, encounters,
discoveries, journeys and projects. But for me
there are also a few incontrovertible facts, or paths
that are more certain than others.

We got through the Covid crisis. It didn't force any major decisions upon us – we had to take it day by day, adapt, remain attentive, stay calm and embody serenity at a time that was chaotic and uncertain. I tried to carry on working the way I have always worked, by having as few meetings as possible so I could adapt and face up to the unexpected, so that nothing was impeded or prevented, by staying agile, curious and knowing how to act each morning in order to move forward. In those uncertain times, you had to be certain of the need to carry on.

It was during that tense, unpredictable period that I visited the Maison du Peuple for the first time, a building that was constructed in the late 1930s in Clichy-la-Garenne by the Communist Party. It was designed and constructed by the architects Beaudouin and Lods and the studios of Jean Prouvé. It is a magnificent building, a masterpiece, an architectural treasure marrying glass and metal. You notice its extraordinary lighting effects when you see it for the first time: the light penetrates everything, producing contrasts and creating depth. Then at the heart of the building there are giant movable partition walls, a retractable floor and a retractable roof. It was classified as a historical monument in 1983 by Jack Lang, then Minister of Culture, but had since been completely abandoned for several years. It has been dominated by pigeons since its semi-closure in 1993, though the ground floor was home to a market until February 2022. Yet when you see it, you can sense the spirit that once brought such a place to life, with the market below, the reception halls, the cinema and the union offices.

I fell in love with the place. And I immediately began to imagine how we could fit into this place, truly respect it, respecting its history and drawing a connection between its industrial look and the world of our factories. I want to collect all our equipment, which also has links to the past, together in that mechanical building, and to produce and think about cuisine and celebrate it. The cuisine of today, and even more so, the cuisine of tomorrow.

I think it is always important to respect the history of a place and what it was originally used for, and not to meddle with this history. That's why I think I would have been an architect if I hadn't been a chef. Working with Patrick Jouin and Sanjit Manku, we want to maintain the building's extraordinary mechanics and restore its façade and roof. You will be able to buy food and dine at restaurants, and it will house production units, offices and all our factories, bringing blue- and white-collar workers together in one space.

I have a dream for this Maison du Peuple, which was once home to all sorts of variety and creation and was so open. I want it to attract everyone, for it to host a chef in residence who can create things and immerse themselves in what we do, refining their cooking with the best equipment available and all the ovens and cooking utensils in the world. I want this 'house of the people' to somehow embody our collective memories of the profession, but also to look towards the world and the future, enabling our chefs and the chefs we host to work differently, to bounce ideas off one another and create the cuisine of the future.

It will have connections to everything we have already done – to the factories, to our restaurants in France and elsewhere, to the École Ducasse, where the chef in residence could give lessons, and to Naturality, since the site is intended to become a global culinary centre with a focus on vegetables, but also on sustainable, responsible cooking that is respectful to the planet and its people. Chefs and restaurateurs across the world must adopt sustainable practices in their cooking. At the Maison du Peuple, and equally at the summit on the future of food we are holding in Monaco this year, we will be able to reflect on developments in gastronomy and on the sustainable, responsible, humanistic style of cooking that we are calling for.

My dream is to bring everything together in this one place, so that it exudes unparalleled energy, creativity and healthy competition.

As soon as I discovered this building, I wanted to renovate it and inaugurate it, and as with everything I set about doing, I wanted things to happen quickly, as quickly as possible – it will be under construction for at least eighteen months if everything goes to plan. I have a conviction that things that drag on are never completed. It is a conviction that I have perhaps drawn from all the construction sites I've seen, from all my projects, from life experience, or perhaps from a book that I often return to: *The Art of War*, by Sun Tzu. That art is about waiting for the right moment, adapting, anticipating, planning for the worst, bouncing back, finding a solution, and always having a couple of solutions to any given problem. This book has guided me through the last few years, and it will continue to guide me through the construction and realising my dream of the Maison du Peuple, through obstacles, criticism, bad surprises, oppositions and disagreements – in short, all the things that can happen when you decide to try something instead of doing nothing.

It has often been said that I enjoy war, that I enjoy conflict and confrontation, but nothing could be further from the truth. I hate it. But I know that some battles and disagreements are useful, and that when they present themselves, you must know how to fight back, overcome them or change tack. We must fight one battle every day: it is the only way to stick to our commitments and to rise to our ambitions and values.

Over the last few months, the meaning of what I have undertaken, of my words and encounters, has often also involved reflecting on what French gastronomy could be, on its place in the world and on the ways in which restaurateurs, artisans and producers might come together, pool their efforts and help one another.

Joël Robuchon, Paul Bocuse and I set up the Collège Culinaire de France in 2011. We wanted to bridge the divide between great chefs and other restaurateurs and create a real community of artisans, chefs, breeders, fishers and winegrowers, a community that had meaning, enabling these professionals to meet and enrich one another, and allowing for unique connections through interaction and sharing food. Today this collective brings together over 2000 'quality restaurants' and over 1000 'quality artisan producers'. The collective has been a success and its effects manifold: a culinary school will soon be set up in Japan, based on the same model. But this collective cannot do everything, and alone it cannot make up for the fragility of our profession and the lack of a real community or federation. The period we have just lived through has only accentuated its risks and fragility. We have to do this together. But at the moment that authority, that dream federation does not exist.

In 2015 we launched the Goût de France / Good France initiative with the Minister of Foreign Affairs. The aim was to introduce people across the world to great French dishes, celebrating French gastronomy through dinners and workshops and highlighting the work of restaurateurs and producers. The initiative ran for six years before it came to an end, and yet, now more than ever, French gastronomy must prove it is innovative, celebratory, receptive, united, and with a global outlook.

French cuisine is an asset with great influence and is a major attraction for France. But we lack a tool powerful enough to promote it, we lack unison and conversations within an institution or a federation. That is what is at stake over the next few years.

Gastronomy *is* France. But to live up to our history and our expertise, for French gastronomy to continue to be influential, for the art of hospitality, dining and the art of living to continue to survive, we must avoid a fixed idea of French gastronomy or the role of chefs. An old-fashioned, backward-looking vision of our gastronomy scares me: it promotes a retreat towards traditions, techniques and dishes, to the detriment of innovation or fusion. It only celebrates the image of the chef in the kitchen, always in the same place and carving just one career out of a few traditional, perfectly executed dishes. That is some people's experience, but it cannot be the only model. Chefs today can have other ambitions, other desires and other interests.

I will always choose experimentation and boldness over perpetuating classics and traditions.

I will always want to leave an impression on and challenge the person who is tasting the food – that which seems obvious or neutral does not interest me.

I know that this risks creating division and misunderstanding, but it is a risk I am willing to take. This is not because I have nothing to lose or because I don't care about the critics, but because this is how I have always done things – taking risks, being alone on a certain path, mapping out that path, even, and sometimes getting it wrong or having to respond to criticism, explain and suggest something else.

The ADMO project was a risk.

We held a 100-day pop-up on the terrace of Les Ombres in the Musée du Quai Branly – Jacques Chirac, which was designed by Jean Nouvel, where we served exceptional cuisine – a dialogue, an osmosis between two strong sets of culinary expertise: ours, with Romain Meder, and that of the Spanish chef Albert Adrià. We also had Jessica Préalpato's desserts. This presented a challenge: the cuisine had to make sense, it had to be rooted in our beliefs, it had to draw on the key features of Naturality and Adrià's creative engagement, and it had to be a composition that was unique, surprising and never-before-tasted. It was, of course, radical and crazy, and neither the criticism nor the silence had ever been so loud.

In cooking, we are feeding our contemporaries, but we are also asking them questions about the times we are living in, about the ways in which we are living, occupying the land, thinking and participating.

ADMO was a daring concept – provocative, even. It came from a desire to shake up French gastronomy, which, like politics, has recently tended to look back on itself, resisting innovation, difference and fusion, and falling back on what are allegedly original values – traditional dishes that should not be questioned, and should be brought back, even. That is the opposite of who I am and what I want to offer.

On the contrary, I believe that by welcoming foreign chefs, by shaking up our dishes, our dining experiences and our food, French gastronomy can maintain its position, its influence and its attractiveness, and can speak to the world.

I try to respond to all the critics and explain our experiments, our stance, our choices and our history. That is why we photographed and recorded our ADMO experiment, including the people, places and recipes involved. It was so these things might become a point of reference and inspire others, so the project might set an example for a whole generation of chefs who dream of being daring, making decisions and moving away from that which is comforting and ordinary. And I am optimistic: I know that this generation exists, that it is there, that they are only asking to be given an opportunity and to be listened to, and it is them I think of now. I am thinking of them and of how we can promote, respect and encourage them.

I too belonged to a generation of chefs who wanted to break the rules of a cuisine that had become too codified. I saw the masters of nouvelle cuisine revolutionise their art, bringing their personalities and souls to it, and I saw an entire profession transform. It was an evolution that was quiet but necessary. But the next generation, the generation currently in their thirties, who I see growing and learning and coming up with ideas, seems to me to have even more personality, and their ideas represent even more of a rupture, a revolution. That is why it is so important to me that I am there for them. For example, I would like them to be able to publish a record of their cuisine, a book that paints a portrait of them and their beliefs, their recipes and their approaches to creation. And I would like the first chef in this series to be Marie-Victorine Manoa, who works at Aux Lyonnais and always impresses me with her boldness and committed stance. There would also be a book on Amaury Bouhours, the chef at Le Meurice. There would be thirty books on the thirty chefs of the present and the future.

I think it is now more difficult for these young chefs than it was before, even though, paradoxically, we have never had so much to say about cooking and gastronomy. But they have to deal with a new type of customer who has a short attention span and is over-informed, busy, fickle, overfed and stressed out. How can one continue to surprise them and how can we hold their attention and make an impression? This requires more creativity and commitment still. These young people also have to get themselves and their cuisine known, and today, one of the only ways of doing this is through television and cooking programmes. This meets a certain demand, which is a very good thing, but how can it be the only way of existing?

What worries me is not that these programmes exist, it is that there is less interest in the other tools and methods of communication that used to work for food and chefs and made it possible to think about gastronomy. Television, critics, guidebooks and Michelin stars are missing out on several talents, and I also feel that they are taking their time, far too much time in fact, to reward them. When I read a restaurant is 'on the young side', for example, I think to myself that it is this very youth that they should be acknowledging and rewarding.

This will require a period of good will, curiosity, effort and attention.

It seems to me all the more crucial that this generation constructs the future and the position of French gastronomy. In order to rise itself up, create, and question the world, it needs critics to tell its story, to inscribe their dishes and methods in history – critics who are able to understand it. We must provide these young chefs with places, the means for expressing themselves, creativity, representation and exchanges.

My restaurant kitchens are now only headed up by young people, but this is not enough: chefs need to be able to thrive off one another, inspire one another, travel, keep an open and curious mind, question themselves and be rewarded in order to have more time, strength and momentum still. I picture the Maison du Peuple with this in mind, as a place of refuge for these young people and this universe, a place for creation and exchange. A place where everyone can read about the history of gastronomy. To me it seems that this is what we are most lacking: on the one hand, a point of reference, archives and a repository of techniques, and on the other hand, a celebration of creativity, of experimentation, of the unique gesture, of firsts.

Guidebooks should not just wait and see, and critics should not lose their curiosity and their good will. Perhaps we will always have to put up a fight to explain, tell a story, stand out from the crowd. Perhaps customers are more reassured by an 'as seen on TV' label than by the CVs of young chefs who have done the rounds of the best kitchens and chosen one restaurant that suits them, and have even decided to miss out on awards and Michelin stars in order to have as much freedom as possible. I am confident that it is worth fighting for this younger generation, for creation, for freedom, and to be able tell the story of good taste and passion over and over again.

We are artisans and interpreters. Everything we undertake, whether it is opening a new restaurant or opening a new factory, requires accepting a certain amount of danger: we are on a tightrope, and everything is very delicate. Nothing is guaranteed. But that is perhaps the most beautiful part – that element of uncertainty, risk and solitude. It makes you humble and teaches you precious life lessons. You have to do things and learn. You have to demonstrate your persistence, like the time I visited 120 sites for the chocolate factory before finding the atelier on Rue de la Roquette, and then decided in five minutes that it was the right place. You have to be a little reckless. And passionate. I enjoy nothing more than discovering things I have never discovered before, seeing things I have never seen before and tasting things I have never tasted before. I enjoy nothing more than meeting enthusiasts all over the world, visiting markets, tasting the food of other chefs and street food. And sometimes, going back to my house by the ocean, existing in silence and solitude with my books and the horizon, before setting off again for new adventures, travelling once again, tasting things, once again and forever.

ACKNOWLEDGEMENTS

This book exists because I had the great fortune of meeting and working with people who are as passionate as they are rich in their differences. I would like to thank them here for their faultless support, and thank the youngest ones who are here to enrich us, strong with their new horizons, their values and their hard work.

To Franck Cerutti, my most precious and oldest collaborator, Gabrielle Aguilo, Xavier Alberti, Mohamed Ali, Luca Allegri, Natalino

Ambra, Laurent André, Olivier Antonioli,
Johnny Aquino, Anais Arbadji, Aruka Atsuji,
Éric Azoug, Anthony Bâcle, Nicolas Bailet,
Noël Bajor, Daniele Baldo, Jacques Bally, Cedric
Barbarat, Pascal Bardet, Julie Bares-Bonneau,
Stéphanie Barral, Bénédicte de Bary, David
Belin, Hafid Benkhouman, Jean-Philippe
Berens, Nicolas Berger, Olivier Berger, Francesco
Bernardinelli, Emmanuel Beuvelet, Olivier
Bikao, Adonis Bioud, Sarah Blanc, Thierry Blanc,
Jean-Philippe Blondet, Mathieu Bloyet, Xavier
Boireau, Margaux Boisseau, Éric Bonneau, Marc
Bonnieu, Albert Boronat i Miro, Jean-Philippe
Borro, Clémentine Bouchon, Ahmed Bouhizeb,
Amaury Bouhours, Moshen Bourguiba, Bruno
Brangea, Jose Bravo, Caroline Briens, Charlotte
Bringant, Alexandre Brochard, Jemmy Brouet,
Anais Caietta, Bruno Caironi, Jean-François
Camarty, Florence Cane, Agathe Canivet, Nicola
Canuti, Yann Capsie, Jean-François Casanova,
Matteo Casone, Sarah Chailan, Marc Chalopin,
Thomas Chambraud, Mohamed Chamour,
Aurore Charoy, Christopher Charraudeau,
Nicolas Chatenier, Jérémy Cheminade, Thomas
Christoux, Christophe Clarigo, Élodie Collombet,
Dimitri Coly, Romain Corbière, Francis Corniot,

Marine Cossard, Damien Couliou, Francis Coulon, Denis Courtiade, Arnaud Coutret, Adrien de Crignis, Patrick Crochet, Alex Cufley, Hélène Darroze, Bruno Davaillon, Flora Davies, Luc Debove, Alban Del Monte, Christian Delouvrier, Helene Denaiffe, Lisa Denis, Anthony Denon, Charlotte Dequeker, François Deshayes, Christophe Devoille, Caroline Dhjan, Niran Di Blasio, Mireille Djob, Madeleine Dubois, Céline Dubourdieu, Stéphane Duchiron, Thierry Dufroux, Arnaud Duhem, Julien Dumas, Arnaud Dutertre, Didier Elena, Tony Esnault, Sylvain Étiévant, Fabienne Eymard, Francis Fauvel, Manon Fays, Olivier Fellous, Pascal Feraud, Louis-Gabriel Fichet, Fabio Fioravanti, Jean-Paul Fontan, Lucas Foudinier, Quentin Francis-Gaigneux, Kiyoko Fujisawa, Didier Fulconis, Pierre Gaborit, Fabrice Gallis, Robert Gamba, Pierre-Charles Gandilhon, Frédéric Garnier, Thomas Gauthier, Hugues Gérard, Thomas Gérard, Georges-Marie Gerini, François-Xavier Germain, Philippe Gollino, Guillaume Gomez, Philippe Gomez, Stéphane Gortina, Antoine Gournac-Poli, Laurent Gras, Frédérick E. Grasser-Hermé, Yanis Geerinck, Alexandre Gregoire, Cédric Grolet, Alice Grossi, William Groult, Alessandro Guardiani, Gianni

Guatieri, Sébastien Guénard, Olivier Guénot,
Mark Guillain-Williams, Matthias Hahn,
Delphine Heraud, Jocelyn Herland, Fanny Herpin,
Jean-Marie Hiblot, Wilfrid Hocquet, Caroline
Jacquelin, Arnaud Jahn, Emmanuel Jirou-Najou,
Kelly Jolivet, Julien Jouhannaud, Patrick Jouin,
Christian Julliard, Laurent Kalkotour, Akihiko
Kamioka, Guillaume Katola, Julien Kientzler,
Takashi Kitahira, Kei Kojima, Shujiro Kono,
Tanaka Kota, Louis Kothe, Jérôme Lacressonnière,
Patrick Laine, Michel Lang, Frédéric Larquemin,
Christophe Larrat, Véronique Lartigue, Julien
Lasseaux, Christian Laval, Sonja Lee, Alexandra
Legrand, Marion Lemarchand, Diane Le
Pennec, Loïc Leplat, Damien Leroux, Gwendal
Le Ruyet, Marc Loiseau, Matteo Lorenzini,
Dominique Lory, Alessandro Lucassino, Vincent
Lung, Dorian Lutzelschwab, Maxime Luvara,
Marcelo Mabilia, Farah Madi, Jean Mahu,
Vincent Maillard, Sanjit Manku, Marie-Victorine
Manoa, Sara Maranzana, Philippe Marc, Alberto
Marcolongo, Gérard Margeon, Nadège Marini
Carriere, Céline Martin, Christophe Martin,
Rui Martins, Pierre Marty, Alexandre Masselin,
Jérémy Masson, Élise Masurel, Josiane Mathias,
Jacques Maximin, Maxime Maze, Romain Meder,

Marvic Medina, Éric Mercier, Julian Mercier, Christophe Michalak, Sandro Micheli, Julien Moreno, Christophe Moret, Alexandre Mousset, Mario Muratore, Angelo Musa, Yoshinori Nagata, Axel Nail, Paule Neyrat, Isabelle Nicolino, Takahiro Noguchi, Jean-Louis Nomicos, Lyonel Nowitz, Douglas Oberson, Patrick Ogheard, Mandy Pan, Massimo Pasquarelli, Maxime Pastor, Benoit Peeters, Georges Pelissier, Robbie Pepin, Emmanuelle Perrier, Antoine Petrus, Jean-François Piège, Nicolas Pierantoni, Emmanuel Pilon, Aymeric Pinard, Martin Pitarque, Giovanni Pitton, Laurent Plantier, Sylvain Portay, Dominique Potier, Carole Pourchet, Jessica Préalpato, Stéphane Prévidi, Franck Profumo, Aymeric Prudhomme, Vincent Puma, Christophe Quantin, Gwenn Raoult, Christophe Raoux, David Rathgeber, Sébastien Rebaudo, Cécile Rebbot, Christian Regouby, Frédéric Rivierre, Adeline Robert, Frédéric Robert, Miguel Rodrigues, Frédéric Roemer, Jean-Éric Roiné, Pierre Stephan Romano, Michelle Romeo, Vito Romeo, Fabrice Laslo Rosso, Michel Roth, Laëtitia Rouabah, Xavier Rouland, Jean-Pierre Rous, Sébastien Rousseau, Nadège Roy, Julie Ruel, Alizée Sagnes, Christophe Saintagne, Éric

Santalucia, Cédric Satabin, Dominique Saugnac, Romane Sauvêtre, Pierre Schaedelin, Jeremy Schotte, Cheongyan See, Rocco Seminara, Alexandre Sempere, Hisanobu Shigeta, Caroline Siri, Habib Soilihi, Alain Solivérès, Claire Sonnet, Alain Soulard, Alain Souliac, Reiko Speciale-Murakami, Yannis Stanisiere, Pierre Tachon, Michael Tan, Mari Tanaka, Katrina Tayo, Laëtitia Teil, David Teillet, Frédéric Thévenet, Silvia Tola, Sonja Toulouse-Martin, Carine Trividic, Célia Tunc, Geoffrey Turpin, Gwenael Van Acker, Tjaco Van Eijken, Frédéric Vardon, Gabriel Veissaire, Nicolas Vernier, Jean-Paul Veziano, Quentin Vicas, Éric Vincent, Sophie Vincent, Veda Viraswami, Karine Wigno, Chantal Wittmann, Benoit Witz, Ugo Wolff, Kohei Yamamoto, Jean-Philippe Zahm, Stéphanie Zara-Morin, Pierre Zerouali, Luca Zvaleni.